SACRED GROUND
ON DE LA SAVANE

Bronze bust of Baron de Hirsch on the grounds of the Cemetery.

Sacred Ground
on de la Savane

Montreal's
Baron de Hirsch Cemetery

Danny Kucharsky

WITH A PORTFOLIO OF PHOTOGRAPHS BY

D.R. Cowles

Véhicule Press

Published with the generous assistance of the Canada Council for
the Arts, the Book Publishing Industry Development Program of the
Department of Canadian Heritage and the Société de développement des
entreprises culturelles du Québec (SODEC).

Cover design: J.W. Stewart
Frontispiece photo: D.R. Cowles
Set in Adobe Minion by Simon Garamond
Printed by Marquis Book Printing Inc.

Special thanks: Bruce Henry

LIBRARY AND ARCHIVES CANADA CATALOGUING IN PUBLICATION

Kucharsky, Danny
Sacred ground on de la Savane : Montreal's Baron de Hirsch
Cemetery / Danny Kucharsky.

Includes index.
ISBN 1-55065-196-X

1. Baron de Hirsch Cemetery (Montréal, Québec)—History.
2. Jewish cemeteries—Québec (Province)—Montréal—History. I. Title.

FC2947.61.K82 2005   971.4'28004924   C2004-906573-4

Published by Véhicule Press, Montréal, Québec, Canada
www.vehiculepress.com

Distribution in Canada by LitDistCo
orders@litdistco.ca

Distribution in U.S. by Independent Publishers Group
www.ipgbook.com

Printed in Canada on 100% post-consumer recycled paper.

Contents

Preface

Sacred Ground on de la Savane celebrates 100 years of history at Montreal's Baron de Hirsch Cemetery—Canada's largest Jewish cemetery in a city that, at one time was Canada's greatest metropolis with the largest Jewish population, next to New York City, in North America.

Over the past century, Montreal Jews have played important and critical roles in influencing and shaping commerce, the arts, and the social history of this great city and beyond. Always connected, in one degree or another, to their religious and their European and North African traditions and principles, the Jews who lived and died here have left us valuable and rich stories that must be told and retold. It falls to us to remember them and keep our heritage alive.

In the pages of this book, you will learn how, long before the last century, the earliest Jews in Quebec bought and donated land to bury family members and those with whom they shared a faith. You will learn how the first synagogues in Montreal coped with the financial burden of burying Jews who died penniless in a new land, of the beginnings of community groups devoted to looking after the welfare of increasing numbers of immigrants, and of the burial societies that, based on common roots in the Old Country, banded together to take care of the needs of "brothers" and families during difficult times. You will read how a community, stressed by overwhelming growth, pleaded for funds from a wealthy benefactor, Baron Maurice de Hirsch, and how the Baron's gift became the genesis of the Baron de Hirsch Institute, the starting point for almost a century and a half of providing support—in life and in death—to the neediest members of Montreal's Jewish community.

Cemeteries are often thought of as a kind of collective, a community resting place, a village of the dead. The Yiddish term for cemetery—*Beth Chaim*, house of life—seems paradoxical, but the Talmud reasons that if we called a cemetery a house of death, it would discourage people from wanting to visit. We like to think that people who are buried in the cemetery have stories that we can bring to life as lessons for the living.

With that idea in mind, in addition to being a history of a venerable institution, this book is also a collection of anecdotes and stories about some of the Cemetery's sixty thousand occupants. There are stories of heroes and angels, poets and novelists, businessmen and scholars, and accounts of the rogues and scoundrels that made up the Jewish community through the twentieth century. Most of those buried in the Cemetery lived in Montreal all or part of their lives but some had their remains transferred here from other places or from battlefields and even sunken ships.

Take the time to read their stories. Learn how many faced the challenge of moving from often harshly inhospitable societies to a new "free" country and how they strove for success. They coped with the burdens, not only of the local issues of the day, but with the insecurities that poverty, upheaval, and the horror of war forced upon them.

As you read this book you may recognize landmarks and historical names from a time when families were large, when people worked hard at physical labour, got sick from diseases easily cured today, and often died in their youth. It was a time when winters seemed harsher, colder and longer. When times were harder, but simpler.

If you visit the cemetery, you can also use this book as a walking tour guide. Let *Sacred Ground on de la Savane* inspire and inform you. Let it be a link to your parents, grandparents, great-grandparents, relatives and friends, and to the Montreal Jewish community in its early days. Encourage your children to read it so they have a better sense of their past and of those who came before them; help them learn how their ancestors lived and died, how they dealt with everyday challenges and achievements, and how they built a community and a cemetery that grew and thrived.

The Baron de Hirsch Cemetery Centennial Book Committee
Jay Aaron
Suzanne Belson, Chair
Jacques Berkowitz
Martin Brook

Acknowledgements

A lot of work went into the research, writing and, publication of this book. Thanks are due to all who contributed their time and who shared their always wonderful, interesting and sometimes quirky stories.

Kudos to the team of dedicated and committed people who came up with the idea and participated in getting this history committed to paper. It was a pleasure to work with them. Many thanks to Suzanne Belson for brilliantly conceiving of the idea for the book; to Jacques Berkowitz for his legal guidance and candid insights into a period of the Baron de Hirsh Executive's inner sanctum; to Jay Aaron for his unflagging interest and for sitting through many editorial meetings; to the Board of Directors of the Cemetery for its support and encouragement; to Rabbi Moshe Glustein for his halachic guidance and input; and to all of the former Board members and generous contributors of stories and recollections of lore passed down from generation to generation. Without all of these people, this book would not have been possible.

Thanks are due especially to Danny Kucharsky, who dug deep into files and archives and who walked the Cemetery's grounds dozens of times, notebook and camera in hand, before writing this book; to David Cowles, whose photographs of monuments and architectural features touchingly evoke the cemetery's mood; to Bruce Henry, whose editing skills are so appreciated, and to Simon Dardick of Véhicule Press, who had the confidence to publish this record of the first hundred years of the Baron de Hirsch Cemetery's story.

Martin Brook, President, Baron de Hirsch Cemetery Inc.

1

The Cemetery's Historical Roots

If all life moves inevitably toward its end, we should during ours
paint it with our colours of life and hope.
–Marc Chagall

Although Montreal's Baron de Hirsch Cemetery opened at the beginning of the twentieth century, its roots lie in the very foundation of the Jewish community in Quebec.

Jewish life sprang up in Montreal in the last third of the eighteenth century, the period following the French and Indian Wars and the Seven Years' War. The British military occupied Montreal on September 8, 1760. There were further battles, until France ceded the northern part of its American empire to England in 1763. The cession was one of the terms of the treaty ending the Seven Years' War.

A number of Jewish officers, soldiers, and military purveyors decided to remain in Quebec. They became merchants and fur traders, and brought their families from England and the Thirteen Colonies. The Montreal community founded the Shearith Israel Spanish & Portuguese Synagogue in 1768; it was the first Jewish congregation in the new British colony of Quebec.

Like the other Jewish communities in North America at the time, the congregation was Sephardic in ritual, although the founding members were Ashkenazi Jews of Dutch, British, and German origin. The members looked to the Spanish & Portuguese congregations of London and New York as parents. The synagogue building was erected in 1777, and Jacob Raphael Cohen of London became its rabbi the following year .

A member of the congregation, Lazarus David, already a landowner in Montreal, bought property on St. Janvier Street in 1775. It was to serve as a cemetery for his family and the community. His wish was that the land was "to serve in perpetuity as a cemetery for individuals of the Jewish faith who may die in the Montreal district." It was outside the city limits, on the southern part of today's Dorchester Square.

Lazarus David's initiative in providing burial space for the Jews of Montreal was in keeping with a major concern of other new Jewish communities in North America—the right to a Jewish grave and the responsibility to respect the dead. In some North American Jewish communities, a cemetery preceded the appearance of a synagogue.

The first person to be interred in the St. Janvier Street Cemetery was Lazarus David himself. He was buried on October 22, 1776, one year after obtaining the ground.

The first written mention of the Jewish cemetery occurs in a 1781 document detailing holdings of the landowning seigneurs of Montreal. The register attests that the St. Janvier Street plot was legally severanced from a larger holding "owned by Les Héritiers Décarris who sold thirty square feet for the Jewish Cemetery."

In 1797, Lazarus David's son David David obtained an adjacent ninety-square-foot plot to enlarge the cemetery. Mr. David ultimately donated it to the Shearith Israel Spanish & Portuguese Congregation for burial of all Jews, irrespective of their affiliation.

Spanish & Portuguese Congregational bylaws of 1838 spoke of "The New Burial Ground, of which ninety feet immediately adjoining the Old Burying Ground remain the possession of the late David David, Esq., and the Ground given the congregation by the executors of the estate of the late David David, Esq."

The right to be buried is complemented by the responsibility to bury all Jews, with a dignity that is their birthright. Recognizing this, its bylaws engage the Shearith Israel to be compassionate to the needy: "In the case of death of poor persons professing Judaism, they shall be buried at the expense of the congregation."

About the same time as the Shearith Israel synagogue was being founded, Jews were also settling outside Montreal. Aaron Hart, either a military purveyor or an officer under General Amherst during the British attack on Montreal in 1760, was one of the first Jewish settlers in Canada. He was English- or German-born, and probably came via the Thirteen Colonies. He settled in Trois-Rivières (Three Rivers), Quebec.

Hart became the postmaster, and was active as a fur merchant and financier. He acquired large estates, including the seigneurie of nearby Bécancour. (Under a semi-feudal system of landholding, which had long been established in France, seigneurs granted habitants the right to work farm plots on the land they owned in exchange for annual dues. The system continued in Quebec for many years after it became a British colony.)

Near the end of the 1700s, Hart decided to set aside a piece of his Alexander Street garden in Trois-Rivières for a cemetery, called in Hebrew, *Beth Haim*, or House of Life. He was following an ancient Jewish tradition of family plot burial.

The earliest interment in what became known as the Alexander Street Cemetery took place in 1796. Hart's seven-month-old granddaughter Julia Hart had passed away. She was the daughter of Ezekiel, one of Aaron Hart's four sons. When Aaron Hart died in 1800, he was buried next to his granddaughter.

In 1827, the Hart family decided to offer their family plot as a cemetery for other Jews as well. By 1850, however, the Alexander Street plot was full. Ezekiel Hart provided a further piece of land on Prison Street in Trois-Rivières for a new cemetery for all Jews who wanted to be buried there.

The Harts kept their cemetery, and even members of the family who died in Montreal were laid to rest there. But as the decades passed, the branch of the Hart family that remained Jewish moved to Montreal and the Alexander Street cemetery fell into disuse for about forty-five years.

More Jews were arriving from Europe. To accommodate these new arrivals the Montreal Jewish community formed the Congregation of English, German and Polish Jews in 1846. It was Ashkenazi, perhaps the first such synagogue in British North America. At first they worshipped in rented quarters. In 1858 the Congregation built the Shaar Hashomayim Synagogue, on St. Constant (now de Bullion) Street; it was dedicated in July 1859.

The St. Janvier Street Cemetery was still the burial site for the Jewish community. However, Montreal's overall population was growing and the built-up area was beginning to surround the cemetery.

In the 1850s, the city was in the midst of a cholera epidemic. In 1853 the authorities placed a ban on burials within city limits. The Jewish community needed a new burial place, and a committee of its members was struck to explore possible new locations.

A year later, the community purchased land from the heirs of a Dr.

McCulloch. It was situated on the north-eastern slope of Mount Royal, beside the Protestant community's Mount Royal Cemetery that had been established there in 1847.

In 1858, the St. Janvier Street Cemetery was closed. Lazarus David's remains and tombstone were removed to the present Spanish & Portuguese Cemetery on Mount Royal. His is probably the oldest existing Jewish grave in Canada.

On November 21, 1858, the Congregation of German and Polish Jews asked whether the Spanish & Portuguese Congregation would consent "to the joint and free use of the burying ground by both congregations." The Spanish & Portuguese Congregation resisted, but it was having trouble paying the bills for the new cemetery land and the McCulloch estate was suing for non-payment of interest on the purchase. The compromise was that the Spanish & Portuguese offered to sell half of the ground to the new congregation. "Members thought it better to operate separate cemeteries than to try to combine, given the different forms of prayer and other customs," explained the Shaar Hashomayim's long-time rabbi, Wilfred Shuchat.

On September 11, 1859, the German and Polish Congregation bought, from the McCulloch widow, a sixty- by one-hundred-and-seventeen-foot plot of ground adjacent to the Spanish & Portuguese cemetery. Although the congregation's financial situation was precarious, the purchase was completed in November 1863.

About ten years after refusing to allow any more burials at the St. Janvier Street cemetery, the City of Montreal decided to expropriate the land for development. In May 1863, a city clerk asked if the Spanish & Portuguese Congregation would sell the old burying ground. This would mean that remains would have to be disinterred and moved to the new site. The cemetery trustees asked the city for $1,000 for the lot and for an additional five hundred dollars to remove the bodies, monuments, and tombstones. It is not clear whether these amounts were accepted by the city, but it is known that the city paid the congregation when the land expropriation was effected.

An 1864 document details the arrangements "to remove the whole of the Bodies Separately (and furnish new coffins where necessary) from the old Jewish cemetery in Montreal" to the new Spanish & Portuguese Jewish cemetery on Mount Royal, "and re-inter them separately under the superintendent of the Spanish & Portuguese congregation for the sum of one dollar fifty cents each." The city contracted with Richard Spriggins, superintendent of the Mount Royal Cemetery, to transfer the remains.

The congregation of German and Polish Jews formally notified the Spanish & Portuguese Congregation that it considered itself entitled to part of the compensation for its members and members' families who had been buried in the old St. Janvier Cemetery. The Ashkenazi wished the remains to be reburied in their own section of the cemetery on Mount Royal, not in the Spanish & Portuguese cemetery.

The Spanish & Portuguese responded that while all Jews had had the right to be buried in the old cemetery, they had not had the right to buy or sell graves. Furthermore, the deed transferring the St. Janvier Cemetery from David David to the Spanish & Portuguese congregation stipulated that, were something to happen to the donated plot of land, the proceeds should revert to the congregation. This led to a debate about who was or was not a member of the Spanish & Portuguese or German and Polish congregations.

The German and Polish Congregation argued that the city should not recognize the right of the Spanish & Portuguese Congregation to negotiate the purchase of the burying ground or the removal of remains, since the cemetery had been set apart "not for any particular denomination of persons professing the Jewish religion, but as a place of burial indiscriminately of all individuals professing the Jewish faith."

The dispute went to court. On August 24, 1868, the German and Polish Congregation won its case. The issue received mainstream press coverage, embarrassing the tiny Jewish community.

Finally, the bodies of all five hundred or so Jews buried at the St. Janvier Street Cemetery—most of them members of the Spanish & Portuguese— were removed at the cost of a dollar fifty each and, in a spirit of compromise, buried at the boundary between the two cemeteries on Mount Royal.

In the 1860s the port of Montreal witnessed a steady flow of Jewish immigrants from Eastern Europe, many of them destitute and in need of help to get established in their new land. To address their needs, at the invitation of the community's leaders, on July 23, 1863, the unmarried male members of the Jewish community met in a room above a Great St. James Street storefront to consider forming an association to assist the new arrivals. Organizers reasoned that the Society should be led by young unmarried men in part to encourage their interest in communal work, and in part because it would relieve married members of the community from the heavy responsibilities involved in helping the newcomers. The men unanimously voted in favour of a motion that proposed the formation of the Young Men's Hebrew Benevolent Society. It was the community's first organized social service, and would assume an important role in assuring proper Jewish burial for the people it served.

However, it got off to a slow start. At its annual meeting in July 1867, four years after its creation, and at the dawn of Canadian Confederation, the Young Men's Hebrew Benevolent Society's treasurer reported a balance of only twenty-nine cents. In 1869, with the Society's treasurer now owed fifty-two dollars, the merits of a bachelors-only society were re-examined. The bylaws were changed to admit "married co-religionists." The Young Men's Hebrew Benevolent Society was incorporated in 1870.

The arrival of indigent Jews in the 1870s put a serious strain on the resources of the Society. The minutes of an 1874 meeting of the Society reported that totally destitute families were arriving from Lithuania, Poland, and Germany. It pleaded with Jewish organizations in London to stop sending Eastern European Jews. To help feed, clothe, and house the newcomers, the Society asked for help from the Russian-Jewish Relief Committee in London and the Alliance Israelite Universelle in Paris. Non-Jewish organizations like the Montreal City and District Savings Bank also contributed to the effort to help the newly arrived establish themselves. Outside donations and the sale of five-dollar memberships—a princely sum at the time—helped the Society look after the needy among the Jewish population of Montreal, which now included just over five hundred people.

The Ladies' Auxiliary of the Young Men's Hebrew Benevolent Society was formed in 1877.

While the needs of the living remained a priority for the Young Men's Hebrew Benevolent Society, they did not neglect people who died without synagogue affiliations and whose families did not have the means to provide burials. Some immigrants had already organized themselves into non-profit societies that would ensure their future burial costs, but caring for the needs of other deceased poor was a responsibility accepted by the Society.

Operation of the Society was in the hands of the leaders of the three major congregations—the Shearith Israel, the Shaar Hashomayim, and

Temple Emanu-El—and on April 28, 1889, Harris Vineberg, president of the Young Men's Hebrew Benevolent Society, convened a meeting "for the purpose of consulting with presidents and ministers of the different synagogues and congregations as to what steps should be taken for the burial of the dead poor, it having come to the notice of this society of the great distress existing in cases of this nature."

Minutes from the meeting note that Reverend Meldola de Sola said the Spanish & Portuguese Congregation was willing to accept burial of the "country poor" in rotation. And if only the poor would attend his synagogue it would have no objection to burying them free, he said.

At a second meeting convened later in 1889, Temple Emanu-El also agreed to give free burial to the dead poor, as long as the different congregations took turns. Its suggestion was approved unanimously. The oldest established synagogue—the Spanish &Portuguese, would go first, fol-lowed by the German and Polish Congregation and Temple Emanu-El.

While the congregations assumed the burden for a while, the costs bore heavily on them. At a board meeting late in 1889, the Benevolent Society concluded that the system of burial by rotation had ended in failure. The Society moved to secure land of its own.

The situation in Montreal intensified when serious persecution of Jews began in Russia after Czar Alexander III acceded to the throne in 1881. Pogroms and other anti-Semitic outbreaks followed in Eastern Europe. To escape the violence and find new opportunities, a wave of Russian, Romanian, Galician, and other Jewish immigrants came to North America. The Montreal community prepared to accept all the Jews who found their way to Canada via various European immigration committees.

By 1890, more Jewish refugees were arriving in Montreal than New York City. (Apparently many of the immigrants to Montreal were not aware that the part of "Amerike" in which they were disembarking was a different country from the United States.) Montreal's Jewish population topped six thousand five hundred in 1890, an almost twelve-fold increase in twenty years. The new arrivals were mostly poor, and challenged the established community's capacity to help. Money was desperately needed. Members of the community met, and decided to write to the great European Jewish philanthropist Baron Maurice de Hirsch and request his assistance.

The Young Men's Hebrew Benevolent Society wrote to the Baron on

May 20, 1890, reminding him that he had endowed co-religionists of the United States with a generous sum to help distressed immigrants. They said that the Young Men's Hebrew Benevolent Society of Montreal operated separately and distinctly from any Societies existing in the U.S. They informed him that, given its direct link by steamer to Liverpool, London, Hamburg, Le Havre, and other European ports, Montreal (total population then two hundred and twenty-five thousand), was receiving the great majority of immigrants, who could then disperse throughout the continent.

Because laws in the United States "prohibited the Steamship Companies from landing pauper immigrants, many of this class are sent by the Agents of the Steamship Lines in European cities to Canada," the letter explained. The steamship companies thereby avoided having to carry them back to Europe at their own expense, which they would have been obliged to do by the U.S. The result was a great influx of arrivals every spring. "These immigrants are all thrown upon our community, who have to furnish them with means, either to make a living here, or to join their friends" in the U.S.

The Society's letter explained that its membership of one hundred and fifty included the "leading Hebrews" of Montreal, "who have taken a warm active interest in helping their destitute brethren." But due to the influx of Russian and other immigrants, they said, "we regret to state that our work has been cramped for want of funds."

The Jewish community, mainly Russian and Romanian refugees, were gaining their livelihood with much difficulty, since few were tradesmen, the letter continued. What's more, "there exists a heavy restrictive tax on what is known as Pedlars; we must however remark that they notwithstanding conduct themselves very well, as it is indeed a rare spectacle to find one of our faith in prisons or jails; the Jews in good circumstances however are very few, and as all calls fall upon the same shoulders, these few are naturally heavily taxed."

With the goal "of elevating the moral culture of our less fortunate Co-religionists, so as to become good and loyal citizens of the Country of their adoption," the Society, with Quebec government aid, had succeeded in opening a night school for the poor of both sexes, attended by over two hundred during the winter season. But more help was needed to establish a home for immigrants until they could find work, to help them learn trades, to establish a free English-language day school during the day and a night school for those who worked, to help the unemployed, and to aid those who wished to take up farming, by providing them with government land grants and the necessary tools.

The letter concluded:

> Should this appeal find favour with you, esteemed sir, and if you consider that the foregoing objects are worthy of your universally recognized philanthropic works, we beg to refer you to the following gentlemen, who have been good enough to append their names, as vouching for the truth of our situation and statements.
>
> Awaiting the favour of your kind consideration and decision, we beg to subscribe ourselves,
>
> On behalf of the Society,
> Harris Vineberg, President
> Arthur D. Moss, Secretary (and several others)

The Baron responded within three weeks with a cheque for the then immense sum of $20,000 for a Jewish school and a house of refuge. He promised more if needed. After much discussion the members decided that the Society should name its school and refuge in recognition of the Baron's generosity. And so, the Baron de Hirsch Institute was formed. A store on St. Elizabeth Street (near what is now St. Antoine Street) was bought, renovated, and dedicated as the Institute in 1891. It included a free day school for orphans "for the purpose of educating the poor children of the Jewish faith," and a home for immigrants and orphans.

Born in Munich, Germany in 1831, Baron Maurice de Hirsch was a member of a distinguished family of landowners and bankers. His grandfather, Jacob von Hirsch, was among the first Jews who were permitted to own land in Bavaria. His father, a banker with the Bavarian court, was made a Baron in 1869. Maurice de Hirsch, who inherited a considerable fortune from both, studied in Jewish schools in Munich and Brussels.

He showed little interest in academic work, took part in several business ventures while still in his teens, and became a clerk in the banking house Bischoffsheim and Goldschmid. When he was twenty-four he married Clara Bischoffsheim, the eldest daughter of the firm's senior partner, Senator Bischoffsheim of Brussels.

Maurice de Hirsch branched out into copper and sugar. He eventually established his own bank in Belgium. His father had been chief builder of the Bavarian Ostbahn, and Maurice shared his father's interest in railway ventures. He financed and constructed railways in Austria, the Balkans and Russia. Although his banker colleagues were sceptical, he secured a concession from the Turkish government for the building of a major railway connecting Turkey with Germany.

He was widely considered one of the captains of industry and finance in Europe. Before he was forty, Baron de Hirsch was one of the wealthiest men in the world. He began to interest himself in helping Jews in distress, particularly those in Russia, and philanthropic work became his main preoccupation. When the Baron's son Lucien died in 1887, he declared "my son I may have lost, but not my heir; humanity is my heir."

In 1891, the Baron's attention was drawn to the wave of Jewish immigration to North America that was caused by the oppressive laws of Russia. He first attempted to improve the lot of Jews in that country by offering the government money to provide a system of secular education to Jews located in the Pale of Settlement. Although the Russian government was willing to accept the Baron's money, it declined to allow him to be involved in its administration.

The Baron developed an emigration scheme that would help Jews who were being persecuted to resettle in agricultural colonies. He established and funded the Jewish Colonization Association in London. which sponsored the resettlement of Eastern Europe's Jewish poor to land in North and South America which he had bought for this purpose. Its charter stated that the Association was "to assist the emigration of Jews from any part of Europe or Asia, principally from countries in which they may for the time being be subjected to any special taxes or political or other disabilities, to any other parts of the world, and to form and establish colonies in various parts of North and South America and other countries for agricultural, commercial and other purposes."

In a publication called *Forum*, the Baron wrote in 1891: "My efforts shall show that the Jews have not lost the agricultural qualities that their forefathers possessed. I shall try to make for them a new home in different lands, where as free farmers, on their own soil, they can make themselves useful to the country."

In 1891, a delegation from the Montreal Baron de Hirsch Institute went to meet him. They asked him to underwrite Jewish settlements in Canada. He proposed that the Baron de Hirsch Institute form a Jewish agricultural colony in Canada, as a relief measure. The Dominion government was in sympathy and granted tracts of land. For years, the Institute was responsible for channelling immigrants westward, and maintaining the Hirsch settlements that formed in Saskatchewan, Manitoba, and Alberta, as well as Ste-Sophie, Quebec, north of Montreal.

Although the Baron was in agreement with Dr. Theodore Herzl, the father of Zionism, that Jews should establish a country of their own, he did not join Dr. Herzl in his plan. The Baron considered the selection of Palestine as the Jewish homeland ill advised "because of the big sea of Arab population" there and in surrounding countries, which he believed would bring about the failure of any Jewish settlement in what is now Israel.

It is estimated that Baron de Hirsch donated about $100 million to philanthropic and charitable activities, an amount that would number in the billions of dollars today. He expressed his view on philanthropy: "It is my utmost conviction that I must consider myself as only the temporary administrator of the wealth I have amassed, and that it is my duty to contribute in my way to the relief of the suffering of those who are pressed by fate."

Baron de Hirsch died in Hungary in 1896.

The financial burden related to the purchase of the new cemeteries on the mountain and disinterment of bodies from the old cemetery weighed heavily on the city's Jewish community for years. The Spanish & Portuguese Congregation wrote to its counterpart in London, seeking a four hundred pound-sterling loan. It explained that the removal of about five hundred bodies from the St. Janvier Street Cemetery, together with tombstones and monuments, had entailed an additional debt to the congre-gation of some $3,000.

A third synagogue was formed in Montreal in 1882, when newcomers founded the Temple Emanu-El (Reform) Congregation of Montreal. Temple Emanu-El purchased land in 1893 on the Back River Road for a cemetery which became known as the Sault aux Récollets or Back River Cemetery. (The site is adjacent to the Sauvé Métro station.) However,

A Bust of the Baron

In 1940, Herbert Levine, chairman of the Joint Cemetery Committee, found that a bust of the Baron de Hirsch (which was probably once on display in the Baron de Hirsch Institute building) was available and suggested it be erected on a pedestal at the entrance gates of the Baron de Hirsch Cemetery. The Committee approved, but not before getting the opinion of Rabbi Hirsch Cohen as to whether this would be against Jewish tradition and practice. It was acceptable, said the Rabbi, and the monument was unveiled September 12, 1941 before leaders of the Jewish community. The bronze bust was mounted on a brown granite column seven feet high and bears the simple inscription: "Baron de Hirsch, December 9, 1831—April 21, 1896."

As newspaper accounts of the event described it, Max Finestone, president of the Baron de Hirsch Institute, presided at the ceremony and Levine unveiled the monument. Lawyer Lazarus Phillips represented the Jewish Colonization Association, and others present included Harris Vineberg, the man who had written the Baron decades earlier seeking funding to assist Montreal's Jewish poor. A prayer was recited by Cantor Efraim Schlepack of the Beth David Synagogue (now Tifereth Beth David Jerusalem).

Finestone said the monument would be "an everlasting memorial to a great Jew and a great humanitarian." The Baron, he said, "moved among the great ones of the earth; kings, emperors, and ministers were his friends; his enterprises were enormous and his powers vast; but his heart was with the little people, the oppressed and the disinherited, and his whole life is a record of his care for those whose lives needed to be rebuilt."

The monument to the Baron can be seen outside the entrance to the Baron de Hirsch Cemetery offices.

because the site turned out to be poorly drained, and as it was too far from the city centre, in the early 1890s the congregation purchased land adjacent to the cemeteries of the Spanish &Portuguese and Shaar Hashomayim congregations on Mount Royal.

The trustees of Temple Emanu-El agreed to give a portion of its Back River land to the Baron de Hirsch Institute. Since the Young Men's Hebrew Benevolent Society "was meeting with great difficulty in securing the necessary burial space for the dead poor, it was resolved that our burying grounds at Back River be offered to the Society for a nominal sum of one hundred dollars—that is, the part fenced in—on condition that the Society secures the transfers of those persons who have acquired lots therein and undertakes to keep the ground in proper condition," read the minutes of a Temple Emanu-El board meeting of September 1892.

The Society's annual report of 1892 counts twenty-six Jews who were buried at Society expense with the women of the Society supplying shrouds and other assistance. The annual report also mentions that, to improve the lives of the living, the Society's board discussed the desirability of forming visiting committees "to inculcate habits of cleanliness, thrift and self-support amongst the poor of the community," and of a reading room, "where the hardworking men and boys could spend their leisure hours in literary occupation and self-improvement."

Problems arose at the Back River Cemetery. The Society's Burial Committee chairman Hiram Levy reported at the Society's 1893 annual meeting that while the land set aside for burial of the dead poor had been measured off, there was no money available "to make any distinctive divisions or to place the grounds in that condition in which your committee would like to see them." The committee also called upon the cemetery to be placed in a proper state as soon as there were funds available. That year, the Burial Committee had a budget of $89.75. Three years earlier, the Society had spent $54 on burial of poor persons.

The Young Men's Hebrew Benevolent Society's responsibility for burial of the Jewish poor was formally entrenched in its 1896 constitution: "The Burial Committee shall have charge of the Burial Ground of the Society, see that it is put and kept in proper order, and supervise the burial of the dead poor of the Hebrew religion in the City of Montreal. They may, if they see fit, grant permission for the interment of the dead Hebrew poor of neighbouring towns. They shall keep a register in which they shall record the names, age, sex, and latest residence of the deceased, and the number of the grave in which the body has been buried."

In 1899, nearly three thousand Jewish immigrants, mostly from Romania, arrived in Montreal. Twenty-four people were buried by the Society that year; eighteen were children, including four new arrivals.

In its 1899 annual report the Young Men's Hebrew Benevolent Society warned, "There is now little room left for the burial of our dead poor, and if this part of the Society's work is to be continued, steps must immediately be taken to acquire additional grounds for the purpose." Expenditures for burials increased that year to $142.50 (burial for adults cost $57.00, and for children, $85.50)—an amount that was outstripped by the Relief Committee's expenditure on Passover matzoth ($147.75).

When Clara de Hirsch died in Paris in 1899, three years after her husband, she left a bequest of six hundred thousand francs (about $89,000) to the Young Men's Hebrew Benevolent Society of Montreal. In appreciation, the Society officially changed its name to the Baron de Hirsch Institute and Hebrew Benevolent Society of Montreal.

It was typical of the era that her name was not included in the title. The short shrift given to Baroness Clara de Hirsch is all the more striking when one reads her biography, which states that "the uninfluenced Baron de Hirsch, cosmopolitan as he was, might have devoted his fortune to totally different purposes, but in philanthropic matters he yielded to his wife's judgment and she would not permit money of which the poor persecuted and oppressed Jews stood in so much need to be deflected into alien channels. She determined that her husband should turn his restless energies to relieving the distress of his co-religionists."

Feathers were ruffled in Montreal in 1900 when a memorial service was held for the Baroness de Hirsch. It turned out that the Reform rabbi had been excluded from participation in the service. That prompted an upset Harris Vineberg to write to Montreal's English-language paper the *Jewish Times* (Canada's first continuing Jewish publication): "I have always contended that the intolerance from within is more injurious to the cause of pure Judaism than even the worst manifestation of anti-Semitism."

In 1899, a situation in which the remains of two Jews were exhumed and moved to a Christian cemetery, rocked the Jewish community. Dame A. Wetzlar (first name unavailable) was the only child of Sarah Wetzlar and

Daniel Noe Wetzlar, members of the Spanish & Portuguese Synagogue. They had been buried in its cemetery in the early 1890s. Wetzlar had married a non-Jew named R.P. McLea and converted to Christianity. She petitioned Quebec Superior Court to allow her parents' bodies to be transferred from the Jewish cemetery to the Protestant Mount Royal Cemetery, so that they could be brought to her family vault. The court granted the request in 1899.

The general Jewish community only knew of the incident after the court judgement was published in *The Gazette*. "Nothing ever occurred in the Jewish community of Montreal which made a more profound and painful impression than this incident," thundered the *Jewish Times*, demanding action be taken against "those who permitted this desecration of the dead without a protest."

The fact the Wetzlars had lived, died, and been buried as members of the Shearith Israel Congregation provided more than sufficient proof that they should be buried as Jews, among Jews, in a Jewish cemetery, the newspaper wrote. They most certainly believed that any attempt to disturb their bodies and move them from what should have been their final resting place "would be repelled with all possible energy." But this was not to be their lot.

Why, asked the newspaper, did the synagogue not do its duty and raise a stink? "We can imagine what a storm would be raised if the daughter of Protestant parents sought an order from a judge to remove their bodies from a Protestant to a Roman Catholic cemetery. Hebrew law forbids removal from even one part of the same burial ground to another. Such a thing as the removal of Jewish dead to a Christian cemetery was never contemplated by the Rabbis who laid down the law concerning disposal of the dead." The newspaper charged the synagogue's rabbi, Reverend Meldola de Sola, with extraordinary neglect of duty to the Jewish community and questioned how any congregation could be guaranteed a Jewish burial in the face of such indifference to solemn obligations.

The "painful scandal" would forever be remembered with grief and shame, the newspaper predicted, not just for the court judgement but also because of the community's neglect in allowing it to happen.

The only bright spot in the whole affair was that the Young Men's Hebrew Benevolent Society took up the newspaper's suggestion to strike a committee to look into the questions involved and, if necessary, secure legislation to prevent a future "desecration of the dead and an outrage on religious feelings of the living."

The Spanish & Portuguese Synagogue fought back against the *Jewish Times*, saying it was not just removal of the dead that was forbidden by Jewish law, but also the spreading of a false report. The newspaper "cast a most unjust reflection upon our congregation and its respected minister," wrote J.L. Samuel, secretary of the Spanish & Portuguese. He had "solemnly protested" against the daughter's actions. But the synagogue board had obtained legal advice that there was no clause in its bylaws prohibiting such a removal of bodies and that Mrs. McLea had a right in civil law to remove her parents' remains.

To prevent a recurrence, a new clause was inserted in the contract that grave purchasers had to sign. The clause prohibited the removal of bodies in the future. "Such a thing was never contemplated by those who framed the By-Laws of our congregation."

Eventually it was revealed that one of the reasons the daughter wanted her parents' bodies moved was the poor condition of the cemetery. Although Mrs. McLea was told a new man had been hired to keep the cemetery "in a thoroughly satisfactory condition," this did not satisfy her, Samuel reported.

"We are more than ever confirmed in the correctness of our attitude," replied the *Jewish Times*. "The conduct of those responsible for the proper care of the cemetery appears all the more reprehensible as we are informed Mrs. McLea has been urging for the last four years or five years that the cemetery be kept in a proper condition. Upon ordinary circumstances the duty of showing respect to the dead by seeing that their last resting place is kept in decent order … devolves upon the congregation to which the cemetery belongs."

There was soon no more room for the poor in the Back River. The 1900 charter of the Baron de Hirsch Institute empowered it to "grant relief to sick and indigent persons of the Hebrew faith, to establish a home or refuge for the distressed, aged and orphans of the said faith, to provide a burial ground for the interment of their dead poor, to conduct schools for general instruction and manual training of the needy of said faith."

The Burial Committee warned in its 1900 annual report, "The condition of the ground is such that the space originally acquired has been nearly all occupied and it is now incumbent upon the Society to make some provision for the future." The following year, the Society reported its Back River "burial accommodation" had become exhausted, making it "absolutely necessary" that new space be acquired.

Although the Society's Burial Committee secured an additional plot of land in the Back River Cemetery that year, this was only a stopgap measure: "The large annual increase in the population, with its usual proportion of poor, will make it necessary to acquire still further land in the near future," warned the annual report.

At the beginning of the twentieth century, the Baron de Hirsch Institute was the hub of Jewish philanthropic and social activity in Montreal and one of the city's most important sites for immigrants. As journalist Israel Medres revealed in Montreal's Yiddish daily newspaper, the *Keneder Adler*, many of the newcomers had been under the impression that poor Jews were only to be found in the old country, something they would soon find was certainly not the case.

Once they saw the Baron's name on the Institute building, some believed it belonged to the Baron himself, as they had been familiar with his name in Europe. But the more established immigrants would tell the newcomers that a small group of Montreal Jews, having heard how the Baron had helped settle Jews on agricultural lands, had sought his assistance. Immigrants who frequented the reading room at the Baron de Hirsch Institute (forerunner of Montreal's Jewish Public Library), admired Harris Vineberg because he had chaired the group, but not all immigrants shared that admiration. To those who didn't attend the Institute, he was known only as a clothing manufacturer and therefore "personified capitalist exploitation," Medres wrote. "It was known that in Vineberg's shop the workers, all of them Jewish, worked long hours while the union waged a constant battle against him."

The night school at the Institute was one of the most important destinations for Jewish newcomers, who could apply themselves zealously to the study of English. The younger people had an additional motivation for attending the night school: it was a great place to meet young immigrants of the opposite gender who were also learning English.

In the summer of 1901, a notice appeared in a Trois-Rivières newspaper that the city had applied to Superior Court for permission to expropriate

The Baron de Hirsch Institute, Bleury Street, circa 1924.
A donation from the late Baroness de Hirsch allowed the Institute to move
from its original St. Elizabeth Street location. On June 3, 1901, the laying
of the cornerstone of the new building was presided over by the
mayor of Montreal "in the presence of a large gathering of citizens
of all creeds and nationalities."
[*The Jew in Canada*, 1926]

the Alexander Street Jewish Cemetery "for sanitary reasons", and to remove all of its graves. Unless there was an objection in the next fifteen days, the petition would be granted. Immediately after he received the news, Hart family descendant Louis A. Hart of Montreal hired a lawyer to fight the application. Investigation revealed that the "sanitary reasons" were a sham. The owner of the adjoining property wished to buy the Jewish cemetery and the action to expropriate was taken to enable transfer of the property to this would-be purchaser. Now Catholic, the descendants of the early Harts left in Trois-Rivières felt no particular attachment to the Jewish burial ground.

The court gave the expropriation permit. The *Jewish Times* took up the issue. "Everybody knows with what commanding fervour the Roman Catholic authorities in this province insist on the 'sacred rite of Christian burial,' and with what supreme indifference they dispose of their graveyards after such are filled up with the dead," noted the paper. "We have seen cemeteries in this city turned over to secular uses, the coffins, bones, cerements dug up, thrown into carts like so much garbage, and dumped among the refuse ... Is it to be expected that a Jewish cemetery will receive more consideration from those people than their own cemeteries have been given?"

Unfortunately, the concerns proved justified. The land was sold to the owner of the adjoining property. The *Jewish Times* was revolted. The individual "guilty of the crime, for it was nothing else, of selling the land sacred as the last resting place of the pioneers of Judaism in Canada, deserves all the reprobation as well as all the legal penalties that can be inflicted on him."

When the challenge to the expropriation had arisen, the owner of the adjoining property had offered to have the bodies removed with "all the rites of the Hebrew religion," and to have the remains reburied on con-secrated land by a minister of the Hebrew faith. But the disinterments took place and the tombstones were moved without the presence of a rabbi to ensure that Jewish ritual was followed. Only one member of the Hart family, a non-Jew, was present and the bodies were buried in an "unconsecrated field."

The news aroused serious disapproval in Montreal's Jewish community. The leaders of the Spanish & Portuguese Congregation convened a meeting with other congregations to determine what action was possible.

Angry delegates asked whether the Superior Court would have allowed this to happen had it been a Christian cemetery. They questioned Trois-Rivières' right to expropriate the land and the right of any member of the Hart family to give or sell land that had been left as a cemetery for all the Jews of the province. And there was outrage that no Jewish ritual or supervision had accompanied the removal of the remains. Had the parties who removed the bodies called in a rabbi to disinter the bodies, consecrate the new ground, and supervise the reburial, the Jewish community would not have been so horrified or felt the need to protest to the same extent. All were aware that the action was irreversible. At the same time, concern mounted that the desecration could be repeated at the remaining Jewish burial ground in Trois-Rivières should the legal owners decide to dispose of that cemetery as well.

Reverend Meldola de Sola—who became the first minister of Canadian birth when he succeeded his father as spiritual leader of the Spanish & Portuguese Congregation—addressed the Trois-Rivières cemetery matter in a sermon on November 2, 1901. He urged Montreal's Jewish community to take vigorous action against those responsible for the "vandalism" involved in moving and dumping the Jewish dead without any guarantee that their bones would be permitted to remain for any length of time in their new quarters.

He recalled that the Jewish cemetery had existed for nearly one hundred years. It was a gift made by one of the first Jewish families, to the Jewish community of Quebec. But "it appears that a descendant of one of the original owners of the cemetery assumed that the land was his own personal property and sold it to the individual who had instigated the expropriation proceedings." Because of "this extraordinary and most high-handed action" the bodies interred in the old cemetery were moved. He continued:

> Not only has the course pursued by these people been outrageous, but a very dangerous precedent will have been established if this sacrilege be permitted to pass unchallenged. As the matter now stands, the owner of the land in which the bodies have been buried may, if he feels so disposed, at any time dump into a ditch the remains of the men who first unfurled the banner of Judaism in this country, or burn them as the old coffin boards were burned on the site of

Dominion Square four decades ago. We have often spoken of the service rendered by the fathers of our community, and have dwelt upon our debt of gratitude to them. Today their remains have not as much as an assured resting place ...

If the Jewish community of Montreal has any true zeal for the cause of Israel's faith, if it is not devoid of all nobility of sentiment, it will not allow such an outrage upon all that it should hold most sacred to pass with impunity.

He recalled to the community its duty to ensure that the final resting place of its deceased members should be respected in perpetuity. "I do not believe the fiercest persecution of our people in Russia or Romania has ever been blackened by anything so infamous as this desecration of the graves in the old Jewish cemetery of Three Rivers," he said.

Contrasting with the currents of anti-Semitism in Quebec that underlay the Superior Court decision to allow expropriation of the Jewish cemetery at Trois-Rivières, a year later, on a sunny May 28, 1902, the Baron de Hirsch Institute of Montreal inaugurated its brand-new Egyptian-style quarters at 250 Bleury Street with a gala celebration.

Invitations to the event were much in demand. The Governor General of Canada, Lord Minto, was present, along with Quebec Premier Napoléon Parent and other provincial and federal politicians. Also present were Montreal Mayor James Cochrane, the principal of McGill University, the French consul, and the *crème de la crème* of Montreal society.

Alas, no one seemed to have noticed that missing on the invitation list were those whom the Institute was to serve, the newly arrived Jewish immigrants. The immigrants noticed, however, and, although appreciative of the efforts of established Jews on their behalf, following the ceremony a small group met with the leaders of the Baron de Hirsch Institute. The immigrants would no longer merely accept being treated as "objects of philanthropy", but wanted a role in the Jewish community's decision-making bodies. There was a serious gap between the uptown Jewish establish-ment and the downtown newcomers.

The Institute continued to provide burial for indigent members of the growing community. Its next annual meeting took place a few months after the gala opening, in October 1902. The Board of Directors was instructed by the membership to find a burial ground "suitable for the purpose of the Society for some years to come, in view of the increasing population." The Board struck a Burial Committee, mandated to report its findings at a special meeting.

People in desperate need of clothing, food, homes, jobs, and eventually burial, were landing in Montreal by thousands. In 1903, the Jewish population of Montreal and suburbs reached 6,876, comprised mostly of poor, Yiddish-speaking immigrants. That year, the city greeted 1,854 Romanian Jews, 729 Russian Jews, and 265 Jews from other nations. "Every incoming vessel from Europe brought its quota of immigrants—from Romania, Russia, Galicia, etc. to find a new home in Canada," the Institute's 1903 annual report noted. "Others came from London where they had resided for three or four years before leaving for Montreal in search of regular employment and better wages."

The annual report went on to say, however, "that the assertion that a large number of immigrants who arrive here are paupers and that Canada is being used as a dumping ground for the undesirables of European countries, cannot be justified, as far as the Hebrew immigrant is concerned … It is the persecution to which they are subjected which makes them emigrate to our free and happy country."

At the present death rate, the Institute warned at its 1904 annual meeting, there would not be sufficient land to last another year for burial of the poor.

2

The New Cemetery

*I often feel that death is not the enemy of life, but its friend, for it is the
knowledge that our years are limited which makes them so precious.*
–Joshua Loth Liebman, *Piece of Mind*, 1946

B etween 1902 and 1905, the Burial Committee of the Baron de Hirsch
Institute made repeated efforts to secure ground suitable for a cemetery.
A potential solution arrived when Life Governor Mr. S. Roman
donated a 130 by 112-foot plot of land in Longueuil on the South Shore of
Montreal, as the 1904 annual report relates. But the Longueuil authorities
raised objections to its being used as a cemetery—and the hunt resumed.
The Longueuil land-holding was appraised at two hundred dollars in 1907,
the Institute reported at its annual meeting that year. At an October 29,
1914 meeting, a committee appointed to ascertain the value of the land
found "it would be worth 25 cents a foot in a year or two" and advised the
Institute to hold onto it. The Institute continued to pay taxes on it until
1952 when it was considered to be of no value whatsoever, as surrounding
property was owned by the Crown. It was given to Longueuil as a gift.

But finally the Committee's efforts bore fruit. They had found land
on the island of Montreal. At a July 26, 1905 Board meeting the Committee
advised of the purchase of "a piece of ground at Côte des Neiges about
eight miles from the Post Office and fronting on a road accessible at all
times of the year." This piece of land was well situated and accessible by
public transit, it argued. "The Park & Island Railway line to Cartierville
runs at a short distance from this ground, and there is rumour of another
line being constructed in the immediate vicinity. Arrangements for the
right of way, if necessary, from such car lines will be a matter of adjustment.
The Board of Health of the Province have examined this piece of land,
have found the same suitable, and have given their official consent as

required by law, to its being used as a cemetery."

Unfortunately, as was noted at that Board meeting, the owners had not initially seemed anxious to sell their ground for use as a cemetery, and they refused a sale of anything less than thirty arpents. (In later years, the land area would be described as thirty acres, although acres are slightly smaller than arpents.) This was a considerably greater area than the Institute felt it required. Fortunately, a number of newly-formed Jewish congregations and burial societies expressed interest in buying twenty-three of the thirty arpents, which would leave the Society seven arpents for its own use. The ground was purchased at $250 per arpent, for a total price of $7,500. For legal reasons, the Institute had to buy all the land in its own name. It obtained a temporary loan to pay for it and then recouped much of the cost from sales to the various congregations and societies.

At its August 6, 1905 meeting, the Board was informed of the approval to purchase a "certain piece of land comprising about 30 arpents, forming part of Lot No. 94 of the incorporated village of Côte des Neiges in the County of Hochelaga, as shown on the plan made by J.P.B. Casgrain, sworn land surveyor, dated 13th July 1905."

At the Institute's fall 1905 annual meeting, the Burial Committee "regret(ted) extremely to report" a large increase in burials—nineteen adults and fifty-three children. "It may of course be anticipated that with ... the increased population there must be an increased number of dead poor. Provision has to be made to supply ground for the burial of new arrivals and the children of immigrants," the Committee explained.

The Back River Cemetery was full, so every effort was being made to prepare the newly-acquired land in what was then called Côte des Neiges West. Money had to be spent on fencing, levelling, and arranging the land in accordance with Quebec government requirements. Attendees at the 1905 annual meeting learned that advice on how to do all this was sought from the superintendent of the Mount Royal Protestant Cemetery. Donations were requested to carry out the work, and to provide a house for a custodian, "with proper accommodation for the proper conduct of the rituals of our faith."

While the 1902 opening of the Baron de Hirsch Institute's new Bleury Street home had been greeted with much fanfare and visits from official-dom, the opening of the Cemetery three years later was met with silence. There is nary a record of any ceremonies for its opening. It may be that the land was available for burials even before the purchase was finalized. One mysterious tombstone in Baron de Hirsch #1, one of the oldest sections of the Cemetery, is dated December 7, 1904, eight months before the land was bought. Sheindel Shneider, "the wife of Rabbi M. Shneider, the daughter of Leibush," was only twenty-two when she died in the month of Kislev of that year. It is not known how her tombstone got there, nor is it listed in the Cemetery's handwritten ledger of burials.

Still, the choice of the Côte des Neiges site proved to be a brilliant one. Although the buyer of the St. Janvier site 127 years earlier had erred in failing to predict that the city would ever move as far north as Dorchester Square, the Baron de Hirsch Institute made a much better choice. Whether it was by fluke or prescience, the purchase of the land for the new cemetery predated the shift of Montreal's Jewish population north-westward by generations.

The mutual benefit and burial societies that participated with the Baron de Hirsch Institute in purchasing the new cemetery were a feature of North American Jewish life. Many Eastern European Jewish immigrants to North America in the late nineteenth and early twentieth centuries formed *landsmanshaften,* mutual aid societies of immigrants from the same European hometown. These and other mutual benefit societies provided services akin to medicare, unemployment insurance, and welfare, long before today's government social safety net was in place. They also provided a social network for lonely immigrants arriving in a new land at a time when there were no social workers to meet them at the docks, and when there was little help available for finding lodgings or work.

The societies collaborated with the synagogues to help members obtain burial plots. To many new immigrants, having a Jewish burial was viewed as the most important function of these groups. As American author Irving Howe once put it, "The necessities of life might force a Jew to spend his days among strangers, but even if no longer Orthodox, he wanted to spend eternity among Jews." The societies were also fulfilling the halachic religious command that a person should prepare for his death during his lifetime, noted Gerald Silverberg, the former general manager of the Baron de Hirsch Cemetery, in an interview.

Many *landsmanshaften* remained fiercely independent, and others affiliated with broader organizations such as the Russian Polish Hebrew

Sick Benefit Association or socialist and labour orders such as the Workmen's Circle.

Joining the societies was easy. One *landsman* would bring in another, according to Israel Medres in the *Keneder Adler*. But since no sick benefit societies had existed in the old country, the concept had to be explained to newcomers. "On this side of the Atlantic," they would say, "a person is alone even if he has relatives. If you fall ill, there is no one to look after you. Here everyone is concerned only with himself." The sick benefit society would provide a doctor, a committee to visit, and weekly sick benefit payments. As recounted in the compilation of translations of Medres's articles, *Montreal of Yesterday: Jewish Life in Montreal 1900-1920*, other compelling reasons to join included the opportunity to meet new friends, the ability for once penniless immigrants to become important people in their societies, and the honour of being referred to as "brother" by the other members.

As Medres related, those who did not belong to a sick benefit society were worthy only of pity. As officers would tell newcomers:

> Such people are lonely and alone, lonely while they live and alone when they die. No one will care when they pass away. However, when a member of the society dies, even in the middle of the night, the secretary is awakened and informed. Even in a storm or blizzard, the secretary can always be reached. The secretary will notify everyone else, whomever should be notified ... Even in thunder and lightning everyone comes to the brother who has died. He is never left by himself. His funeral is arranged, a brotherly funeral.

Medres added that one of the most common topics of any sick benefit society meeting was the cemetery:

> In the course of this discussion the newcomer came to realize that even here, in Montreal, Jews still had to confront the problem of death. He discovered that once in a while the Jewish immigrant would die before he had the opportunity to become financially successful and fully Canadian. A tailor or a cloak-maker died of consumption, which he had contracted while working in a sweatshop. A country pedlar was killed when his horse and wagon were run

Register of Deaths for Hebrew Sick Benefit Association of Montreal.

No. *1*

Name of deceased *Eva Rexel (Braunstein)* Age *43*

Date of deceased's death *February 7th* 190*6*

Place of death —City *Montreal* Country *Hochalago*

Place of birth —City _____ Country _____

His (or her) Father's name _____ of _____

His (or her) Mother's name _____ of _____

How long a resident of this country *one year*

Doctor's name *L D Mignault* Cause of death *Phthisis*

Duration of sickness *9 months* Date of Burial *February 8th* 190*6*

Interred in No. *1* Section *1* Family Lot No. _____

Officiating Minister _____

Witness { _____ Hebrew } _____
{ _____ Date }

No. _____

Name of deceased *Moses Kornberg* Age *1 year 2 ___*

Date of deceased's death *Sept 19* 190*6*

Place of death—City _____ Country _____

Place of birth—City _____ Country _____

His (or her) Father's name _____ of _____

His (or her) Mother's name _____ of _____

How long a resident of this country _____

Doctor's name _____ Cause of death _____

Duration of sickness _____ Date of Burial _____ 19

Interred in No. _____ Section *1* Family Lot No. _____

Officiating Minister _____

Witness { _____ Hebrew } _____
{ _____ Date }

No. *3*

Name of deceased *Leib Hart* Age *22 month*

Date of deceased's death *June 12* 19*06*

Place of death—City *Montreal* Country _____

Place of birth—City *Montreal* Country _____

The first entries in the Hebrew Sick Benefit Association's
Register of Deaths, 1906.

HEBREW SICK BENEFIT ASSOCIATION

SOUVENIR
BROCHURE
OF THEIR

75th JUBILEE BANQUET

IN THE
SPANISH
AND
PORTUGUESE
SYNAGOGUE
MONTREAL

SATURDAY EVENING, DECEMBER 7TH, 1968

At its peak the Hebrew Sick Benefit Association was the largest
society of its kind in Canada.

over by a train at a railway crossing. On another occasion, a bricklayer met his death when he fell off a high wall, his arms full of bricks. These incidents made a profound impression on the immigrant. He was even more keenly aware of the need for the protection of the society although he personally felt far from death and the cemetery. For someone who had recently arrived in this country and about to begin a new life, the idea of the cemetery was the furthest from his mind.

Various benefit societies and congregations have been partners in the Baron de Hirsch Cemetery over the years.

The Hebrew Sick Benefit Association was founded in 1892 by seven Russian immigrants, nearly all of whom worked in the clothing industry. At its peak after the First World War, the "Hebrew Sick" had twelve hundred members, making it the largest society of its kind in Canada.

"Most of the early members were poor, unskilled workers, such as pedlars or factory employees who shared the hardships of making their way in the new world," said its final financial secretary Jacob Rubinson in a 1989 interview in *The Canadian Jewish News*.

When it was incorporated in 1920 by the Quebec Legislature, the Hebrew Sick was described as "a corporation for the purpose of assisting its members in case of sickness, accident, inability to work, reverse of fortune and death, and to grant assistance and aid and confer all other benefits upon the widowers, widows, children, heirs or legatees of all members, including funeral and cemetery benefits."

Applicants to the Hebrew Sick Benefit Association were asked a number of medical questions. Among the questions in 1952 were the following:

Have you ever been obliged to change residence for the benefit of your health? Has any physician given an unfavourable opinion on your life with reference to life insurance, or admission into a society? Have your parents, brothers, sisters been affected with any hereditary disease (tuberculosis, epilepsy, insanity, cancer, etc.)? What are your habits with regard to alcoholic stimulants or narcotics? Are you ruptured? Do you wear a truss?

Questions to be answered by the wife included:

> Did you ever have any Menstrual disorder, Ovarian, Uterine or Breast trouble? Have you ever had any serious complication in labour? Have you ever had any abortion or miscarriage?

Members of the Hebrew Sick were entitled to the following cemetery benefits:

> Every member shall be entitled to cemetery ground for himself and his family, that is to say for his wife and unmarried children, males to the age of 20 and females until married. In the event a member's wife predeceases him, and such member remarries a second time, such member shall be entitled to cemetery ground for his second wife provided he has registered her with this association, and paid the required registration fee. Upon the death of a member, only his widow shall be entitled to cemetery ground provided she does not remarry; the cemetery benefit for the children will automatically lapse upon such death occurring.

The Association's aim, as members were told at the Seventy-fifth Jubilee Banquet in 1968, was to create

> the idea of a fraternal friendly society which would provide some sort of security for its members in adversity and also maintain that spirit of brotherhood and Yiddishkeit which were the normal thing in the Old Country but which might wither and die in the hurly-burly struggle for existence in a foreign land.

In the beginning, dues were five cents a week, a bargain considering the benefits. Association meetings were held in a number of venues, including the Globe Theatre on St. Laurent Boulevard near Duluth and the Montefiore Hebrew Orphan's Home on Jeanne Mance. Aside from discussing internal affairs, meetings covered a wide gamut of topics. For example, at the March 23, 1938 meeting, the topic for discussion was "Shall we combat anti-Semitism and how?" with speaker Hannaniah Caiserman, general secretary of the Canadian Jewish Congress.

By the 1960s, the Association was facing a major problem recruiting younger members. "It is one of the anomalies of modern living that it may be more difficult to obtain new members in good times than in bad. In other words, young people growing up in the affluent society and living under the wing of the Welfare State, do not feel the same need for protection that motivated their fathers and grandfathers," the Hebrew Sick noted on the occasion of its Seventy-fifth Jubilee. However, "government pension plans or unemployment insurance, admirable though they may be, cannot of themselves be a substitute for the principles of fraternity and service to one's fellow men." An unnamed Quebec government official agreed, writing on the occasion that while sick or death benefits were less needed than they used to be, other activities remained very useful. "One of these functions is to make sure that one does not live in isolation of his fellow citizens and does not feel alone. There is no doubt in my mind that as our materialistic society keeps getting more and more impersonal and run by bureaucrats, there is a role for an organization like yours."

With money raised from dues and the sales of cemetery plots, the Hebrew Sick gave "hundreds of thousands of dollars" over the years to charities, former president Morris Pascal told *The Canadian Jewish News* in 1989. Causes supported by the Association included the Jewish People's and Peretz Schools, Israel's Magen David Adom for ambulances, Histadrut, State of Israel Bonds, the Lubavitcher yeshiva, Maimonides Hospital, and Jewish refugees during the Second World War.

As the Association's bylaws noted, starting in 1964 an endowment benefit of $1,000 became payable to any member of the association upon reaching age seventy. Mortuary benefits starting that year were $1,500 to the wife or children, in the event of a member's death. If the member died after receiving the endowment benefit, the mortuary benefit was reduced by that amount. By 1970, the endowment benefit was given to members reaching the age of sixty-five.

In 1974, annual dues were thirty dollars. New members were charged two hundred dollars for a double plot, with the understanding this "exceptionally low price" was available only to members of good standing. Applicants for new membership could not be more than forty-five years old. Benefits included ten dollars per week for Sick Benefit, payable for a maximum of ten weeks during any calendar year.

Membership was frozen in 1983, when it appeared the Association's days were numbered. By the time it wound down completely, in 1989, only eighty-six members remained. But when it sold its holdings at the Baron de Hirsch Cemetery, the Hebrew Sick was second only to the Baron de Hirsch Institute in the amount of space it held—a constant throughout most of the Cemetery's history.

The Russian Polish Hebrew Sick Benefit Association was formed in 1907. At its first general meeting held at 54 Main Street (St. Laurent Boulevard), the Association described its purpose with the Mishnah proverb "These are deeds that never end." Among these deeds:

> If a Society member becomes sick there is a special committee assigned to visit him—said visit easing his pain and loneliness. In case of the death of a member, there is an appointed committee to pay respect to the deceased by attending his funeral, visiting the family, and partly covering the expense of burial ground as well as bestowing upon the family of the deceased a compensatory sum of money.

In 1933, representatives of the Association founded the Federation of Polish Jews in Canada, which aimed to lobby governments about the situation of the Jews in Poland and to send money to Polish Jews. In 1939, when the Nazis invaded Poland, Jews in Vilna received "a substantial sum" from the Federation. Vilna Rabbi Pinchas Hirschprung, who was later a refugee in Shanghai, China and who then made his way to Canada, wrote:

> I will never forget the joy that this gift brought to us. What joy! The hungry were fed, their torn rags changed to decent clothes, their bare feet were shod and above all, they were conscious of the feeling that across the ocean there were brethren organized in a Federation who sent them aid. That feeling actually kept us alive, kept our courage and strength in our wanderings.

In 1940 the Russian Polish Hebrew Sick Benefit Association held a raffle to raise funds.

> Our organization is now raffling an electric refrigerator, a radio and a vacuum cleaner. The cost per raffle is fifty cents. Every brother

must take upon himself to sell at least one book of raffles for Five Dollars ($5.00). The money derived from the sale of these raffles will be used for the following three purposes: 1. To help our unfortunate brethren here, who need our assistance. 2. To establish a Free Loan Fund to re-establish themselves in their businesses. 3. For the relief of Polish Jewry.

Another of the Association's activities was a social evening and money shower held on May 11, 1943 at 4114 St. Laurent, arranged by the Ladies' Auxiliary. The meeting notice reads

> We assure you of a very interesting and pleasant evening. You will spend an enjoyable evening and at the same time help our brave Soldiers who are fighting against the Nazi barbarism. Please bring your friends.

By the late 1950s, with the community dispersing throughout the growing city, it was becoming much more difficult to attract members to Russian-Polish meetings, as I. Poplinger related in 1957 in the Association's fiftieth anniversary book:

> Members, up to a few years ago, were concentrated and located in a few streets within easy close reach of each other, and no matter where one lived he was still a few minutes within the association's reach, that resulted in the meetings being so well attended that some latecomers found it difficult to get a seat.

But with members scattered in various new districts it took some a few hours' travelling time to and from the meetings, "which is a burden to a person after a hard day's work." However, the Russian-Polish lives on, one of the few mutual benefit societies to do so.

The Workmen's Circle, or Arbeiter Ring, made its Montreal debut in 1907, as part of a loose network of socialist, anti-communist groups head-quartered in New York. It was the most important fraternal group among Jewish workers in the world.

In its heyday the Montreal group had four thousand members, but by the 1990s membership had slipped to the hundreds, with the average age over eighty. Among those active in the Workmen's Circle over the years were poet A.M. Klein and politicians David Lewis and Joseph Schubert.

Many Jewish immigrants who were attracted to radical politics or were involved in socialist politics in the old country joined the Arbeiter Ring, which stated in its constitution that it is "striving for the complete emancipation of the working class." A large number of members toiled in the sweatshops of the garment trade, at a time when organized Jewish workers in the clothing industry exerted a strong influence on community matters.

As a 1936 souvenir book explained, "the Workmen's Circle is a labor fraternal organization whose establishment became a necessity when industrial conditions became, under capitalism, a threat and a menace to the health and living conditions of the workers."

While it provided the same benefits as any sick benefit society, its social environment was entirely different. During many social occasions, money was collected to support Russian revolutionaries languishing in prison. As Israel Medres described it, "A new member of the Arbeiter Ring often heard lectures and speeches on socialist themes. In those days socialist leaders believed that once the struggle for the forty-four hour work week was won, a social revolution would follow."

The organization became involved in elections, endorsing the Co-operative Commonwealth Federation (CCF), which became the New Democratic Party.

Along with lectures and speeches, members packed the Association's rooms at 4848 St. Laurent (until 1961) for card games, plays, dances, concerts, dinners, and teas and fundraisers for Israel. It promoted Yiddish literature, established a Yiddish afternoon school for children, and was home to a theatre group and sixty-voice choir.

In the 1920s, a split within the Circle reflected division over the question of affiliation with the Communist International (the Comintern or Third International), created in 1919. A group favouring communist ideology broke away from the Workmen's Circle to form the Canadian Labour Circle. For a while, the breakaway communist faction in Montreal was known informally as the Left Workmen's Circle while the existing Workmen's Circle was known as the Right Workmen's Circle, notes Eiran Harris, long-time archivist at the Jewish Public Library of Montreal. The

"Even In Death They Are Not Divided" „בחייהם ובמותם לא נפרדו"

Top: From the 1937 Jubilee book of the Russian Polish Hebrew Sick Benefit Association. *Bottom:* From the Twentieth Anniversary album of the Hebrew Protective Association of Montreal.
[Jewish Public Library]

communist breakaway group obtained its own section in the Baron de Hirsch Cemetery and for a few years obituary notices in the *Keneder Adler* would read that the deceased "will be buried at Left Workmen's Circle." The section is known today as Jewish Assistance.

With the creation of the communist faction, the Workmen's Circle was hit by a large drop in members, and relations between once-united Jewish workers were poisoned. However, the Workmen's Circle was given a new lease on life from post-Second World War immigration which included many people who had formerly been affiliated with the labour movement.

The Circle continues today albeit in much smaller form and under a different name. Since it split from the New York headquarters of Workmen's Circle, the Montreal branch, now based in a Snowdon home, is known as the Workers Circle. April 2003 saw the Workers Circle commemorate the sixtieth anniversary of the Warsaw Ghetto Uprising.

A receipt for a plot at the Workmen's Circle reads:

> The grave will be kept in reserve, until necessary, with no extra charge as long as you are a member in good standing of the Workmen's Circle in Montreal. The only charge will be for the foundation, which will have to be paid before a stone is erected.

The Jewish National Workers' Alliance, the Farband, was organized in 1913, following a resolution adopted at a convention in Montreal for the Poale Zionist party. The goal was to create a broader base for the party, which aimed to foster a positive attitude toward Israel. Comprising a large part of the Jewish intelligentsia, the Poale Zion and Farband were active in all aspects of Jewish nationalism and culture. They fought on behalf of the Histadrut labour movement in Israel, which later became a collective and grew into the economic backbone of Israel. Mass meetings were held in Montreal to raise funds for the Histadrut. During the Depression, activists from the Farband, Poale Zion, and Arbeiter Ring opened a people's kitchen (or soup kitchen) in Montreal.

Until the Second World War, the Sunday Open Forum was an important cultural activity in the Jewish community. Held in both Yiddish and English, the forums attracted the Jewish intelligentsia and dealt with issues ranging from politics to science. Some of these meetings were quite stormy, particularly when politics or Jewish questions were brought up. Particularly stormy was a crowded meeting discussing the Stalin-Hitler Pact of 1939 which was addressed by former leading communists. Farband is known today as Farband Labor Zionist Alliance.

There were eight sick benefit societies in existence by 1911, but recently arrived Jewish immigrants from England felt the need for a ninth. These were, after all, "people imbued with British tradition and way of life, who desired to continue their association in an organization to the mutual benefit of all concerned."

The first meeting of the then King George Sick Benefit Association was held that year at 12 Roy Street, in what is today the Plateau Mont-Royal, at the home of one of the founding treasurers, Davis Cohen. The first col-lection at that meeting brought in six dollars.

As related in its thirty-fifth anniversary program in 1946, the Associ-ation was able to begin paying out sick benefits after only eighteen months of existence—a maximum of five dollars weekly, for a maximum of thirteen weeks.

Finances improved dramatically, however, and by 1914 the King George was able to buy one acre of land at Baron de Hirsch Cemetery for $3,000 from the Bassarabier Sick Benefit Society. Another section was bought in 1927 for $6,500.

In 1930 a group met to discuss the need for supplying spiritual nourish-ment for the fast-growing Jewish community in Outremont. The newly-born Adath Israel Synagogue rented premises on Van Horne Avenue. Groundbreaking for Outremont premises the congregation could call its own began in 1939. The synagogue moved to its current Hampstead location in 1981.

In 1940, Adath Israel appointed Rabbi Charles Bender, and he would remain the congregation's rabbi until 1975. In the 1940s, the congregation was so large "we had people in the sanctuary, the assembly hall and the auditorium, all at once," recalled Rabbi Bender in an interview in 1990. "Each day, I alternated from room to room. I was a busy boy."

Adath Israel later opened a Hebrew Day School, one of the first of its kind for a North American congregation. Shortly after the end of the Second World War, Adath Israel dedicated a special plaque in the front foyer of the synagogue, memorializing the six million Jews killed in the Holocaust. In 1952, a cenotaph in memory of the Holocaust victims was placed on the Adath Israel's grounds at Baron de Hirsch Cemetery—the first such Holocaust memorial in the Cemetery.

Shomrim Laboker—officially Congregation Shomrim Laboker, Beth Yehuda, Shaare Tefilah, Beth Hamedrash Hagodol-Tifereth Israel—represents the amalgamation of some of Montreal's oldest congregations.

The synagogue stands today at the corner of Westbury and Plamondon in the Snowdon area, but its origins, like so many others, are in the Plateau Mont-Royal area. The Shomrim Laboker, believed to have been established in 1906, was formerly located at 3675 St. Dominique. Its Honorary Rabbi was Jacob Leib Colton, but he made most of his living as one of the city's most popular *mohels* (a person certified to perform a *bris*, the Jewish ritual of circumcision, on baby boys) and as a successful *shochet* (a person who conducts kosher slaughter of animals).

Rabbi Colton wore a top hat and used a walking stick, "a stick which he did not hesitate to wield against the neighbourhood's hooligans," as a history of the congregations notes. One particular Kol Nidre night shortly after the creation of the State of Israel in 1948, stood out in the memory of his son, Yoel Colton. As a souvenir booklet written for the Shomrim Laboker's hundredth anniversary described:

> During the Kol Nidre appeal, the youngsters would run outside to play. (But) on the Kol Nidre evening after the creation of the State of Israel my father locked the doors of the sanctuary. 'No one is going out,' he announced. 'I know what you all earn. This is what you are going to give, and this is what you are going to give.' And so he went around the room and no one refused him.

Another of the synagogue's well-known rabbis was Chaim Denburg. Denburg, who became the longest-serving pulpit rabbi in Montreal, joined the Shomrim Laboker in 1956 and was the congregation's rabbi for the next thirty-five years until his death in 1991.

The Shaare Tefilah or Austro-Hungarian Shul once stood at the corner of Milton and Clark streets and may have been the first synagogue in the Plateau Mont-Royal. It featured a green velvet curtain covering the gaps of the railing surrounding the women's gallery, protecting women's legs from immodest view. The Beth Yehudah Synagogue, on the corner of Hôtel de Ville and Duluth, was heralded as one of the most beautiful synagogues in Canada at its 1921 opening. The synagogue served its congregation until its 1957 amalgamation with the Shomrim Laboker. It was subsequently converted into apartments.

Much more recently, in 1995 the Beth Hamedrash Hagodol merged with the Shomrim Laboker.

A product of several mergers, the Tifereth Beth David Jerusalem Synagogue is now commonly known by its initials TBDJ or as the Baily Shul, after the street on which it is located.

The Beth David, named after the father of the first president, was formed by Romanian Jews who came to Canada in the late nineteenth century. In 1886, a congregation was organized and two years later began to hold services in rented quarters on Fortification Lane. In 1890, when the Shearith Israel (Spanish and Portuguese) Synagogue moved from Cheneville Street to Stanley Street, the Beth David rented the vacated building for twenty dollars per month. In 1894, the synagogue spent $8,000 to buy the building, then the oldest synagogue building in Canada, and used it until 1929, when the congregation moved to St. Joseph Boulevard. The Cheneville building was demolished in 1979; on the site today stands the federal government's Complexe Guy-Favreau.

The congregation voted in 1891 that in the event of a member's death, the widow was to receive fifty dollars. A decade later, the congregation decided to grant the use of two carriages at funerals, as a means "to alleviate the problems of a bereaved family." The synagogue eventually acquired its own hearse, which was later shared with the Baron de Hirsch Institute, before it was sold to Paperman & Sons, funeral directors .

Rabbi J. Herschorn joined the congregation in the 1920s and later became Chief Rabbi of Montreal. After ten years, Rabbi Herschorn left the congregation.

Records exist from 1904 for the Tifereth Jerusalem, which was composed primarily of Russian immigrants. It was known as the Papineau, or the Rossland Synagogue in honour of the donors; the synagogue was built on land donated to Jewish residents by the Ross Realty Co. The family real estate firm owned vast parcels of land in the suburbs of Montreal but fell on hard times in the Depression when the city failed to expand outside its core.

A 1998 souvenir booklet for the Tifereth Beth David Jerusalem notes that the congregation "was clearly an enigma." It was united by a very strong sense of community. Services would be followed by *kiddish* in homes of different members. Special delegations would visit the sick. However, at the same time, the congregation was severely fragmented by internal squabbles over such things as the presidency. "Who would lead services? Who would read from the Torah? Why did the first minyan finish late?" So intense were these arguments that a second Tifereth Jerusalem Synagogue had to be opened to accommodate one of the factions.

The first Tifereth Jerusalem was called The Red Shul because of its red bricks while the new synagogue was known as The White Shul because of its white exterior bricks.

Beth Yitzchok was established in 1904 in a building owned by Abraham Yitzchok Luterman, which also served as his family home in the early years. Years later, for a membership fee of twelve dollars, members were entitled to a cemetery plot, a casket, a vehicle from Paperman & Sons Inc., and shrouds.

Established in 1904 on St. Catherine Street, Kehal Yeshurun Synagogue later moved to Colonial Avenue and then Fairmount Avenue. Reverend Fishel Avrutick was the spiritual leader. When he passed away, "he requested that only Shomrei Shabbat Jews [Jews who observed the Sabbath] be buried in his line." The request was honoured and was written on the Cemetery plan.

The Beth Yitzchok joined the Beth David in the mid-1950s and was followed by the Kehal Yeshurun. In 1964, Beth David and its amalgamated congregations joined the Tifereth Jerusalem. The Jewish Community of Eastern Côte Saint-Luc and Hampstead was formed in 1958, and joined by the Tifereth Jerusalem in 1962. The Tifereth Beth David Jerusalem Synagogue, as it is known today, was established in 1965.

A compromise was reached between the Tifereth Jerusalem and Beth David congregations over the synagogue's new name. The merged congregations took the first word of Tifereth Jerusalem first, Beth David in the middle, and Jerusalem last, to create Tifereth Beth David Jerusalem.

The Poale Zedek (meaning "workers for justice") used to be known as the "working man's shul" or the Mile End synagogue. Its building on St. Urbain

Street in the Mile End district was built by the immigrant workers and merchants who founded it. They were mainly carpenters, plumbers, and other railway workers for the Canadian National and Canadian Pacific Railways at nearby Mile End station. It was a project they started in 1910 and completed in 1922.

Historian David Rome contended that the synagogue was the setting for the world's first Jewish National Radical School, started in 1910, although that title is contested. Inspired by the social and national ideals of Labour Zionism, the Jewish school later became the Jewish People's Schools and Peretz Schools.

Noted for its chandeliers and candelabras, stained-glass windows, columns, hanging balconies and wood finishing, the three hundred and fifty-seat Poale Zedek was believed to be the oldest continuously functioning synagogue in Montreal. Weekly services were held there until it was damaged by arson in 1988.

In 1992, the synagogue began life anew as the temple of the CaoDaists of Montreal, a Vietnamese religion dedicated to the unity of all creeds.

As time passed, the children of immigrants lost their ties to the Old Country, and gradually the members of the Montreal Jewish community shifted their interests from membership in the *landsmanshaften* or other sick benefit societies. Increasing prosperity and a widening social safety net also meant that fewer people depended on the societies' services. The result was a decline in membership.

As the decades passed, many of the sick benefit societies closed their doors. "We've reached a certain time and place where the society has no time or place," noted Martin Brook, who was a long-time member and the last president of the Independent Hebrew Sick Benefit Association, which only recently closed its doors after 102 years. The Association sold its cemetery holdings to Baron de Hirsch in 2003 for $212,500. "There's no longevity in the group today—there's no reason to exist."

As early as October 1983, the Hebrew Sick Benefit Association (a separate organization from the Independent Hebrew Sick Benefit Association) was telling members its days were numbered: "It has become readily apparent that we are, willingly or not, in the twilight of our existence."

Not only had the organization declined dramatically in numbers by the 1980s, but because of the nature of the benefits they provided members, the societies were increasingly being treated by the government as insurance companies, subject to the same laws and regulations as the insurance industry. The government was encouraging societies to get out of the insurance business. While many of the services they provided were once revolutionary, such benefits were now widely available.

Government officials were also beginning to make visits to the societies, something that did not go down very well. Describing an "inspection by the Department of Assurance," Brother Morris Pascal, then president of the Hebrew Sick and who would later go on to become president of the Baron de Hirsch Cemetery, told Hebrew Sick members, "We now have new impetus to get out of the cemetery business and should do so to give out benefits to members."

Visits from government officials were also greeted with less than enthusiasm by other burial societies. A representative of the Russian Polish Hebrew Sick Benefit Association described a visit to his organization by two bureaucrats: "The attitude of these men was one of rudeness and harassment." He said the men told the Russian Polish that the purchase of Israel Bonds by such organizations was illegal and that minutes were to be written in French.

By the late 1980s, the Hebrew Sick was engaged in serious negotiations to sell its Cemetery holdings to Baron de Hirsch. As Brother Nutkevitch noted at a June 1988 meeting of the Hebrew Sick, "We are an aged society, closed to new membership. We must consider who will look after the Cemetery when we are not around."

In a March 1987 letter to Hebrew Sick Benefit Association members, past president Morris Pascal had outlined the advantages they could obtain "by getting out of the cemetery business" while keeping the society afloat to provide other services.

> Each member can get his "rightful share" while he can still enjoy it. Our responsibilities for the current and perpetual maintenance of the Cemetery will have been met, forever. This is an obligation we owe to all of our dear departed, as well as our Jewish community.
>
> The society would be able to return "to its original fraternal priorities and begin to function as it did in the past. More like a brotherhood."

Pascal bemoaned the fact some board members wanted to launch the organization on a new course of action that would get it into the cemetery operation and maintenance business. "In my humble opinion this could well cost us everything and would destroy the good name of our society," he wrote.

"Finally, aren't we all getting a little too old to be involved in this complex business of running a cemetery?" Pascal asked. "Let's get out while we can. We have a very good offer of settlement and we can retain our dignity and the Society's standing in the community."

Later that year an offer was on the table. Baron de Hirsch would pay the Hebrew Sick Benefit Association $300,000 for its Cemetery holdings. As the minutes of the September 6, 1988 meeting state, "after a period of unruly behaviour and shouting" a motion was passed that the Hebrew Sick would accept the Baron de Hirsch's written offer to purchase. "The meeting then disintegrated in chaos at 9:30 p.m."

At the next meeting, on September 28, in which minutes of the previous meeting were read, Brother Sperber corrected the word "kaos" (*sic*) to "awful, vulture behaviour." He suggested that action be taken to change the general behaviour of the brothers during meetings, and suggested another meeting to deal with the matter. But another member suggested a meeting on the matter would result only in aggravation.

Amid the wrangling, the Baron de Hirsch began to worry that the people it was negotiating with might not have been mandated to make the sale. In an October 1988 letter to the Hebrew Sick's lawyer, Baron de Hirsch representatives wrote: "You will understand that your client or its members have a variety of opinions and expectations and have publicly voiced these in the past and consequently, we must be assured that the land being offered for sale is being offered by a group authorized by proper resolution so to sell."

On October 31, 1988, the Hebrew Sick board approved the land sale. The vote had to be ratified at a general meeting of members. Members were urged to accept the sale. Plot reservations of every member and his wife would be honoured by the Baron de Hirsch and "the name of our society will continue to be displayed to identify our Cemetery into perpetuity."

Despite the board's approval of the sale, suspicion lingered. At a meeting two weeks later, on November 13, Brother Nutkevitch accused the Baron de Hirsch of doing things "under the table". Enough is enough, Brother Ribovitch replied. "At all of our meetings, we discuss the Baron de Hirsch and the Cemetery; we attack ourselves and Baron de Hirsch continuously. We must leave the cemetery business. Let us treat the Baron de Hirsch offer without animosity." At the following meeting, Brother Nutkevich sought assurances that the Hebrew Sick land would "be used as a cemetery for Jewish people only and not for a parking lot or such other use." Such assurances were received, apparently, because by June 1989, members were being invited to their last meeting concerning "perhaps, one of the most important events in the history of our society ... You will be served a meal and we'll have 'schnapps' to commemorate this event."

Contrary to Pascal's hope that the Association could renew itself, the final meeting of the Hebrew Sick Benefit Association was held at the Spanish & Portuguese Synagogue on September 17, 1989. The winding up of the Association had to be decided by an affirmative vote of three-quarters of the members attending. It was unanimously approved and the ninety-seven-year-old Hebrew Sick was history.

With the disappearance of most of the sick benefit societies, much has been lost—including planning for death. "Cemetery is a very difficult thing to talk about," Jacques Berkowitz, former president of the Baron de Hirsch Cemetery and a long-time member of its Board of Directors, said in an interview. "People hesitate. They don't want to know about it. People don't plan properly. Comes the time, they're so distraught." The advantage of the old sick benefit societies, Berkowitz said, was the "Don't worry" factor. "When you are sick we'll send you to a doctor. When you die, we have a place for you to be buried. Today, we don't have that any more. I say to people 'Have you made arrangements for your burial? What's going to be? Are you going to leave it to your kids to do it at the last minute?'"

The total square footage of the Baron de Hirsch Cemetery now stands at 1.97 million square feet or about forty-five acres with the inclusion of the former United Hebrew Cemeteries grounds. While the Baron de Hirsch Institute holds 39.1 per cent of the Cemetery land today, in 1982 it owned only 14.2 per cent of the Cemetery, just slightly ahead of the Hebrew Sick Benefit Association's 12.9 per cent. The smallest of the thirty-six affiliates that year owned 0.2 percent.

3

The Cemetery's Early
Operations

*When the dead are buried among their people and families, and
their names are remembered by them, it is as though they
continue to participate in life upon earth.*
–Yechezkel Kaufmann, *The Religion of Israel*, 1937.

From the time it opened in 1905, the new cemetery served Montreal's
Jewish community as the final resting place for the Jewish poor.

During its first full year of operation, eighty indigents (the term used
for those who could not afford to pay for burial costs) were buried, sixty-
two of whom were children. "The majority of these were the bodies of
newly-arrived emigrants, especially the children who suffered from the
strain and close confinement of their long journeys," the Institute's 1906
annual report notes. The burials cost $554.16, or $6.93 each. Four hundred
and ten dollars and fifteen cents was contributed by the Baron de Hirsch
Institute and the rest by friends.

Arrangements were made for the Chevra Kadisha Congregation to
conduct funeral services for indigents, as well as supply shrouds, coffins,
and transportation to the Cemetery at a cost ranging from $3.00 for babies
up to two years of age, to $12.00 for those ten and up. By 1915, the prices
had increased to $3.50 for those up to age two, $7.00 for two- to ten-year-
olds, and $14.00 for all others.

"The wisdom of the purchase of the new cemetery ... becomes more
evident as time goes on," reads the Institute's 1907 annual report. Burials
that year had increased again, this time to ninety-eight; seventy-nine were
children. The cost rose to $919.90 for all burials.

Cemetery costs in 1908 increased to $1,321. Because of high unemployment rates, many were compelled to seek burial assistance for loved ones, even though they may not have required any other aid, the 1908 annual report notes. These included people who would have previously been able to secure plots from one of the many burial societies, but could no longer afford to do so.

Sadly, the death toll for children far outstripped that of adults in the Cemetery's first few decades. Montreal was hit with an alarming increase in "consumption" (tuberculosis). Infant mortality continued to rise. Of the 177 people buried in the Cemetery in 1908, 139 were children, states the annual report from that year. Hardest hit in the Jewish community were the poor. While Montreal was home to much of Canada's wealth in the early twentieth century, its slums for some time had the highest infant mortality rate in the Western world and Jewish children were far from exempt. It would not be until 1927 that the number of adult burials would begin to surpass those of childen.

A move was made to send those afflicted to the healthy atmosphere of Ste-Agathe in the Laurentians. At its April 13, 1909 Board meeting, the Baron de Hirsch Institute approved the purchase of the Laurentide Inn in Ste-Agathe for $16,000. It was renamed, and so the Mount Sinai Hospital began in 1909 with a humble twelve-bed facility. The hospital grew over the years and moved to its current one hundred and seven-bed facility in Côte Saint-Luc in 1990.

In 1918, with an influenza epidemic raging, the Baron de Hirsch Institute had to scramble to make sure that indigent Jewish victims were not buried in Christian cemeteries—stricken Jewish patients had been dispersed to several hospitals and institutions. For example, three adults died during the epidemic that year at the St-Vincent-de-Paul Penitentiary and three others at the Protestant Hospital for the Insane. All were subsequently buried at the Baron de Hirsch Cemetery.

The second annual report of the Federation of Jewish Philanthropies notes three cases where Jewish patients had been found in the public hospitals, the superintendent of the Baron de Hirsch Cemetery Department arriving just in time to avoid their being buried as Christians. The three were buried at Baron de Hirsch, and only later were their relatives informed.

* * *

On September 5, 1909, Reverend H.S. Stuart, rector of St. James Anglican Cathedral in Trois-Rivières, was concerned enough to write to Chief Rabbi Glazer of Montreal, to inform him that Trois-Rivières' small Jewish cemetery "finds itself in a state of scandalous depredation." Located behind the LaSalle Academy of the Christian Brothers and surrounded by a broken stone wall, the cemetery had not seen a burial for thirty years and was in "a horrible state". A decade earlier there had been as many as twenty "fine tombstones of coloured granite," erected mainly by members of the Hart-Judah families (Aaron Hart was married to Dorothy Judah), but they had been thrown down by vandals. "Since no one cares about this cemetery, and it appears that the Montreal congregation has even forgotten that it exists, I have decided to write you about it and the condition it finds itself in today," Stuart wrote.

The leaders of the Spanish & Portuguese Congregation responded to this embarrassing and unacceptable situation by dispatching one of its members to Trois-Rivières. Upon receiving his report, a decision was made: to prevent the further violation of the remains and the memory of the early Canadian Jewish pioneers, all the Jewish graves and broken head-stones would be transferred to the Shearith Israel Synagogue's cemetery in Montreal. The remains of Aaron Hart and other family members buried in Trois-Rivières were brought to Montreal in 1909 and buried in the Spanish & Portuguese Cemetery on Mount Royal.

In 1977, the founding families of the Canadian Jewish community were commemorated by the Spanish & Portuguese Congregation with the dedication in the synagogue's cemetery on Mount Royal of a monu-ment bearing their names. The eight-foot obelisk is inscribed with the names of the Hart family as they appeared on the original tombstones.

Between 1906 and 1914 the mighty Canadian Pacific steamship *Empress of Ireland* plied the North Atlantic between Liverpool and Quebec. During those years it shuttled nearly one hundred and twenty thousand European immigrants to new lives in the New World. It is now estimated that as many as five hundred thousand Canadians are descended from people who came over on the *Empress* between 1906 and 1914.

On May 29, 1914, the *Empress of Ireland* was headed from Quebec City to Liverpool, when it collided with the Norwegian coal ship *Storstad*, in the St. Lawrence River near Rimouski, in extremely foggy conditions. The impact of the collision was deceptively gentle, but the wound was fatal. A mere fourteen minutes after the collision, the *Empress* sank. More than one thousand passengers and crew died—the second-worst peacetime disaster in maritime history after the sinking of the *Titanic* two years earlier.

Within days, the Baron de Hirsch Institute received notice that several Jewish victims of the shipwreck had been given Christian funeral services and been buried in Christian cemeteries. Although the matter was out of its jurisdiction, the Institute thought it advisable to send a representative to help Jewish survivors and make inquiries about the disposition of recovered Jewish bodies. Mrs. B. Groner was sent to Quebec City. In her June 1914 report to the Board, she wrote: "I desire to inform you that there was no truth whatever in the rumour which was circulated to the effect that Jewish bodies had been buried on Christian burial grounds."

In fact, no Jewish body had gone unclaimed. A Quebec City-based representative of the Montreal Baron de Hirsch Institute, Mr. Bennett-English, had attended all twelve funerals of identifiable Jewish victims in the Quebec City Jewish cemetery. "What's more," reported Mrs. Groner, "I am glad to be able to report that my investigation showed that there were no grounds whatever for supposing that Jewish survivors were being neglected, i.e., Jewish survivors of the poorer class, the others needing no such attention."

However, the burial of Jewish victims of the disaster weighed heavily on the Quebec City Jewish community, and a special meeting of the Baron de Hirsch was called June 13, 1914 to receive a delegation from Quebec City. A letter from Congregation Beth Yisroel of Quebec City notes: "Our cemetery here in Quebec is unfortunately too well filled. Had it not been for the sad *Empress of Ireland* disaster, it might have lasted us some five or ten years longer. But with the unfortunate accident that overwhelmed our waters two weeks ago and with the consequent burial of some twelve Jewish souls, which was an entirely unforeseen accident, our cemetery has been taxed to its utmost capacity and the immediate purchase of new ground is now most necessary. It is for this that we are now appealing to you, and we would earnestly solicit your assistance to the extent of $500.00 towards the purchase of this ground."

The Baron de Hirsch Institute said no to the Quebec City delegation, arguing that each city had a responsibility to its Jewish poor. And since Quebec's Jewish community had only been burying an average of two people a year for the last fifteen years, it had "not been overburdened in that direction." The delegation was advised to make a request to the Jewish Colonization Association that had been founded by Baron Maurice de Hirsch for reimbursement for burials of victims of the *Empress* disaster.

The living conditions of the Jewish settlers in Montreal were a concern. In the face of a health crisis and a growing population, Baron de Hirsch Institute president Lyon Cohen called upon the city, in a speech to the 1910 annual meeting, "to regulate the tenement and slum districts." Better paved streets and improved garbage collection would improve the situation, but better housing for the poor was of key importance. Cohen asked members to "impress upon your wives and sisters" the importance of organizing "lady workers who would unselfishly devote themselves to the work of visiting the poor in their own homes. It is scarcely possible to realize what effect true-hearted, energetic, sensible, and sympathetic women could have on the lives of those who are dependent upon charity. They could instruct them how to make the most of the allowance granted, they could encourage them to take a pride in their homes no matter how unattractive these might be, and what is of vital importance, they could watch over the moral upbringing of their children."

By 1915, armed with estimates that fifty per cent of sicknesses were due to preventable causes like bad home surroundings and overcrowding, the Baron de Hirsch Institute continued to call the larger community to action. At its annual meeting, it was noted that "if the community at large could realize the amount that could be saved by the prevention of these sources of poverty, instead of waiting to spend far larger sums in actual relief work, there would be a general awakening of the need of more energetic measures for good housing and home control in crowded districts."

It would not be until 1923 that the Cemetery Committee of the Baron de Hirsch could announce at the annual meeting a year "of great satisfaction", due to the death rate having shown a sizable decrease.

Funeral costs were also a preoccupation. Paperman & Sons Inc. began conducting funeral services for Jews whose families could not afford to pay for them during the duration of the First Great War. By 1950, the Paperman funeral home had been conducting funeral services for indigents at Baron de Hirsch for close to thirty-five years. However, changes were necessary in the way services were conducted, Sam Paperman informed the Cemetery Board at an August 1950 meeting.

The Paperman company was being paid $22.50 by the Baron de Hirsch for each funeral service. Sam Paperman explained that this meant that funeral services were being offered for indigents at a loss. The amount only represented the furnishing of the shrouds, coffin, and hearse, and did not include other required items such as *shomer* (the watchman who stays with the body until burial), Torah, limousine, and chapel service, all of them necessary elements for a proper Jewish funeral.

"Since no provisions had been made by the Baron de Hirsch Institute for the payment of such a complete service, it was found necessary to approach the relatives of the deceased for such payment," the minutes of the Board meeting explain. "Such an approach was very unpleasant and unprofitable."

Sam Paperman requested $65 for each funeral service for indigent clients of the Baron de Hirsch Institute. This would result in truly free funeral services to the families of the deceased. The Board decided to increase the fee paid to $45—covering the coffin ($10), shrouds ($10), *shomer* ($3), Torah ($3), limousine ($4), chapel service ($5) and hearse ($10)—with an additional charge of $5 for the transfer of a body to the funeral parlour. The charge for infants was to remain at $5.

The real estate adage "location, location, location" holds true even in death. That's seen, for example, in prices the Independent Hebrew Sick Benefit Association charged non-members for single plots in 1983. It cost $450 that year for a plot in a section of the Cemetery located near apartment buildings, but $650 for a plot in a rear section with trees. Prices could also differ within sections. In 1960, rates for individual plots in Baron de Hirsch's Memorial Park section ranged from $150 to $250.

In 1952, the Baron de Hirsch Institute became aware that the City of Montreal had contracted with several undertakers and cemeteries to take care of burials of Roman Catholic and Protestant indigents. It had never made provision to do so for Jews.

"I believe that it is the duty of the municipal authorities to look after the dead indigents, whether they be Roman Catholic, Protestant or Jewish," William Gittes, president of the Baron de Hirsch Institute, wrote in a

January 28, 1952 letter to Max Seigler, then the senior Jewish city councillor in Montreal. "Due to its financial difficulties and other circumstances beyond its control, the Baron de Hirsch Institute finds itself unable any longer to underwrite the total expenses of burials of Jewish indigents, and must appeal to the Municipal authorities for financial assistance to provide such service in the future."

The city took heed and authorized its Social Welfare Service to make payments to the Baron de Hirsch Institute "for the burial of persons of the Hebrew faith recognized as indigents by the department," as a late November 1952 letter notes. The Institute would be paid $15 for the burial of still-born babies and children less than twelve months old and $50 for all others. The Institute reckoned this would bring in additional revenue to its Cemetery Department of twelve to fifteen hundred dollars annually. This payment system is no longer in force today.

While most people buried as indigents by the Baron de Hirsch Institute (and later by the Jewish Family Services of the Baron de Hirsch Institute) were deserving recipients of free burials, a few have taken advantage of the service, as subsequent investigations showed.

In 1961, a man was buried at Baron de Hirsch as an indigent member of the Jewish community. Afterwards, it was discovered through the deceased's landlady that the man had a bank account under an assumed name and that there was plenty of money in the account. The bank manager agreed to withdraw four hundred and seventy-five dollars for the funeral service, grave opening and closing, and tombstone, as an internal letter from the Cemetery noted in November 1961.

In another instance in the early 1980s, former Cemetery president Herbert Isenberg recalls in an interview, the family of a deceased person told the Cemetery it could only afford to pay for a part of the burial cost. Several months later, monument-maker Smith Bros. arrived with a tombstone worth $11,000 for the man's grave. Monument-makers must obtain a permit to install a tombstone. Isenberg told Smith Bros. to take the stone back, and had the family pay the balance of the funeral costs before being allowed to install the stone. And they did. "We took the attitude that if people cheat the Cemetery it comes out of the community," he said.

The Cemetery has a commitment that the graves of people whose families could not afford to pay burial costs should not be identifiable as such. By the mid-1970s, the section called New Memorial Park had been opened at Baron de Hirsch Cemetery. Some thought that the new section should be reserved for indigent burials only, but most felt this would turn the section into an easily-identified paupers' field. This could only be avoided by selling plots in the section to anyone.

To this day, the Baron de Hirsch Cemetery provides persons who are identified as indigent Jews with more dignified burials than is afforded to others in Montreal. Non-Jewish destitutes from the Montreal area are buried in the Cimetière de Laval. Unclaimed bodies are placed in the ground in an area where hundreds of small, round metal plaques, each with two letter-and-number markings, identify the graves.

By contrast, indigent Jews buried at Baron de Hirsch are given full funeral services and respectful burials. As minutes from a December 1977 Cemetery Board meeting note, "all Jews deserve dignity in burial." And so, instead of being buried in a paupers' field, they are interred throughout the Cemetery grounds, together with people from all social classes and backgrounds. Instead of being buried in unmarked graves, their names live on in stone monuments that are barely distinguishable from all others. And only those who are truly in the know, know where the indigent are buried.

"There is absolutely no indication that a person is a pauper," said Jacques Berkowitz. "That would be terrible."

In 1973, to ensure indigent burials were scattered throughout the Cemetery, a new plan for indigent burial was presented in which each organization or synagogue would, in turn, donate one burial plot per year for indigent burials in their section. Not all affiliates agreed, however, and plans called for a $350 assessment to be charged to affiliates who would or could not offer a free plot for burial of the poor. This led to complaints from some of those who were likely to be charged the fee. One Board member summed up his feelings:

> The donation of a grave was in effect a charity or mitzvah. In dealing with charities, some give and some do not. Because a few prefer not to give does not deter others from making donations. Therefore, a tax of $350 should be forgotten. Those with a desire to help indigents will still do so.

The proposal to charge the assessment was dropped.

In 1988, in a move aimed at ensuring that it would have burial plots for indigents as long as possible, the Baron de Hirsch Cemetery ceased selling plots to the general Jewish community. At the time, the Cemetery estimated it had about three thousand plots that were unsold or unreserved. Sale of plots is still allowed to the near kin of those already buried on Baron de Hirsch-owned grounds, including parents, spouses, and siblings. Still-active burial societies or congregations can continue to sell plots.

By the early 1990s, the process for qualifying for indigent burial at Baron de Hirsch Cemetery had become standardized. Family members seeking an indigent burial for a loved one go through a multi-step process, although measures are taken to make the required paperwork less onerous.

"As this is a very delicate and emotional time for the family, it is usually not possible to gather the proper documents to determine financial resources of the deceased," notes a 1991 memo from the Community Assistance Program (CAP) of the Jewish Family Services of the Baron de Hirsch Institute. "The family should therefore be told they will be contacted after Shiva in order to complete the assessment." It is CAP policy, in accordance with Jewish law, to keep to an absolute minimum the amount of time between death and burial, making it often difficult to explore the deceased's financial situation in depth when burial requests are made.

Funeral costs are now determined by funeral homes, which often waive all expenses to indigents. "We do indigent cases *gratis* for the community," Herbert Paperman said in an interview.

The Community Assistance Program will consider the burial application for "any Jewish person whose circumstances initially indicate that either the individual's estate or next-of-kin is unable to pay for the complete cost of burial." Among the questions asked are: Did the deceased have a plot? Is there a possibility of a will? Is there a possibility of a pension plan from work? Did they belong to any organization or synagogue which makes them eligible for a plot? In addition, applicants are asked to provide documents establishing their situation.

The distinction of being the first name in the Baron de Hirsch Cemetery Register belongs to a man named Simon, whose last name is possibly Kastin. He is listed as having lived at 113 Argyle Avenue in Montreal. He died November 4, 1905. Ten other individuals were buried that year, including Mrs. Schneider (first name not mentioned) of 322 St. Dominique Street. Her listing is memorable in that it is the first to mention an occupation: she was a glazier.

The first listing in the register of deaths of the Hebrew Sick Benefit Society is for forty-three-year-old (first name illegible) Braumstein, who died February 7, 1906. He had been in Canada for only a year. The cause of death was phthisis, a wasting form of tuberculosis that had lasted for nine months.

One of the first persons to have a cause of death listed was five-year-old Rubin Sheinfeld, of 245 Lagauchetière, who on July 10, 1907 was "killed by electric car." Other listings for 1907 tell other stories: dead at four days, dead at eleven weeks, dead at one month five days, or six months, or three hours.

Other causes of death are mentioned in the handwritten ledger. Presser Emil Mariasch, of 23 Leduc Lane, died at age fifty of pneumonia. Typhoid fever felled thirty-five-year-old A. Steamer at the "Clarke St. Foundling Home." Meningitis killed a two-month-old. Tuberculosis, bronchial pneumonia, miscarriage, "pressure of trachea," burns, diphtheria, and scarlet fever are among the causes of death entered.

Occupations of the deceased who are listed in the register included glasscutter, labourer, tailor, presser, cabinet-maker, peddler, schoolboy, and clerk. Well into the late 1950s, the forms of work listed included many tradespersons: shoemaker, fur operator, printer, shoe-shiner, laundry operator, shipper, merchant, traveller, bellboy. *Titanic* victim Leopold Weisz (listed as "Leopold Weis") was entered as a "married sculptor" who died at sea.

Not surprisingly, most early entries into the ledger were people who lived in the primarily Jewish neighbourhood off the Main, when street addresses were numbered in the hundreds rather than the thousands. By the early 1960s, home addresses reflect the Jewish community's shift north-westward. Where once Duluth, City Hall, Cadieux, St. Urbain and St. Lawrence in Plateau Mont-Royal were listed, streets like Linton, St. Kevin, Westbury and Dupuis in Snowdon make their appearance.

Records allow us to review the Cemetery's budget over the years. According to annual reports:

In 1918, cemetery expenses of $1,759.62 included $720 for janitorial service, $26.97 for road repairs and $30 for "cemetery sticks" (markers).

In 1920, cemetery expenditures (not including wages) totalled $1,537.80, including $5.70 for carfare, $5 for laundry, $3.15 for hardware and $15.34 for a light fixture and electrical installation.

In 2003, expenses topped $833,555, including labour of $381,598, monument repairs costing $62,176, and $59,620 for security guards. Revenues in 2003 reached $875,125, including grave openings of $338,268 and assessments to affiliates of $99,180.

Burial costs on Baron de Hirsch grounds (burial plots not included):

In 1961, a grave opening cost $31.50, while a foundation cost $25.

In 1977, a grave opening cost $145, foundations were $95 and unveilings $15.

In 1989, a grave opening cost $300, foundations cost $250, gravesite preparation was $125 and perpetual cemetery maintenance $75.

In 1996, a grave opening cost $470, foundations were $330 and gravesite preparations $190.

In 2003, a grave opening cost $560, foundations were $400 and gravesite preparations $230.

In 2004, a grave opening cost $875 and foundations $525.

4

The Evolving Organization
of the Cemetery

Two men came to Rabbi Moshe Yitzhak of Ponovezh. They had
both bought plots in the cemetery, and each wanted the better of the two.
After they had argued back and forth for some time, Rabbi Moshe Yitzchak
rendered his verdict: "Whoever dies first gets the better plot."
Never again did they argue the issue.
–Shmuel Himelstein, *A Touch of Wisdom, a Touch of Wit*

Throughout its history, the Baron de Hirsch Cemetery has administered the entire Cemetery on behalf of all of the affiliate burial societies and congregations which owned parts of the burial ground, although the Baron de Hirsch Institute was only a minority owner of the land until recently.

For the first sixty-six years of its operation, the Cemetery was managed by a committee of a much larger organization. When it opened in 1905, this larger organization was initially the Baron de Hirsch Institute, which has served as the genesis of many of today's Jewish community organizations in Montreal. As other organizations and institutions began to form, the Federation of Jewish Philanthropies was formed in 1916 to coordinate fund-raising for these groups. It was renamed the Federation of Jewish Community Services in 1951, then Allied Jewish Community Services in 1965.

A 1970 Quebec government report and the subsequent Bill 65 changed the entire structure and funding of health care and social services in Quebec. The Jewish community of Montreal was immediately faced with the question of how the changes would affect its agencies. There were major concerns that the Bill would challenge the continuing existence of the Jewish community's health services (including the Jewish General Hospital and the Mount Sinai Hospital). It was uncertain how the Bill would affect what is now Jewish Family Services of the Baron de Hirsch Institute. Fears were expressed that control of Jewish institutions could be watered down or even lost to the Jewish community.

Despite assurances from the Quebec government that the Bill would not cause any substantial changes to the operation of Jewish agencies, there were fundamental changes in the composition of health and social service agency boards. One such change led to the Baron de Hirsch Institute adopting the name Jewish Family Services. The pioneer agency became divided in two. Government-funded services would continue to be provided under the Jewish Family Services Social Services Centre, while community-underwritten services would be provided through Jewish Family Services of the Baron de Hirsch Institute. As part of this move, the Baron de Hirsch Cemetery was re-organized as a non-profit corporation in 1971; as such, it has continued to operate within the framework of Jewish Family Services of the Baron de Hirsch Institute. A majority of Cemetery Board appointments have come from Jewish Family Services. Such changes were unimaginable in the Cemetery's early years.

Minutes document the relations between the various groups that have made up the Cemetery Committee. For example, "Our Cemetery Committee functions. No decision necessary is quibbled or equivocated with, delayed or pigeon-holed," the Committee reported at the ninth annual meeting of the Federation of Jewish Philanthropies in 1926. "Cordial relationship is maintained with our associate societies—grounds (are) held in appropriate condition and resting places supplied to those answering the last call." As to sharing expenses and upkeep, the "neighbouring societies" of the Cemetery "cooperate with us in that respect with the greatest harmony," said Herbert M. Levine, chair of the Cemetery Committee.

However, despite such statements of cordiality, there had been some conflict as early as 1907. The Baron de Hirsch Institute complained that the new burial societies were refusing to sign the deeds of sale prepared by its notary for their grounds. The Institute's lawyer was instructed at the December 8, 1907 Board meeting to take whatever proceedings he saw fit to protect its interests.

In 1934, affiliates who had few graves in their sections complained about being charged the same assessment as those with more graves, but it was pointed out to them that the only satisfactory method for levying charges was according to the amount of land held.

The collection of assessments for Cemetery maintenance "has always been a difficult task," notes a 1950 memo describing the activities of the Institute's Cemetery Committee. Some of the affiliates required numerous notices to be sent "to remind them of their obligations."

In a June 1951 letter, Cemetery Committee chairman Max Finestone bemoaned the fact that, while he had done everything possible to eliminate friction and provide representation to the various societies, he had still been unable to avoid strife. "I find that you gentlemen forget that we are all working for one common cause, the poor indigents of Montreal, and that Baron de Hirsch is only a part of a great organization. It is very disappointing indeed to find that instead of the wholehearted cooperation which I expected … I find that everyone looks out for himself only."

Finestone expressed dismay at the conduct during meetings. "There is to be no arguing when the Chairman calls 'Out of order.' Most of the Societies have the habit of calling 'out of order' and disrupting the entire meeting, when this is only the prerogative of the Chairman." Finestone went on to give notice in a letter to late-payers that "unless payments in accord with statements are made promptly a lock will be put on the gate and no burial will be permitted until same is paid up."

A 1952 internal letter within the Baron de Hirsch Institute accuses some of the congregations and burial societies of encouraging membership by charging extortionate prices to non-members seeking to buy cemetery plots. The Hebrew Sick Benefit Association, for one, "has sold approximately half of its acreage to other societies and synagogues at a great profit, since available sites within reasonable distance of the city upon which the development of cemeteries will be permitted are not plentiful."

A year later, a memo outlined problems involving affiliates who were allegedly charging too much to non-members for burial plots. It called for an "attempt to put a ceiling on the sale price of graves, so that the high cost of living shall not be translated into the high cost of dying."

The affiliates' frustrations were clearly outlined in a 1951 letter from lawyer E. Michael Berger, chairman of the Cemetery Committee, to Baron de Hirsch Institute president William Gittes. During meetings, "there seems to be basic hostility," directed against the Baron de Hirsch Institute and its representatives, Berger noted. As a result meetings bogged down on points of order and minute details. "Most of the meeting time was devoted to a discussion of the minutes of earlier meetings," he noted.

Wrote Berger: "They feel that the Baron de Hirsch Institute is treating them as stepchildren and adopts towards them an attitude of tolerance and indulgence bordering on contempt ... They feel that they are victims of Baron de Hirsch Institute bureaucracy... They feel that the cemeteries which they represent do not receive the care and attention which they should receive and which they are entitled to in view of their contributions to the general maintenance fund."

Aside from the Baron de Hirsch Institute, the earliest burial societies or congregations to own land at the Cemetery included the Hebrew Sick Benefit Association, Congregation Beth Yehuda, Beth David Congregation, Beth Yitzchok Congregation, the Independent Hebrew Sick Benefit Association, Chevra Shaas Congregation, Rabbi Hirsch Cohen, Ohel Moshe Congregation, and the English, German and Polish Congregation.

The ink was barely dry on the 1905 land purchase agreement before various lot owners began to sell and others to buy. Such has been the case throughout the Cemetery's history, as various affiliates have grown or entered the scene, while others have disappeared or reduced their holdings in exchange for cash. The Baron de Hirsch Institute has always maintained the ability to formulate rules and regulations governing the Cemetery as a whole.

The earliest seller is believed to have been the Ohel Moshe Congregation (later to become the Beth Yehuda Congregation), which in January 1907 asked for permission to sell its acre of land. Chevra Shaas Congregation followed in June 1909 when it sought to sell one of its two acres to Adath Yeshurun Congregation.

Among the early sellers was the English, German and Polish Congregation (Shaar Hashomayim Synagogue), which already had its own cemetery grounds on Mount Royal. In 1910, the Shaar Hashomayim sold six acres back to Baron de Hirsch for the original purchase price. Reported Lyon Cohen of the Baron de Hirsch Institute at the 1910 annual meeting: "This will add to our assets what must in time become a valuable property."

In 1910 three lots were sold to the Independent Hebrew Sick Benefit Association for $500, two to the Hebrew Sick Benefit Society for $1,250, three to the Austro-Galician Society for five hundred dollars and three to Baron de Hirsch Institute board member Lazarus Cohen, for $250.

And so it would go for several decades. In recent years, however, the selling has been a one-way street—to Jewish Family Services of the Baron de Hirsch Institute—as burial societies seek to get out of the cemetery business or can no longer make ends meet.

There were particular tensions between the Baron de Hirsch Institute and the Hebrew Sick Benefit Association, perhaps not surprising, given that the two were the biggest landowners of the Cemetery. In 1959, the two groups attempted to make peace, but not before bringing up past and present grievances. As an example, for decades the two had been at odds with each other about Cemetery land sales. In 1933 and in 1944 the Hebrew Sick had sold some of its land holdings to the adjacent United Hebrew Cemeteries. That, according to the Baron de Hirsch Institute, was done without permission and in violation of a 1909 deed of sale between the Institute and the Hebrew Sick.

At a special meeting of the Cemetery Committee on September 29, 1959, Hebrew Sick president Paul Hopkins questioned the right of Baron de Hirsch to build a stone wall on de la Savane Street without having consulted the Hebrew Sick. The Baron de Hirsch replied that an agreement had been reached between the two about the division of costs for the stone fence, only to be promptly turned down the next day by the Hebrew Sick.

"This incident was typical of the lack of performance and cooperation by the Hebrew Sick Benefit Association," said Abe Nissenson, chairman of the Cemetery Committee. Referring to the "many disappointments and aggravations suffered in the past" in dealings with the Hebrew Sick, Nissenson added, "It is useless to deal with a group of apparently irresponsible people."

Hopkins continued that the Hebrew Sick did not wish to go it alone and separate from the Baron de Hirsch, and that it would like to forget the past and begin anew. A past president of the Hebrew Sick Benefit Association spoke of the "old times when the Hebrew Sick worked in harmony with the Baron de Hirsch." Several members of his Association were responsible for misunderstandings between the two, he said, and it was time to "come back into the fold." Alas, two years later, the "come back into the fold" meetings were still being held. However, "this group, as usual, is unable to follow through on commitments," said Baron de

Hirsch Institute executive director David Weiss. "Present internal strife has made it impossible for them to move."

Tempers subsided, and by January 1967, a motion of the Cemetery's Joint Advisory Committee marvelled at the harmony which now existed between Baron de Hirsch and several affiliates.

Prior to the 1970s, Baron de Hirsch Institute representatives "took a hard line with the 'affiliates,'" concluded a 1979 task force set up by the Baron de Hirsch Cemetery to discuss future orientations for the Cemetery. The affiliates felt that the Baron de Hirsch Institute was somewhat dictatorial and a certain animosity was created. "The animosity and distrust have not been totally dissolved."

The Cemetery's incorporation as a separate entity in the 1970s led to hopes for better times ahead. Under its new board structure, the Cemetery Board was comprised in its majority of ten representatives named from Jewish Family Services. A minority of board members (five) were chosen by the affiliated burial societies and congregations.

"In previous years, the Cemetery was operated as a part of the Baron de Hirsch and the affiliates played the role of 'absentee landlords' who incurred profits but who did not enjoy a happy relationship with Baron de Hirsch," read the minutes of a November 28, 1977 meeting of the Cemetery and the Jewish community's Planning and Allocation Committee. "Since the Cemetery was independently incorporated, they feel more a part of the whole." But affiliates still felt their assessments continued to be imposed from above. When affiliates' assessments were doubled that year in the face of a deficit, they were told, "We want you to feel assured that this was done only after many hours of head-breaking thought and planning."

At an October 1979 Cemetery Board meeting, Maurice Sohmer, auditor of the Hebrew Sick Benefit Association, asked: "Why are not the affiliates true partners in everything instead of allowing themselves to be dominated by Baron de Hirsch?" He "then exhorted the affiliates to throw off the yoke of Baron de Hirsch domination and run the Cemetery on their own."

One Board member pointed out that Baron de Hirsch was entirely willing to hand over its control of the Cemetery to Hebrew Sick, should that be the general wish of the affiliates. Another mentioned that Sohmer's facts were erroneous and that Hebrew Sick had "a long history of wanting to control the entire Cemetery."

Entrance to the Jewish Assistance Social
Organization section of the Cemetery.
[Photo: D.R. Cowles]

The friction continued, even as burial societies began to fall by the wayside in the latter decades of the twentieth century. The affiliates' goal was to protect their interests and make sure money on the Cemetery was properly spent, said Herbert Isenberg, a Cemetery president in the early 1980s. "Hey, let *them* pay," was the prevailing attitude. "Baron de Hirsch is rich." Affiliates had to increase their members' dues in the face of higher assessments. They were more enthusiastic about being able to disburse dividends to their members, than spending money on Cemetery maintenance or infrastructure. "They knew we didn't line our pockets. They just didn't want us to squander the money and the Cemetery was dead last on (their) list of priorities."

Among the affiliates, there were haves and have-nots, Isenberg pointed out. Most of the have-nots only had enough land to bury their members. But the haves had far more burial plots than members and could sell plots, often at a tremendous profit, given how little they had originally paid for the land. The money from plot sales went into their treasuries.

It was common for affiliates to balk when they received their assessments. The affiliates eyed any money accumulated by Baron de Hirsch and felt it should be spent, instead of their being charged monthly or annual dues. It came to the point where one of the burial societies just wouldn't pay. Said Isenberg, "We told them that we would stop providing services to them. We wouldn't cut their grass; we would only open and close graves. And we'll send them a registered letter and we'll see how their members like it when they would show up at their Cemetery and see the grass wasn't cut, the leaves weren't raked and so on. Toward the end, they all fell into line, because they knew with their heart of hearts that we only tried to do the best for the Cemetery and the community."

Burial can be an emotional issue, and there have been colourful meetings. "We have had to expel people from the room because they were obnoxious to the point that we could not tolerate them," former Cemetery Board president Jacques Berkowitz said. He recalls walking out of meetings "practically with tears in my eyes" in the face of comments likening Baron de Hirsch board members to crooks. But "it wasn't meant like that. We had to grow up and understand that these people were covering their own organizations. What's important is that a lot of the tears were caused by individuals who by and large were well meaning. They wanted to protect their organizations as much as possible."

The volunteer Board members from Jewish Family Services who have controlled the Cemetery since its 1971 incorporation were often left dismayed by "this feeling that Jewish Family Services was trying to screw the other affiliates," Berkowitz said.

As the Cemetery's condition improved over the years, the assets of burial societies were increasing and those with plots to sell could raise their prices. In 1987, for example, the Hebrew Sick Benefit Association's revenue from plot sales totalled about $65,000. "It felt really uncomfortable, to be really polite about it, that certain people were benefitting from the work that we were doing," said Berkowitz. "We felt offended that they were making a profit out of the operations of the Cemetery."

When it becomes painfully clear that a Cemetery affiliate (either a burial society or congregation) is nearing the end of its existence—most of its members have died or it is having difficulty paying its assessments—the Baron de Hirsch Cemetery will make overtures to work out an arrangement.

"Sometimes we get assets, sometimes we get land, sometimes we get cash, sometimes we get nothing," said Cemetery executive director Jay Aaron. "The bottom line is we try to do the deal as soon as possible. Most of the affiliates recognize when they're approached that it's in everyone's best interests to do something. Generally the response is good."

To make the passage of the inevitable less painful, affiliates' names are retained on their former sections after they cease to exist. Today, the Baron de Hirsch Cemetery has numerous sections named after their original burial societies or congregations, but owned by Jewish Family Services of the Baron de Hirsch Institute.

Since 2001, the Cemetery Board has consisted of twenty members, fifteen appointed by Jewish Family Services and five representing the affiliates. Under other 2001 changes, the immediate past-president as well as the two most recent past presidents present at a meeting have voting rights. In addition, all past presidents remain honourary members of the board and have speaking privileges at meetings.

The Baron de Hirsch Community Foundation was incorporated in 1976 as a charitable organization. It holds all funds of the Baron de Hirsch Institute in separate accounts, including the Cemetery Capital Fund, which derives from the sale of plots, and the Perpetual Care Fund.

Board members have always "sincerely believed that they were fulfilling the highest level of giving" for people who obviously could not repay, said Steven Tabac, a Cemetery president in the mid-1970s. Long-time Board member and Cemetery chaplain Rabbi Moishe Glustein deems it an honour to have been a member of the Board for the last twenty years. "It's thankless for the people that you are serving. You are serving the deceased and they're not there to thank you or reward you financially, emotionally, personally, anything else."

A cemetery is known as a *chesed shel emes*—a society that doesn't expect remuneration, Rabbi Glustein notes. "People are never going to come back and tell you 'thank you'. They're not going to get up tomorrow morning and give you a fifty-dollar bill. What you're dealing with here are people dedicated to the cause."

5

The Land

Humility and sadness fill my soul when I enter this mournful abode of the
dead. Here all human project and desires, all passions of pride and
power end. Wealth and poverty, love and hate, are all here
levelled within the bosom of mother earth.
—From a Paperman & Sons booklet

The Baron de Hirsch Cemetery today consists of more land than was originally acquired when it was formed in 1905 because a few years after its founding a group of burial societies and congregations banded together to buy several adjacent acres of land that now form the northwest corner of the Cemetery. The Bassarabier Hebrew Sick Benefit Association, Canadian Hebrew Sick Benefit Association, Chevra Mishnayes Congregation, and Chevra T'Hilim Congregation were among the earliest buyers.

The new area as a whole was often referred to as "the Hebrew Sick side". It would become the United Hebrew Cemeteries and was incorporated as such in 1930. United Hebrew Cemeteries for several years operated with its own caretaker and had its own office building on de la Savane Street. Minutes mention that the Baron de Hirsch's Cemetery Department either maintained, supervised, or administered the Hebrew Sick Benefit Association "grounds immediately adjoining our own burial ground," comprising a variety of different organizations.

By 1963, the United Hebrew Cemeteries was comprised of the following associated organizations: Bassarabier Hebrew Sick Benefit Association, Pinsker Synagogue, Congregation Chevra T'Hilim, King George Hebrew Sick Benefit Association, Canadian Hebrew Sick Benefit Association, Workmen's Circle, Congregation Adath Yeshurun-Hadrath Kodesh, North End Wilkomirer Sick Benefit Association, Russian Polish Hebrew Sick Benefit Association, and Congregation Beth Yitzhok.

With the gradual disappearance of benefit societies, the United Hebrew Cemeteries gradually fell into decline. The Baron de Hirsch assumed operations of United Hebrew Cemeteries in March 1978, after its caretaker Max Wolman suddenly passed away. By the February 20, 1980 Board meeting, the United Hebrew Cemeteries was offering its building to Baron de Hirsch for $45,000 and was seeking to join the Cemetery on an equal basis with other affiliates. However, the Baron de Hirsch complained that maintenance standards at United Hebrew Cemeteries had fallen below its own in recent years. The Baron de Hirsch therefore insisted that the United Hebrew's level of upkeep be raised before a merger could be considered.

In January 1981, Smith Brothers monument-makers offered to buy the United Hebrew Cemeteries building as their place of business. There were considerable objections to this move because it would entail the display of Christian monuments on land which is within a Jewish cemetery. Instead, it was recommended that the Cemetery buy the house for caretaker Yves Lahaie, who was living with his family in the tiny basement apartment of the present Baron de Hirsch office building. Finally, in March 1981, Baron de Hirsch Cemetery leased the building for one dollar and renovated it, and Lahaie and his family moved in. The Lahaies continue to live in the only residential building situated on the Cemetery grounds.

The Lahaie family has had a long history at the Baron de Hirsch Cemetery. Yves Lahaie has been working at the Cemetery since 1975. His uncle Gaetan Lahaie died at age thirty-nine in October 1976, after being employed by the Cemetery for over twenty years as foreman. Yves' father and grandfather worked in cemeteries. Although Yves Lahaie is a francophone Québécois, he is so well-versed in Jewish burial ritual that he knows the words to the Hebrew prayers by heart. In June 2005, he was fêted for his thirty years of services to the Cemetery at its annual meeting.

Shortly after buying the United Hebrew Cemeteries office, the Cemetery assumed ownership of the entire United Hebrew Cemeteries. The former United Hebrew Cemeteries now represents about sixteen per cent of the Baron de Hirsch Cemetery's total land area.

Land boundary disputes sometimes cropped up between the many affiliates that have made up the Baron de Hirsch Cemetery. Sometimes disputes over land or other issues would make their way to the Rabbinical Court of Greater Montreal, whose decisions were binding.

One such dispute in 1982 pitted several burial societies and congregations against each other over the calculation of accurate land boundaries. It involved the Dominion Hebrew Sick Benefit Association, Anshei Ukraina (Zichron Kedoshim Congregation), Canadian Hebrew Sick Benefit Association, Congregation Nusach Hoari and the North End Wilkomirer Hebrew Sick Benefit Association.

As the office of the Chief Rabbi explained on September 15, 1982, the court ruled there had been "no deliberate attempt on the part of any of these organizations or of the Baron de Hirsch Institute to defraud, conceal or otherwise usurp any property belonging to another organization." However, there had been errors in boundary calculations over the years, meaning some organizations derived benefits while others suffered losses.

To rectify the situation, the court ruled that the Baron de Hirsch Cemetery had to give the equivalent of thirty grave sites to the Anshei Ukraina–Zichron Kedoshim Congregation.

The Dominion Hebrew Sick Benefit Association, as a result of its having gained the equivalent of twelve grave sites in the miscalculation of boundaries, had to pay the Baron de Hirsch Cemetery $36,000, based on a calculation of three hundred dollars per grave. This sum was an average of the fair market value of a grave site (one hundred dollars) in 1964, when the first miscalculation of boundaries occurred, and the 1982 fair market value (five hundred dollars).

Since the Anshei Ukraina–Zichron Kedoshim Congregation used four gravesites on land owned by the Canadian Hebrew Sick Benefit Association, it had to pay $1,200 to Canadian Hebrew Sick based on the same calculation. The Canadian Hebrew Sick Benefit Association used six gravesites on land owned by the Congregation Nusach Hoari, and had to pay $1,800 to Nusach Hoari.

The North End Wilkomirer Hebrew Sick Benefit Association was exempt from any action, since it was not encroached upon and did not suffer any losses nor derive any gains.

In the mid-1930s, the Baron de Hirsch Cemetery developed the section called Memorial Park. People who were not affiliated with congregations or burial societies could buy plots there. "This new part of our Cemetery has been excellently constructed, and should be visited by those of our community desirous of knowing the work done by our institution," the

Baron de Hirsch Institute crowed in its 1934 annual report.

In the mid-1970s initial plans for development of another section of the Cemetery to be known as New Memorial Park called for something much different than the first Memorial Park. The elimination of all upright monuments was considered, "in accordance with more modern arrangements in North America," Cemetery executive director Philip Finkel wrote in a letter to affiliates. "This will be far less costly for the bereaved, and far easier for us to maintain."

Plans were briefly floated to divide the New Memorial Park in two sections, one for men and one for women. For ease of operation, no tombstones above ground level would be permitted and only ground markers would be used. This would allow for the elimination of foundations, and for maintenance and grave openings to be done entirely by machine.

Those plans were dropped in the end, however, and the section ended up accepting conventional tombstones.

The Baron de Hirsch Cemetery could be excused if it were diagnosed with an identity crisis. After all, the Cemetery has been given all sorts of names over the years and has seemingly been located in several neighbourhoods and suburbs of Montreal, even though it has never moved an inch.

First, when the land was bought, the area was known as Côte des Neiges, the name of the old incorporated village in which it was located. But it wasn't long before the Cemetery became known to people as Cartierville, even though the municipality of Cartierville is situated miles to the north. That is undoubtedly due to the fact the Park & Island Railway tram, known as the Cartierville line, later the No. 17 bus, stopped near the Cemetery. In the Cemetery's early years, the tram served as the main form of transportation for visitors.

However, by 1907 the Baron de Hirsch Institute was referring to the Cemetery as being located in Notre Dame de Grâce, despite the fact that the Montreal neighbourhood of NDG is a few miles to the southwest. To add to the confusion, Cemetery societies took to calling the Cemetery's home as Côte Saint Laurent or Côte St. Lawrence. Finally, the Côte des Neiges West name gained favour for several decades, and was included in newspaper accounts that mentioned the Cemetery. "Years and years ago, when we had to write where the burial took place, it was 'this and this

Entrance to the Beth Hachnesses Nusach Hoari (North End)
section of the Cemetery.
[Photo: D.R. Cowles]

section of the Côte des Neiges West cemetery,'" Herbert Paperman explained. That was done to differentiate the Cemetery from the Catholic Côte des Neiges Cemetery on the west side of Mount Royal.

The popular nomenclature was complicated by the existence of the United Hebrew Cemeteries next to Baron de Hirsch Cemetery. In 1938, the Cemetery adopted the official name Baron de Hirsch United Cemeteries, combining the Baron de Hirsch and United Hebrew Cemetery names. Bronze plates were erected at the entrance with that name.

But the Cemetery has also been known as the Baron de Hirsch and Affiliated Cemeteries. And in 1980, it was given an official French corporate name, Le Cimetière Baron de Hirsch Inc.–Baron de Hirsch Cemetery Inc.

Even the street that the Cemetery calls home took a circuitous route before obtaining its name. While a 1778 plan of part of the island of Montreal called the road Chemin de la Savane, the road took on the name de la Petite-Liesse followed by rue Saint-Jean-Baptiste at an unknown date. In 1912, it became rue Boudria. It was named rue Namur in 1914 and finally rue de la Savane on March 14, 1947. Small wonder then that many Montrealers are familiar with the Cemetery but remain unaware its name is Baron de Hirsch Cemetery. For many people, it is "de la Savane".

Fulfilling the responsibility to tend the graves has presented various challenges over the years.

A report to a Cemetery Committee meeting in early May 1922 indicated that fallen tombstones were a problem. A committee was appointed to ensure that workers would straighten them. At a November 1924 meeting, the caretaker was asked to make a list of all fallen tombstones. Two-and-a half years had gone by since the problem had been raised, yet the caretaker came up with a list of seventy-nine monuments that had to be fixed.

A large part of the problem stemmed from the fact the underground cement foundations needed to provide support to monuments were often not poured below the frost line, leaving them susceptible to the effects of heaving earth. Sometimes, the cement used was of poor quality, which left the foundations susceptible to cracking.

In 1926, a representative of the Nusach Hoari Congregation reported that foundations should be at least three-and-a-half feet deep. In fact, even three and a half feet (about one metre) was not deep enough, as Aaron

Paltiel, past president of the Adath Jeshurun Congregation, noted in 1934. He suggested that foundations be dug to a depth of at least five feet. He was thanked and told his idea would receive serious attention. By the standards of the building codes of 2005, Paltiel was right—foundations should be dug to a level of five feet, which is below the frost line. However, even in the early 1940s, the Cemetery moved that the caretaker should place the foundations at a depth of four feet. Meanwhile, the Baron de Hirsch Institute warned affiliates to look after tombstones that had fallen or were otherwise out of position "as it was an eyesore to the community."

More concerted efforts to improve the monument situation began to be made in the late 1970s, when the Cemetery authorities realized that many monuments had fallen because they were set without foundations. That led former Cemetery president Steven Tabac to warn monument-makers in a June 1977 letter that "in future, no more monuments can be installed before a foundation has been installed. This action will avoid possible difficulties arising from falling tombstones."

The Cemetery also urged affiliates to repair tombstones in their sections. In a letter to affiliates in May 1977, Philip Finkel said the large number of fallen monuments in the Cemetery "creates a situation which is unsightly and undignified. Raising monuments is an expensive undertaking and we tend to say, 'Let it wait!' But we cannot wait, for the problem will increase year by year. We must do it now even if it hurts."

At the May 1980 Board meeting, after counting about twenty-five hundred fallen and leaning monuments and complaining that for years, affiliates had been urged to raise fallen monuments but with little response, the Board decided to notify affiliates by registered letter that "because of the hazards involved and the deleterious appearance to our Cemetery we will start immediately to raise all fallen and leaning monuments and perform the necessary repairs involved, the costs for this to be charged to our general maintenance fund."

The challenge was still an issue in 1988. That year, the Cemetery made a "very bold move," Jacques Berkowitz, who was president at the time, said in an interview. "We had so many stones that were leaners and tilters, we said 'Okay, we're going to take the heat,' and decided to put several hundred stones down on the ground. Ads calling attention to fallen monuments were placed in *The Gazette*, *The Suburban* and *The Canadian Jewish News*. The heat was not that bad," Berkowitz said. "There were only a few calls from families demanding, 'What did you do? You didn't look after it.' We had to do something."

In the fall of 1992, a young girl and her aunt were visiting a relative's grave at the Baron de Hirsch Cemetery; the girl's leg was injured when a leaning monument toppled and fell on her. "It could have been a lot worse," Jay Aaron explained.

Before the end of the year, after the monument injured the girl, a Special Monument Repair Assessment was implemented by means of a one-year fee of $35,000 for repairs, prorated among affiliates. "We'd been talking about it, and arguing about it, for years, and just not doing anything," Jay Aaron said. The Cemetery reluctantly decided to proceed with monument repairs at its own expense if families could not be contacted or were unwilling or unable to pay.

"When a family buries a loved one and purchases a monument, they do not realize the maintenance work that may be necessary in the future," Berkowitz explained. For their part, burial societies and congregations are technically responsible for the repairs in areas they still own. But "the answer inevitably is going to be 'We don't have the money,' but it is the family's responsibility."

In 2002, a test was conducted on four rows of an old section in terrible condition. Monuments were temporarily removed and foundations rebuilt to current standards, using reinforcement rods and top-quality cement. The test worked well and a solution to the falling monument problem appeared to have been found.

"Straightening monuments is not enough," explained former general manager Gerald Silverberg. "They'll fall again unless you get to the foundation of the problem, the foundations themselves. Doing anything less is a band-aid solution."

On May 21, 2003, the Cemetery Board passed a resolution authorizing the spending of one million dollars over ten years to repair foundations in the old United Hebrew Cemeteries sections, with the money coming out of the Perpetual Care Fund.

"You remove the old monument, dig up the old foundation, pour a new foundation, and replace the monument," Aaron said.

The first section to be repaired in 2003 was North End Wilkomirer. Monuments and ledgers were removed, new foundations were poured, and the monuments were put back into place. Similar repairs have been made in the King George, Hadrath Kodesh, and Montreal Workers Circle sections of the old United Hebrew Cemeteries.

Board members speculate as to how foundations could have been built improperly over the years. "I don't generalize that (people) were ill-intentioned, but I have a feeling that they didn't think, they didn't know," said Berkowitz. "A lot of people worked in factories and they were not as well educated. They didn't have the thinking and experience we would have." Former president Herbert Isenberg speculated in an interview that burial societies gave foundation-building jobs to workers who may have cheated them because there was no supervision.

In any event, the process of restoring the monuments of long-gone people "is a beautiful thing," said Rabbi Glustein. "We have no obligation (to do the work) because the people have passed away. But out of respect to them—they are helpless—we do it. It's not respectful if you come into a cemetery and find toppled monuments."

Water was a problem in the Cemetery for many years. When people came to the Baron de Hirsch Cemetery after a rainfall, "they would be slopping in water," said Joe Alter, a Board member since the 1980s who works in the construction industry. "People would be walking in puddles to a burial because the grounds would not take the water fast enough."

The reason is that a subterranean stream passes about twenty-five feet under the land, and the terrain has a high water table.

While the French term "la savane" means "grassland" or "prairie" in English, Cemetery lore has long associated it with grassy swampland. "That's where the name de la Savane comes from," said Silverberg. "You don't have to go down too far before you hit water." He said the water starts at the corner of Kindersley Avenue and Lucerne Road in the Town of Mount Royal, cuts diagonally through the Cemetery and ends on de Sorel in Montreal. Workers digging for core samples on a Cemetery road have hit it.

To try to absorb the water, the Cemetery authorities came up with the ingenious solution early in the twentieth century of planting water-loving poplar trees. "To keep water down to a minimum, someone dug trenches, the water flowed into the trenches, the trees drank the water and the trees grew to enormous heights," said Silverberg.

As early as 1915, the City of Montreal's Health Department was warning the Cemetery to remove lavatories that were in close proximity to the ditches. In 1917 a special committee was appointed with the main responsibility of repairing drains and ditches.

As described in a souvenir book of Tifereth Beth David Jerusalem, "the Chaluzic (pioneer) spirit" of members of the Tifereth Jerusalem was evident in the 1930s, when it came to the Cemetery's "swamp-filled" land. "The order of the day for Sunday used to be salami sandwiches, whiskey, and shovels as the younger members would hike to the Cemetery to dig ditches to drain the swamps!"

In late February 1966, the Bassarabier Hebrew Sick Benefit Association complained in a registered letter that "the water problem has now become so acute that we are no longer able to utilize this land to service our members and carry out other obligations that involve its use." The Association asked that a permanent solution be found.

Drainage pipes were put down on several occasions, sometimes resulting in the loss of land for burials. At a January 1967 meeting, for example, it was revealed that the laying of a drainage pipe resulted in the loss of some land to the Hebrew Sick Benefit Association and King George Benefit Society. They were reimbursed at a cost of one hundred and seventy-five dollars per square foot. Still, the problem lingered.

"They would open a grave for a burial, and by the time the casket was lowered, it was full of water," said former president Herbert Isenberg. And so, "every meeting was about drainage."

In 1981, the Board spent $35,000 on drainage but the problem remained. It was pointed out at an April 21, 1982 Board meeting that poor drainage could create a serious health hazard for people living close to the Cemetery. If the problem was not addressed, there were fears that the City of Montreal would intervene and do the repairs itself.

A few years later, a long-term solution appeared to have been found. The work included closing up all roadside ditches and open gullies and streams running through the Cemetery. This was to allow greater pedestrian mobility, and reduce insects and weeds. Perforated pipe was placed underground along all the roads, along with French drains. Some sections of the Cemetery were raised and levelled to allow the entire Cemetery to drain freely. The cost to perform all this work was about $150,000. The situation has vastly improved, then president Herbert Isenberg explained in a September 1983 letter to affiliates.

***

For many years, winter driving conditions within the Cemetery grounds were a challenge. Herbert Paperman recalls burials during winter storms in the 1940s at Baron de Hirsch:

"We used to get a big snowstorm and they couldn't open the roads in the Cemetery. We used to come down as far as the gate. [Caretaker] Harry Rabinovitch would have a sleigh with a horse. The snow was knee deep. [We'd] put the casket on top of the sleigh and the family would try to get a minyan together and the horse would take us into the Cemetery. The family would also get in by sleigh."

In the 1950s, the Paperman funeral home gave the Cemetery a 1934 Packard hearse. Harry Rabinovitch adapted it by putting large concrete blocks in the back (there was no such thing as four-wheel drive in those days), and then attached a snow plough in the front, and used it to clear the snow. "That thing would go through three, four feet of snow like nothing. That, I think, was their first snow plough besides the horses."

In an aside, Mr. Paperman describes how Paperman's ordered graves from the Cemetery in the early days: "My uncle used to tell me, when he was a youngster and got an order for a grave he had to go out to the Cemetery. Telephones not everybody had." Doing so required confronting a big dog. "He was afraid to go up and give the order because of the dog, so he used to carry a hidden baseball bat or stick."

The roads were much narrower than they are today. "We used to have problems in the winter," recalls Herbert Paperman, because snow would often hide the ditches and people would drive right into them. "They used to have to go and get a horse to pull them out."

The Cemetery Board warned in an "Information for Next of Kin" brochure that "extreme caution should be taken to avoid the ditches at the sides of the roads, especially during winter when these ditches are filled with snow and cannot be seen." When the Cemetery filled in all the roadside ditches, affiliates were told it would result in "minimizing accidents and preventing vehicles from falling in, especially during the winter months."

The ditches are now gone, but speeding remains a problem.

"Unfortunately, there's no shortage of people who have very heavy feet and it doesn't matter if they're driving on the Cemetery roadway or street roadway—they go barrelling down," said Jay Aaron. "It always has been a problem and it always will be." At least boorish drivers no longer plummet into the ditches, as used to be the case.

"I myself have witnessed people getting knocked down by cars," said Jacques Berkowitz. "The drivers then turn around and blame the victims by blurting out things like, 'What are you doing walking in the middle of the road?'"

Funeral processions take precedence over other vehicular traffic on Cemetery grounds. And on Sundays during the peak holiday periods of Passover and the High Holidays, security guards attempt to restrict traffic to vehicles bearing a valid handicapped sign. But the clergy have the right to drive in the Cemetery at all times.

To eliminate the car problem, the Board has toyed with the idea of having mini-buses that would circulate throughout the grounds, allowing people to board or hop off at will. "I think that it would avoid a lot of problems. But it's just never come to fruition," said Berkowitz.

Baron de Hirsch Cemetery has been endowed with a large stand of cottonwood poplar trees—approximately thirteen hundred—that were planted about eighty years ago. The trees were certainly nice to look at, as the Baron de Hirsch's Philip Finkel pointed out in an April 1976 letter to affiliates: "Our Cemetery is made beautiful by the fact that we have magnificent lines of poplars bordering our roads. When everything is in order, we will have an outstandingly fine Cemetery."

However, trees, like people, can die. At the August 18, 1982 Board meeting it was reported that twenty-one trees in dangerous rotting condition had to be removed on the grounds of two affiliates at a cost of $6,500. Both groups were notified repeatedly but claimed to have insufficient funds to meet the costs. "As you are aware the present situation is most grave, urgent and dangerous, and as the administrators of the entire Cemetery it is our responsibility that the safety of the public is continuously protected," read a registered letter. "Fortunately up to the present time of writing nobody has been injured or killed." To pay its costs, one of the affiliates, North End Wilkomirer, decided in September 1982 to give the Cemetery nine plots in exchange for the cutting down of ten trees.

The trees have large root systems that constantly search for water, which can cause damage to foundations and drainage systems. When proper drainage was installed and the last ditches were covered in 1984, the thirsty poplar trees had started to die because they were cut off from their water supply. They are now being replaced with long-life columnar oaks. The new trees don't grow as high as poplars, but they don't require vast quantities of water, and they have smaller root systems that don't spread greatly.

The Board has also discussed other plans in recent years to beautify the Cemetery, although they have yet to be realized. In 2002, Silverberg outlined an estimated $20,000 plan to transform an asphalt road surrounding the Children's Monument with brick, a floral and shrub garden, benches, and flowering trees. Groves of trees in addition to the columnar oaks have also been considered in various areas of the Cemetery. "Right now the Cemetery is large fields of tombstones, which is not the most pleasant sight when somebody walks in," Silverberg said.

"Making the Cemetery more beautiful is possible, but it'll never be mistaken for another Mount Royal Cemetery," said Berkowitz. From the outset, the Cemetery on the mountain "was designed in such a way that you would have trees and flower beds and gardens." Baron de Hirsch Cemetery, by contrast, "has one tombstone after the other and doesn't lend itself to much beautification."

Jewish law requires cemeteries to be fenced or walled. In the early days, the Baron de Hirsch Cemetery met that requirement with wooden fences. In September 1913, the "United Cemeteries of Côte des Neiges—Côte St. Lawrence" advertised with much hoopla the dedication of a new fence. Translated, the Yiddish ad from the *Keneder Adler* reads:

> We are dedicating the fence we have been building on Sunday at 9 a.m. Celebrations to last all day. The best speakers, all the rabbis of Montreal, Chazan Yudelson with his choir, refreshments. All are welcome to attend. Take the mountain car and transfer to the Cartierville car, which will take you right there. A committee will greet every streetcar.

Similar excitement greeted the October 1919 dedication of a road by what was now called the "United Cemeteries of Côte St. Laurent", then comprised of eleven sick benefit societies and congregations.

> The celebration will take place on the Cemetery grounds (read the ad in the *Keneder Adler*). If the weather is bad this Sunday, we will have the celebrations at Rachel Market Hall. The banquet will

begin at 2 p.m. Big-band music will play. Rabbis and others will speak and a chazan with a choir will sing. A raffle for silver lights (candle holders) will take place at the banquet.

When tenders to paint the fence were issued in 1930, the lowest price that came in was ninety dollars. But it was agreed that the caretaker could do it for less and the job was given to him, as minutes from a September 15, 1930 meeting show.

By 1950, however, the Cemetery decided to erect a stone fence. In 1960, after ten years of study and planning, a sixteen-hundred-foot-long linear stone fence was built on either side of the main entrance on de la Savane. Affiliates were expected to pay percentages of costs based on their Cemetery holdings. "There was a feeling that this matter should be resolved quickly without any of the usual repercussions and hysteria which some of the societies will want to express," said Cemetery Committee chair Abe Nissenson. Most agreed that the stone wall greatly enhanced the Cemetery's appearance, but there was a dispute with the Hebrew Sick Benefit Association over costs.

Plans that year also called for a steel fence to enclose the rest of the Cemetery, but this was postponed because of disagreement with the Hebrew Sick. The latter was toying with the notion of building an inside fence that would separate the Baron de Hirsch and United Hebrew Cemeteries' grounds from each other. The Baron de Hirsch Institute's David Weiss expressed the hope in a September 21, 1960 letter that the Hebrew Sick might change its attitude and eventually participate in the exterior fence-building, "despite the previous irresponsible behaviour of this group." Fortunately, the fence segregation plan was dropped and steel fences were erected. One such steel fence, on the west side of the Cemetery, was built in 1965 for $8,375, according to the minutes of an October Board meeting that year.

The stone wall erected on de la Savane in 1960 did not fare too well. By 1975, it was desperately in need of repair with stones "dangerously loose" in some sections, a monthly letter to affiliates noted. A patch-up job cost $4,900. Alas, a decade later, fears were again being expressed that the crumbling stone fence would have to be repaired or injuries were possible.

"Everything that would help deteriorate the stability of a wall was going on," said Joe Alter, who became involved in the project because of his construction industry experience. The mortar was giving out because snow was improperly being dumped against the fence, which couldn't support the weight. Ground movements from burials along the inside of the stone wall were causing problems. As well, the concrete sill on top of the fence was too narrow and let rain fall down both sides, resulting in further damage. Stone work on the outside was staggered with stone work on the inside and new concrete was poured on top of old, meaning a temporary fence was never needed. The six-foot-high fence should be good for another thirty years without needing repairs, Alter predicted.

While workers were repairing the stone wall fronting the Cemetery on de la Savane in 1993, they made a surprising find. "We were demolishing the columns in front to rebuild the stone, [and] the guy with the jackhammer realized he hit metal," recalled Alter. "That's when we realized a time capsule was put in when the original stone wall was put up," in 1937.

A sealed, rusted steel box had been found. Among the discoveries: crumbling copies of the *Keneder Adler, The Canadian Jewish Review* (headlined "Present Regime Cannot Continue in Palestine") and *The Gazette* of July 29, 1937 ("Deliberate Plot Revealed in Belfast Bomb Explosion"), minutes of the Board meeting in which plans to build a stone gate and fence were concluded, and the 1932 and 1935 annual reports of the Federation of Jewish Philanthropies of Montreal. "We absolutely had no idea," said Jay Aaron, who was president of the Cemetery Board at the time. "We'd never seen any papers to indicate that this was there."

Baron de Hirsch Institute Board minutes from June 1937 reveal that the total cost of the stone fence along de la Savane was $1,600. Contributions from the affiliated congregations and mutual aid societies ranged from the twenty dollars of the Ukrainer Jewish Congregation to the Baron de Hirsch's five hundred and twenty dollars.

When the new wall was completed, a new time capsule with pieces of information from 1993 was placed under the new gate of the main entrance.

Gravesites are considered sacred in Judaism and people around Jewish cemeteries are careful where they walk. One way of preventing people from unintentionally desecrating gravesites was through the use of cement or granite ledgers (commonly known as slabs) over the grave. "They're there because it was an edict in Halacha that no one could walk on a grave," said Gerald Silverberg.

But the slabs, which transformed graves into semi-mausoleums, have caused a lot of problems in the Cemetery. "They sink, they shift, they crack," resulting in broken foundations, Brandee Berson of Berson & Son Monuments, explained.

On August 8, 1961 the Cemetery Board addressed the issue, and decided that "these slabs deface the appearance of the Cemetery." Confronted with increasing numbers of people contracting for slabs instead of decorations for graves, the Board decided to ban further use of slabs in new graves. However, many of the slabs remain today, particularly in older sections of the Cemetery.

Other features of the Cemetery which were once standard are long gone. In 1912, H. Rosenthal, the Cemetery's caretaker, who was living on the Cemetery grounds, applied to the Baron de Hirsch Institute for a fifty-dollar loan to buy a cow. Adolphe Goldstein, chairman of the Cemetery Committee, recommended to the Baron de Hirsch Board on March 7, 1912 that the loan be approved, and the treasurer was authorized to issue a cheque in that amount. Rosenthal went on to build barns, sheds, stables, a summer kitchen, chicken coops, and an annex to the washhouse. They were mostly for his and his family's use, but the Board found the installations useful, and it paid him three hundred dollars for them. A new barn was erected in 1930.

In 1922 the City of Montreal condemned the caretaker's residence. It was demolished and a new caretaker's residence was built at a cost of about $7,000. (Over the years, the position of caretaker has had a variety of titles, ranging from janitor to superintendent to foreman.)

A room in the new residence was dedicated to the memory of Goldstein, the late Chair of the Cemetery Committee. Previous plans had called for construction of the Goldstein Memorial Gateway at the Cemetery entrance, but it could not be built because of a shortage of funds.

Things improved in 1926 when Herbert M. Levine, chair of the Cemetery Committee, praised the Independent Hebrew Sick Benefit Society for building an archway at the entrance of the society's burial grounds. At the annual meeting that year of the Federation of Jewish Philanthropies, he urged all other societies "to endeavour to improve the appearance of their respective lots by erecting archway divisions." In 1930 several old buildings were demolished, which served, as the Cemetery

Committee noted at the 1930 annual meeting, to enhance its appearance.

In 1931 "a long-felt want" was finally accomplished, namely the building of a modern greenhouse, located in what is now the New Memorial Park section of the Cemetery. It would enable all those interested in improving and beautifying the plots of their departed relatives and friends, to secure flowers and shrubs at a nominal cost, the 1931 annual meeting noted. "With such facilities the Cemetery property itself will be beautified and improved." By 1937, the Board was boasting in an annual report that it was "one of the finest public owned institutions in our community."

Unfortunately, the caretaker's residence built in the 1920s wasn't much of an improvement; it was condemned in 1950. It had long been considered an embarrassment, with numerous out-of-town visitors complaining about the lack of facilities at the caretaker's building. At a special meeting to discuss the issue on December 25, 1950 the various affiliates could not reach a consensus. Isaac Eiley of the Russian Polish Sick Benefit Association said he could not see what benefit societies who purchased land on "the Hebrew Sick side" would derive from the construction of a building on the Baron de Hirsch side. The residence and barn were demolished that year.

Superintendent Harry Rabinovitch, who had built an extension to the greenhouse without permission, was informed that the extension was subject to removal at any time as was the "janitor's shack" which housed the janitor and his family. Complaints continued into the 1950s that there was only one water tap to serve the public and no suitable washrooms.

In May 1963, a gold key was used to open the new administration building of what was then the Baron de Hirsch Institute's Cemetery Department. Rabbi Charles Bender officiated at the outdoor service, which included the gold key door opening by Max Kaufman, the Institute's vice-president. The indoor part of the ceremony included the unveiling of two special plaques. One was in honour of Abraham Nissenson, in recognition of his services as chairman of the Institute's Cemetery Committee. The second recorded the official inscription *Chesed Shel Emes*, a traditional Hebrew title for a burial place.

The original idea in 1960 was that the Baron de Hirsch Institute would finance the building and allow burial societies to use it based on a proportion of their holdings, as David Weiss noted. This was changed and affiliates were charged a percentage based on the cemetery land they held. Tenders were accepted to construct the new building for $67,428.

The caretaker had continued to live in the "shack" until the early 1960s, when a decision was made to demolish both it and a "dangerously crumbling" equipment shed. Finally, he was invited to move into an apartment in the new Cemetery office building, an arrangement that was supposed to be temporary but lasted for years. Conditions in the basement apartment weren't much better, former Board members say. A new residence arrived in the early 1980s when the former United Hebrew Cemeteries building on de la Savane was renovated and transformed into a residence. It is now the home of caretaker Yves Lahaie.

In 1984, the Cemetery received zoning approval from the city to demolish a barn behind the main office that served as the maintenance building, and to replace it by a modern two-storey building at a cost of $139,000. A dedication ceremony for the still-existing and much used Perpetual Care Maintenance Building, with garage and maintenance facilities, took place on May 21, 1986.

In 2000, the office building was renovated. Office space was added in the basement for the general manager, as well as a lunchroom for staff and improved public washroom facilities with access for the disabled.

And so, a Cemetery that was once home to sheds and shacks, can now boast of modern office, residential, and maintenance buildings.

Time was when the "cutting of hay" around tombstones on Cemetery grounds was done almost entirely by hand. "As far back as I could remember, grass was cut but they weren't manicured like they are today. It requires a lot of labour," said Herbert Paperman.

In a January 1947 Committee meeting, Cemetery Committee chair Herbert Levine "pointed out with pardonable pride that the development of land at Côte des Neiges from a mud swamp to its present state was in keeping with Jewish tradition and that the last resting place was not only for those who had departed but also for the living who from time to time came to pay their last tribute to those who were near and dear to them."

But caretaker Harry Rabinovitch had had enough of manual labour. Stating "it was very difficult to cut the hay around the tombstones under the present conditions," at a June 23, 1949 Committee meeting, he urged the purchase of a "cutting machine" without further delay and presented a catalogue showing the type of machines available. But the matter was tabled when a Board member expressed doubt whether such a machine would be suitable for work between the graves. By the 1950s, however, the Cemetery purchased an automotive hay machine, grass cutters, and a snow thrower.

Until 1976, the Cemetery was impeded by not having an efficient way of transporting earth. "Many of you were familiar with the sight of men using wheelbarrows for this purpose," reported Philip Finkel in a letter to affiliates. Fortunately, one of the monument setters of the time donated a dump truck to the Cemetery.

And in 1990, Cemetery General Manager Jerry Glantz recommended the purchase of a casket carriage to ease the burden for the family when burying a loved one. "Our community is aging and it is becoming very difficult to take the casket from the hearse onto the Cemetery for burial," he reported at a January 10, 1990 Board meeting.

For several decades, complaints were made about people attending funerals, unveilings or visiting loved ones at the Cemetery being accosted by individuals collecting money for various charities or causes, or for themselves. A complaint arose as early as a January 1925 Cemetery Committee meeting "that several people were going around with boxes and making collections at funerals and annoying people." Letters were sent to all burial societies and congregations in an attempt to stop these collections.

The letters didn't work for long, because by the early 1930s inquiries were being made as to whether anything could be done to regulate charity requests at the Cemetery as visitors were being "pestered by professional collectors."

By the early 1940s, complaints were voiced that mourners coming to pay their respects to their departed ones "were molested on their visits there" by charity-seekers. At a 1941 Cemetery Committee meeting, Jacob H. Wener, a former president of the Baron de Hirsch Institute, said collections were being made prior to the High Holidays by people, some without proper authorization, and appealed for the cooperation of burial societies and synagogues "to eradicate this evil." Among those making collections were members of the Malbish Arumim Society and the Hebrew Consumptive Aid Society.

Rabbi Moishe Glustein recalls raising money at the Cemetery shortly after the State of Israel was founded. "I remember to get out to the Cemetery from any part of the city would take at least an hour. You had to take the 17 streetcar and get off at de la Savane, which really wasn't a street then. It was a plain field and you had to walk down the field to get to the Cemetery. I remember as a kid, I was a member of a Zionist organization called the B'nei Akiva and in order for us to raise funds for the State of Israel we would go out before the High Holidays to raise money for JNF [Jewish National Fund]. One time (in) 1948, right after the beginning of the state of Israel, we took Israeli flags by the door (cemetery entrance) and came back with a hundred and one dollars. It was a tremendous accomplish-ment."

In 1954, the topic reared its head once more. E.M. Berger, chairman of the Baron de Hirsch Cemetery Committee, complained of the presence of "beggars," especially during the High Holiday season, and expressed his view that fund solicitations should be completely barred, with an announcement to that effect placed in Jewish newspapers.

At a 1961 Committee meeting, the Cemetery again ruled that soli-citation of funds was forbidden and that "proper personnel be hired, such as members of the Corps des Commissionaires … with instructions to rigidly enforce this rule." Strict regulations would also be placed "to curb 'begging' on cemeteries, especially during holiday season," along with "strict supervision of persons performing memorial services and prayers on the cemeteries."

By May 1980, the Board was being told the Cemetery was being "plagued" by people soliciting for money. "Not only have these solicitors made their requests amongst the mourners at funerals, in addition, their requests have been dishonest in that the stated purpose of the request has not been the true one." A motion was passed at a May 14, 1980 meeting that no solici-tations could be made on Cemetery grounds by unauthorized persons.

Today, the problem has been largely quelled. For the most part, only people who have been authorized to do so, collect money inside the Cemetery. In a brochure, relatives are told only two groups can solicit within the Cemetery: the Independent Hebrew Sick Benefit Association and the Veterans Field of Remembrance. On virtually every Sunday, and on high-traffic periods like the High Holidays, Mother's Day, and Father's Day, volunteers like Arthur Schwartz of the now-defunct Independent

Hebrew Sick Benefit Society are at the Cemetery collecting money for disabled Israeli veterans. In 2002 alone, they collected $6,000.

Trying to find the site of a loved one's grave at Baron de Hirsch Cemetery is often a challenge to visitors, but it is much easier than it used to be. As former Cemetery president Herbert Isenberg said, people would come to the Cemetery and ask "where's Mr. So-and-So buried?" Often, the Cemetery was hard-pressed to find the answer. "Nobody knew where anybody was buried."

In 1976, Philip Finkel noted in a letter to affiliates that the complicated situation was "typical of most old cemeteries which have grown without too much planning. At funerals and unveilings, much unnecessary confusion is caused by the fact that precise information concerning location is not given." As well, Hebrew names were often spelled in a variety of ways, he said.

There was a filing system for burials, but most of the cards weren't up to date. To limit the confusion, medal-sporting veterans would set up a table on Sundays and direct people who were lost. Eventually, people were hired to record the names on most of the tombstones and to note their locations.

A computer system has been in place since the late 1990s to make it easier to find people's graves. In some sections of the Cemetery, however, there is no apparent system in the layout of graves. The practice used to be "to use every available inch of space for a grave," said Silverberg. "If they found they could create a space behind a monument, they would create the space. It was the European tradition where every inch was used."

Personalities also came into play, Silverberg explained. A president or chairman of an affiliate would give a good friend a choice location, wherever it may have been. This practice made it impossible to bury people in straight lines. Some people were buried along designated paths, others were buried too close to one another in an attempt to sell more plots. Occasionally in older sections, foundations had to be broken to make way for new burials. "People may have been very well meaning," said Jacques Berkowitz, "but they lacked foresight."

Today it's possible to locate the exact burial location of any individual buried in either the Baron de Hirsch or Back River Cemeteries. Both cemeteries have data on the JewishGen Online Worldwide Burial Registry (www.jewishgen.org).

***

Fund-raising has always been a challenge for the Cemetery. Lawyer and long-time board member Jacques Berkowitz once found a novel way to add some funds to the coffers of the non-profit Baron de Hirsch Cemetery. "Maybe I'm a schnorrer, I don't know," he said. One day he was walking down the path facing Mountain Sights Road, on the western extremity, looking at the industrial properties that overlook the Cemetery on that side. "I see one of the buildings and I say, 'Look at that—they have illegal views on the Cemetery.'" The building had windows opening onto the Cemetery, contrary to Quebec's Civil Code. It turned out that the building belonged to one of his clients.

Berkowitz picked up the phone and told his client he had an illegal view on the Cemetery grounds. "Make you a deal," he told the client. "We're not going to talk about illegal views," in exchange for a $5,000 contribution to the Cemetery. The Cemetery got its five thousand.

Board members have gone to extremes in other ways to save the Cemetery money. When the Cemetery needed a new loader to dig and break the ground in the winter, former president Herbert Isenberg called the dealer, brought him to the Cemetery, and said "Look, it's a cemetery, it's community, we don't have the money." The dealer agreed to sell the Cemetery the $50,000 machine at dealer cost. "This is the way things went."

It is a sad fact of life that when a Jewish cemetery makes the news, it is usually because the sacred ground has fallen victim to vandalism or desecration. On several occasions, especially in recent decades, the Cemetery has had tombstones overturned or defaced with graffiti. And not all such acts of sometimes anti-Semitic vandalism make the news. In 1983, teens overturned monuments and pulled floral arrangements from several graves. In the late 1990s, a couple of gunshots were fired from de la Savane Road at the Cemetery office building, "and you can still see a bullet hole in the wall," pointed out Jay Aaron.

In a 1987 letter to Jewish community institutions, the Chief Rabbi of Montreal called for all necessary steps to be taken to avoid vandalism:

> It often occurs that a Jewish cemetery remains without supervision
> and/or people to take care of such needs as keeping the fences in
> repair in order to prevent vandalism or natural damage from

occurring, resulting in a desecration of these holy places ... It is, therefore, incumbent on any communal body or individual who has the wherewithal, to intervene for the maintenance and protection of these cemeteries, and to take all necessary steps to ensure that these eternal resting places of our honoured, departed fellow Jews are maintained with befitting dignity, in perpetuity.

> Signed first day of Shevat, 5748
> Montreal
> Rabbi Pinchas Hirschprung

One of the most serious acts of vandalism at the Cemetery, and one that did receive large-scale media attention, occurred in April 1990. Twenty-five monuments were overturned and desecrated with swastikas and skinhead slogans, such as "Die Jews", "Skins", and "oi-oi", as a report in *The Suburban* described. Out of respect for the dead, garbage bags were placed over the headstones until they could be repaired. The reaction was swift. The Canadian Jewish Congress called for an immediate consultation among leaders of cultural communities and public security officials to discuss ways to control an "insidious threat posed to our city by the marginal, but nevertheless dangerous, racist skinhead movement." Frank Dimant, executive vice-president of B'nai Brith Canada's League for Human Rights, added "I am deeply saddened by this display of hate," and noted that his father and father-in-law are buried in the cemetery.

The Executive Committee of the City of Montreal and the Quebec Human Rights Commission denounced the attack. Sophia Florakas, vice-president of the Quebec Human Rights Commission, called on "all of Quebec society not to ignore the gravity of these hateful, despicable acts, because we are convinced that we must act against manifestations of intolerance, hatred and contempt towards religion, racial, and ethnic minorities."

One Saturday night, Jacques Berkowitz recalls getting a phone call that there had been vandalism at the Cemetery. He arrived to a sad scene of toppled tombstones and broken beer bottles. When tombstones are toppled over onto flowers in the summer, cleaning must be done quickly. Several Board members and Cemetery staffers were immediately enlisted to reset the tombstones in place and to wash them, so that they would not become impregnated with the red and orange colours from the flowers.

There have been other strange incidents. One hears about people having sex in a cemetery and it's rare but all too true, said Berkowitz, who has found used condoms and packaging near cement slabs in the Cemetery.

Once, Jacques Berkowitz was attending a meeting at the Cemetery at night after public visiting hours were over. "All of a sudden, I see somebody jumping over the wall," he reported. Berkowitz and Gerald Silverberg apprehended the man. His excuse: "Well, I missed Father's Day and I wanted to visit him."

In the wake of vandalism, the Cemetery moves quickly. Tombstones that are broken or turned over are always repaired and repositioned; spray-painted slogans are cleaned off as soon as possible.

As well, steps have been taken to curtail vandalism. Security patrols the Cemetery when it is closed to the public. The police provide frequent surveillance. And vandalism insurance coverage has been increased on several occasions.

With all the effort, care, and importance that so many people have dedicated to the Cemetery for so many years, it was natural that a concern for the proper maintenance of the Cemetery grounds, long into the future, would arise. Who would look after the Cemetery when it was full and families are no longer around to look after loved ones' graves? Avoiding what has happened at other cemeteries was the primary concern, explained Jay Aaron. "You look at cemeteries throughout the world: when they're full, people walk away and they go into neglect."

In the 1970s, Cemetery representatives were becom-ing increasingly concerned that no funding or plan had been put in place to provide for the ongoing maintenance of the Cemetery after all the graves had been filled. This is noted in a memo from Jewish Family Services of the Baron de Hirsch Institute:

> There is a religious and moral obligation on the part of the community to provide for the proper maintenance of Jewish Cemeteries, and to ensure that in perpetuity, the maintenance remains at a quality level consistent with the dignity our community must accord its deceased members.

At the very first annual meeting of the newly incorporated Cemetery, in 1973, this idea was raised by the executive director of the Baron de Hirsch

Institute, Solomon Brownstein, when he stressed the need for "a development of a perpetual maintenance reserve to care for the defunct cemeteries." In 1977 Cemetery president Steve Tabac wrote a brief in which he stated, "The way we care for our dead is important and significant to our religious heritage ... Many congregations and sick benefit associations are becoming less viable. Due to declining and aging memberships, the responsibility will increasingly rest on the community for the maintenance of their burial grounds."

In January 1979 the Perpetual Care Fund was created. The Cemetery mandated that all the proceeds from the sale of flowers would be segregated to this fund. As well, a special fee began to be charged to each family at the time of burial. Actuarial studies were commissioned to determine the precise amounts that would be required to maintain the Cemetery after all burial activity ceased. From the inception of this fund Cemetery authorities have maintained the discipline and foresight to allow it to grow to levels that will ensure the continued maintenance of the grounds in perpetuity.

Over the years this resolve has been tested. Member affiliates, themselves experiencing financial difficulties, have at times pressed for these new funds to be used to ease the difficulties they were having, or for their yearly assessments to be reduced. Shortly after the fund was created, the Cemetery's second-largest landowner, the Hebrew Sick, insisted that the proceeds from the sale of florals be placed in the Cemetery's operating fund and that affiliate assessments be reduced accordingly. When this suggestion was ignored by the Cemetery Board, the Hebrew Sick threatened to create their own fund and to stop paying assessments. Though this threat never materialized, the tension remained.

In 1985, just six years after the fund's creation, the Hebrew Sick and other affiliates proposed that interest generated by the fund along with monies from the sale of florals be used to eliminate the annual assessments paid by the affiliates. This proposal was rejected by the Cemetery Board. The Board noted that actuarial studies had recommended that the fund not be used for a minimum of ten years. This was not well received by these affiliates. In December they said they would stop paying assessments. Legal opinions were sought, lawsuits were threatened, and there were discussions of discontinuing maintenance. However, the one threat that was never considered was to stop performing burials; this was outside any consideration. Eventually, consensus was reached. As would happen time and again, members came together, including those having difficulties. There was always a forward-looking attitude around the table.

In recent years the fund has grown in value and additional actuarial studies have been commissioned, confirming earlier projections. Efforts have been made to reduce the financial burden on member affiliates. Beginning in 1999, the yearly assessments were reduced by nearly fifty per cent.

The Board's efforts have been successful in creating a fund to protect the future well-being of the Cemetery grounds and to maintain the dignity and respect that are so fundamental to this community. Those responsible for managing the Cemetery and its perpetual care fund are determined to leave a legacy that will ensure its long-term future maintenance.

The Baron de Hirsch Cemetery's future is more than secure. Thanks to decisions made in the 1970s, a well-financed Perpetual Care Fund guarantees the Cemetery will be looked after long after its current administrators are gone.

"The reality is, in twenty years when the Cemetery is full, and the affiliates have walked away or been taken over, the Cemetery's going to be maintained," said Jay Aaron. "It will all be due to the vision of previous Board members who said, 'It's not enough to do what we're doing today.' We have to go to the future to protect that Cemetery."

Although the Cemetery's administrators run it as a business, it is in fact much more, said Jacques Berkowitz. "We have an obligation as Jews toward the dead, toward the members of our family," he said. "It's a very precious responsibility that we have to safeguard and maintain."

The Baron de Hirsch Cemetery has met that obligation and will continue to do so.

"Keep your loved one's memory fresh … all summer long … or for years to come," reads the text from a brochure about floral arrangements at the Baron de Hirsch Cemetery. "Honour your loved one's gravesite with a choice of tasteful floral arrangements that declare your memories are strong, and your love endures."

In 1997, the Board formed a marketing committee to encourage floral sales. A new brochure, order form, and information package explaining prepaid plans were created, and credit card payments began to be accepted.

"In the past, order forms were very complex and they shouldn't have been," said Board member Suzanne Belson, former chair of the Marketing

Committee. "Many of them go to older people who shouldn't have to spend a lot of time trying to fill them out."

People who wish to buy floral arrangements are given three to choose from in a range of prices. They can buy arrangements every year or make an investment in a prepaid plan that will last many years. A floral order form is sent out annually to all next-of-kin on record who have previously bought floral arrangements.

Occasionally, people are confused about the difference between pre-paid floral plans and the kind of "perpetual" floral accounts that used to be available. In past years, buyers could pay a lump sum to buy flowers in perpetuity for their loved ones' graves, but such practices at cemeteries have been disallowed by the Quebec government since the 1990s. (However, the Cemetery continues to honour the plans bought by about eighty-five individuals before the change took place.) The Cemetery staff now explain to buyers that prepaid floral plans may last many years, but "long-term" doesn't mean "forever". Prepaid floral plan funds are invested in a trust fund and, as long as there are sufficient funds in an account, the interest earned pays for planting every spring and maintenance all summer.

Some people prefer to plant their own arrangements on loved ones' graves. But individual planting sometimes becomes a problem. While the flowers planted by the Cemetery gardeners are annuals that are tended by the Cemetery and don't overwhelm the space, individual flower arrangements must be looked after by the families who plant them.

A sign outside the Cemetery office advises people they can plant their own arrangements "provided they follow our regulations governing 'private horticultural planting' available at our office. The Cemetery reserves the right to remove any plantings that do not adhere to these regulations."

While the guidelines are reasonable—people have to water the plants, clean debris, and dispose of the flowers at the end of the season—they're sometimes ignored. "It can become a little bit unruly," said Gerald Silverberg. "Some families don't report that they're planting. Some of the things they plant are not appropriate to a small space. They overgrow the adjacent graves, which is not fair to the people on either side." Some people have even planted their own trees on gravesites, Herbert Isenberg notes.

People who don't abide by floral regulations are now told to remove their plants, failing which, the Cemetery will remove them.

In January 1979 the Perpetual Care Fund was created.
The Cemetery Board mandated that this fund would receive the
proceeds from the sale of flowers.
[Photo: Danny Kucharsky]

In 1997, the Cemetery Board formed a marketing committee to encourage floral sales. A new brochure, order form, and information package explaining prepaid plans were created, and credit card payments began to be accepted.
[Photo: Danny Kucharsky]

6

The Future of the Cemetery

No man tells lies at death's door.
–Talmud Yerushalmi, Bava Qamma

As the Baron de Hirsch Cemetery moves into its second century it does so on a stronger footing than at any time in its existence. The Cemetery on de la Savane is professionally managed, increasingly well-maintained, and looking better than ever thanks, in part, to the growing number of floral displays that adorn its graves in the warmer months.

But given the realities of supply and demand, the Cemetery's days are numbered for a major part of its "business". With space slowly running out—over 60,000 individuals are buried there—it's only a matter of time until there will be no more room. The question is "When?" Will it be twenty years until all the plots are spoken for? Twenty-five? Or a bit longer? In any event, a time will come when a new cemetery will have to be found if the Jewish community is to continue to fulfill its honourable obligation of providing respectable burials for its poor. That means the Jewish community will have come full circle and will be in a position it was in over a hundred years ago—looking for a new burial ground for indigents and for the general community.

To ensure that its plots for indigent burials last as long as possible, the Baron de Hirsch Cemetery is tightly controlling the sale of plots in the parts of the Cemetery it owns outright. As of August 31, 2003, the Baron de Hirsch Cemetery had 2,230 available plots in sections it owns outright either for burial of indigents or for the next of kin of those already buried in those areas. People who wish to buy a plot and can afford to do so have to seek out one of the affiliates willing to sell or go to another cemetery, explained Gerald Silverberg. It is a stop-gap measure until a decision is made to buy new land.

To date, there has only been talk about securing new land. And securing

securing that land may be harder than it was for the Baron de Hirsch more than a hundred years ago: no additional cemeteries are allowed on the Island of Montreal. That means any new Jewish cemetery will not be easily accessible, possibly making burials or visits even more of a challenge than they were in the days of horses and tramways.

In 1911, six years after obtaining its current cemetery grounds, the Baron de Hirsch Institute considered the idea of obtaining another cemetery site and abandoning at least part of its existing one, because of what was described as a large increase in the land's value. Notary A. Lighthall suggested that another burying ground be acquired at Bout de L'Isle on the eastern tip of the Island of Montreal at a cost of around five hundred dollars per acre, but discussion on the matter was postponed.

In 1913, the subject arose again and "had become advisable by reason of the enhanced value of the present plot." The chairman of the Cemetery Committee, Mr. A. Goldstein, reported at a January 29, 1913 meeting that the Quebec Mausoleum Co. Ltd. was interested in buying about eight acres of the Cemetery for the purpose of erecting a mausoleum. (The propriety of selling the land for such purposes does not seem to have been discussed. Jewish law requires that bodies be buried in the earth.) In September 1913, the Baron de Hirsch Institute Board decided that the company should be given an option to buy six acres, seven if board member Lazarus Cohen decided to include land he owned in the Cemetery.

As well, Goldstein noted, Baron de Hirsch had been offered an eighteen-arpent piece of land at east-end Pointe aux Trembles for $24,000. However, for reasons that are not clear, the Board decided not to entertain this proposal and instead requested the chair of the Committee to obtain more information about smaller plots in the vicinity of Bout de L'Ile.

At the 1913 annual meeting, the Committee reported it had not "as yet selected a new site for cemetery purposes but is making careful enquiries (about) suitable locations." Enquiries had been received about selling the present land, "but the Committee is not yet in position to place the board with a definite offer." Later that year, a letter from a Mr. W.A. Moreau was read, offering the Board land in Ahuntsic. The Board decided the time was inopportune for purchase and Moreau was told the Institute was "not in the market at the present time."

In 1927, the Baron de Hirsch Institute was offered twenty-one acres of land adjacent to the Cemetery at $1,200 per acre, as minutes of the annual meeting of the Federation of Jewish Philanthropies indicate. Both the Cemetery Committee and the Board unanimously approved the purchase. But the bylaws also called for approval by Life Governors and three-quarters of members present at a meeting. Twenty-five voted in favour of the purchase, fourteen against, and with only sixty-four per cent approval, the opportunity to buy the land was lost. Those in favour of the purchase lashed out at the opposition:

> We feel that the sponsors of the opposition have erred in their judgement. We do not seek to achieve credit by this error, now or when time and experience will have confirmed the merit of our opportunity of developing a Community Cemetery entirely under our supervision, which not only would have, in our opinion handsomely paid as a financial venture, but of greater significance safeguarded for a hundred years and more—burial rights for those entitled to its possession, and the unique pride that might have surrounded a worthwhile community cemetery. We trust that with the new owners some plan may be possible whereby our vision in the matter may yet bear fruition in some measure.

The Baron de Hirsch Cemetery no longer has the option of expanding at its present site, as it is now surrounded on three sides by industrial buildings, single-family homes, and apartment buildings.

In the mid-1970s and again in the following decade, the Board considered expanding for future needs by purchasing land at other sites. Under consideration were acreages in Beaconsfield on the West Island, and Duvernay on the North Shore, as well as the Kehal Israel Cemetery in Dollard des Ormeaux. However, the main stumbling block was that "it was felt a non-profit, community-based group couldn't do it," said Jay Aaron. The Paperman family bought the Kehal Israel Cemetery.

The Baron de Hirsch Cemetery has been helping to revitalize and rebuild the Back River Memorial Gardens Cemetery. For many years it was the main cemetery for the Jewish community and many families have an ancestor buried there. It went into a state of neglect for several reasons. A number of the burial societies connected to the Back River Cemetery had gone into decline. A large non-Jewish community grew up around the cemetery, and there were continual difficulties caused by ground and water problems at the site. The Mount Royal and the Baron de Hirsch cemeteries grew in importance.

By the 1990s, hundreds of monuments at the Back River Cemetery had fallen over, some from neglect or poor construction. The cemetery grounds had become an easy target for vandals. As well, thousands of monuments were precariously close to falling, and if repairs weren't done they would have to be laid down. The problem was serious.

But for the efforts of Seymour Frank and Steve Tabac, the situation would have continued for years. Seymour Frank came from the Chevra Kadisha B'nai Jacob Synagogue and Steve Tabac had been president of the Baron de Hirsch Cemetery. They worked tirelessly and often without thanks to try and convince others to become involved.

In 1993 they approached the Baron de Hirsch Cemetery with the idea of having these two cemeteries become one, in some fashion. That year, Baron de Hirsch Cemetery president Jay Aaron met to discuss the Back River Cemetery with Harvey Wolfe, president of Federation CJA. The Federation could not see itself getting involved. In the words of Harvey Wolfe, Seymour Frank and Steve Tabac should "turn it over to the Papermans," who at that time were stretching their resources to do minimal maintenance at the cemetery. Aaron disagreed, but he also realized that the Baron de Hirsch Cemetery could not become involved because it could not put its funds at risk, given the tremendous amount of work that needed to be done at the Back River Cemetery, and the costs that would be involved.

In the late 1990s Seymour Frank and Steve Tabac's efforts were beginning to see positive results. The discussions now were about how change could be effected. Everyone, including the Federation and the Baron de Hirsch Cemetery, realized that a solution needed to be found. The community couldn't allow this cemetery to continue to decline. It embarrassed the community and it dishonoured those buried there.

After many months of sometimes difficult discussions between the Baron de Hirsch Cemetery Board, Jewish Family Services, the Back River Cemetery, and Federation CJA, a new board of fifteen individuals was structured. Though the Baron de Hirsch Cemetery Board would not be officially involved, some of its members would be. There would be five members representing Federation CJA, five members from the old Back River Cemetery and five members, sitting as individuals, from the Baron de Hirsch Cemetery.

What made this new board structure important was what each of the groups brought to the table. The Federation representatives brought the clout of the community and the ability to raise the necessary funds. The Back River representatives brought the history and ownership of the cemetery, and the Baron de Hirsch representatives brought the needed expertise in managing and running the cemetery. They also brought something more important, though less tangible: they brought the connection between the two cemeteries. This is what the Back River had always wanted and now it was within sight.

The new board quickly went to work, assessing what needed to be done, determining the costs involved, and putting together a fund-raising campaign. An initial goal of $6 million was set. With a contribution from the government of Quebec of $1 million and even more raised from the community, work was finally begun on restoration of the Back River Cemetery. The involvement of the Federation was crucial for the project to go forward. They were able to provide the necessary start-up funding. Although the government's contribution was also significant, the Back River board still required a partner to provide the necessary bridge financing and the Federation was that partner.

More than three thousand five hundred new foundations were poured, new more secure fencing was erected, a new garage/office facility was built, roadways were paved and drainage improved. Jay Aaron oversaw the Back River restoration before becoming executive director of Baron de Hirsch Cemetery in 2004.

In 2003 the Baron de Hirsch Cemetery entered into a contract with the Back River Cemetery to manage and operate the cemetery, reinforcing the historical connection between the two Jewish burial grounds. "We are proud to offer you and the community professional and caring service and the benefit of our many years of experience," read a Baron de Hirsch ad announcing the change in *The Canadian Jewish News* in January 2004.

More work needs to be done, but the cemetery is once again a dignified place of rest and a source of pride for the Montreal Jewish community.

7

Burial Practices

For you are dust and you shall return to dust.
–Bereishit (Genesis) 3:19

The rituals of Jewish burial indicate that all humans are created equal and all are equal in death. This notion of democracy in death is taught in the Talmud:

> Formerly, the expense of the burial was harder to bear by the family than the death itself, so that sometimes they fled to escape the expense. This was so until Rabban Gamliel insisted that he be buried in a plain linen shroud instead of costly garments. And since then we follow the principle of burial in a simple manner.
> –*Moed Katan* 27 a-b

Jews consider the last resting place of their departed to be sacred ground. And, whether they're held at Baron de Hirsch or elsewhere, Jewish burials follow a remarkably similar process. When the hearse reaches the cemetery, pallbearers carry the casket, or roll it on a conveyance, to the gravesite. This follows a practice conducted since biblical times, when Jacob's children carried him to the grave. Seven stops are made while Psalm 91, which speaks of God's sheltering presence, is recited. The stops represent the seven stages of life. After the casket is lowered into the ground, the El Moleh Rachamim (God, full of compassion)—a prayer for the peace of the departed soul—and Kaddish memorial prayers are recited.

Kevurah, the shovelling of earth into the grave, is usually considered the most emotional and striking element of a Jewish funeral, and possibly the most healing. Just before filling the grave, the rabbi hands the principal mourners a shovel, or tells them to pick one up, and they taking turns dropping newly dug up soil onto the coffin.

In one little-known custom, mourners initially use the back of the shovel to demonstrate reluctance. In some places each mourner replaces the shovel back in the earth rather than hand it from one person to the next, perhaps to symbolize that death is somehow contagious. For the most part, the shovel is simply handed to the next person.

After the immediate family has symbolically buried their loved one, others who wish to do so come forward to take a turn. It is felt that the act of shovelling earth into the grave—and the terrible sound the earth makes when it falls on a wooden coffin—is a dose of reality and an act of closure. There can be no denying that death has occurred, meaning that healing can begin. In addition, this filling in of the grave serves as a sign that the dead are not left uncovered or unattended. "According to Halacha, you should not leave the cemetery until the casket is covered with earth," said Rabbi Moshe Glustein. "There has to be a grave and there's a grave when there's a mound. That's when you can say Kaddish."

Following the burial, non-family members form two parallel lines and, as the mourners pass by them, they recite in Hebrew the traditional condolence "May God comfort you among all the mourners of Zion and Jerusalem." Before leaving the Cemetery, it is customary to wash one's hands, which serves as a symbolic cleansing and an indication that burial honours have been fulfilled.

Of course, a cemetery is involved with much more than burial itself. Several other matters need to be considered—from monuments, unveilings and visits to the grave, to interpretation of Jewish law for special cases and bizarre requests. Here's a look at some of the serious (and occasionally not so serious) burial matters dealt with by Baron de Hirsch Cemetery.

Since ancient times, it has been the custom for Jews to mark graves with a monument. After Rachel died, "Jacob erected a monument on Rachel's grave" (Genesis 35:20). In more practical terms, the monument serves to honour the memory of the deceased, identify the grave so that relatives will find it when they visit, and identify a place of burial so that the grave will not be desecrated and kohanim (priests) will avoid it as required by Jewish law.

Jewish tradition makes no stipulation as to the size of the monument, but most cemeteries have specific guidelines. These guidelines are related in part to the Jewish teaching that all are equal in death. In the early years of Baron de Hirsch Cemetery there were no height restrictions. Some of the monuments in the older sections in the rear of the Cemetery are as tall as eight or nine feet (nearly three metres).

"It used to be you could go in there, buy your spot, and put a monument on it as big as you liked," noted the late Mendy Berson of Berson & Son Monuments noted in the Edward Hillel book *The Main, Portrait of a Neighbourhood.* "When the Jews got richer, we started getting stones six feet high and over. Finally, Baron de Hirsch said: 'Maximum four feet, no higher.' So now it doesn't matter how many millions you have in the bank. You can't build 'em over four feet."

In fact, the latest regulations say single monuments can be no more than three feet high (not including a one-foot base), while double or triple monuments can be no more than thirty-two inches high. Monument-makers used to be allowed to install one-piece monuments comprising both the monument and the base, but this practice has been disallowed.

The monument usually includes the English and Hebrew name of the deceased (with the traditional Hebrew "son of" or "daughter of"), the dates of birth and death (according to the Jewish calendar and usually by the Christian calendar), and the relationship to other family members, such as father or mother. As well, there are the Hebrew letters *pay nun*, standing for *po nikbar(ah)*, or "here is buried," and the letters *tav, nun, tzadeek bet, hay*, standing for the phrase "*teheye nishmato tsrurah b'tsror ha-chayyim*," or "May his/her soul be bound up in the bond of eternal life."

Aside from those traditional inclusions, there are no regulations for what goes on the monument. "You don't think in terms of what's allowed, what's not allowed," said Brandee Berson, who now runs Berson & Son Monuments. Rather, "you have to think of what's appropriate, what's inappropriate."

Still, when it comes to monuments, most people "will lean more toward tradition versus uniqueness or individuality," Brandee Berson said. "I've had people who wanted funky stuff, but the majority are traditionalists. A lot of families say 'You made such and such monument for my grandmother. We want the same thing for our parents.'"

Many monuments at Baron de Hirsch go well beyond the traditional, however.

To an ever-increasing extent, it is being recommended that Holocaust survivors include that information on their tombstones, as a reminder for future generations. Monuments with Holocaust information can be seen throughout Baron de Hirsch.

While regulations about the wording of monuments are few, that's not the case when it comes to putting things *on* a monument. According to halachic law, embellishments are not allowed on monuments. However, "some people do things clandestinely, and once it's done, it's very difficult for us to tell them to take it away," Gerald Silverberg said in an interview. For example, it is a Sephardic tradition to post metal lanterns in the ground beside tombstones, which is perfectly acceptable at the Cemetery. However, some people have attached the metal lanterns directly to tombstones, a practice the Cemetery now forbids.

Photographs are also forbidden, although the practice used to be popular early in the twentieth century. The practice of putting pictures on tombstones was so prevalent in 1917 that the Cemetery sent registered letters to each burial society requesting them not to allow pictures on monuments. By 1918, the Board was threatening to remove photographs from tombstones if families warned about them did not do so themselves within thirty days. In 1919, tombstone-makers were warned by registered mail to remove photographs from eight tombstones, or face the refusal to be allowed to erect any other tombstones.

Still, in older sections of Baron de Hirsch, it is not uncommon to find tombstones with poignant photographs on them, usually printed on porcelain and chipped away by time.

A formal unveiling ceremony is generally held to reveal the tombstone put in place to remember the deceased. There are no hard and fast rules as to when this ceremony takes place. While many families wait until almost a full year after death to do the unveiling, others hold it soon after *sheloshim* (the first thirty days of mourning). The unveiling ceremony usually consists of the recitation of Psalms, a brief eulogy, removal of the cloth covering the headstone, the *El Moleh Rahamim* and the Mourner's Kaddish.

People can visit loved ones' graves at any time—within visiting hours, of course. However, excessive visits are discouraged. "The rabbis were apprehensive that frequent visiting to the cemetery might become a pattern of living thus preventing the bereaved from placing their dead in proper perspective," writes Maurice Lamm in *The Jewish Way in Death and Mourning*.

It is considered especially appropriate to visit the graves of family members on the last day of shiva (the first seven days of intensive mourning) and the last day of *sheloshim* (the thirty-day mourning period), on Yahrzeit (the yearly anniversary of a person's death), as well as on Jewish fast days.

It is customary to visit the graves of loved ones during the month of *Elul* prior to Rosh Hashanah or during the ten days of repentance before Yom Kippur. The custom of *Kever Avot*—visiting the graves of dear ones prior to the High Holy Days—is believed to help us confront our own mortality and help us face the future with a sense of purpose.

The harsh reality is that many of the elderly and infirm are unable to visit the graves of loved ones. Some efforts are being made to improve this situation. During the High Holiday period of 2002, for example, twelve residents of Maimonides Hospital, accompanied by a rabbi, two social workers, one nurse, volunteers, and staff from the Volunteer Department, visited Baron de Hirsch Cemetery. Most of the residents had not been to a cemetery for several years, and the experience was one that moved many to tears.

One of the Hebrew names for a cemetery is *beit ha-chaim* (house of living). People who visit a grave at a cemetery help the cemetery live up to its mystifying Hebrew name by helping bring memories back to life.

On busy days at Baron de Hirsch Cemetery, it used to be common to see *moleh machers*—observant Jews who would chant the prayer for the departed, *El Moleh Rachamim*, in exchange for a shekel or two from visitors. Apparently, this situation could get out of hand, as a 1961 memo sent out to affiliates by the Cemetery Board noted that "it is urgently recommended that in the future only accredited persons be permitted to perform this service." In an attempt "to reduce undesirable mendicants," a suggestion was made at a 1977 board meeting that badges be issued by the Cemetery to those who wished to charge money to say prayers. It is rare to see *moleh machers* at Baron de Hirsch today.

Stones on tombstones at the Baron de Hirsch—and at any Jewish cemetery, for that matter (although it is not customary among ultra-Orthodox Jews)—are a familiar sight. It is not uncommon to see people at the Cemetery looking for pebbles, so that they can put stones on loved ones' graves.

So why do people place pebbles on tombstones? The answers are many as to how the custom originated.

According to Rabbi Maurice Lamm in *The Jewish Way in Death and Mourning*, it "probably serves as a reminder of the family's presence." The stones are a sign of respect for the deceased and act as evidence that the grave is visited and cared for.

The custom may hearken to biblical days when the monument was a heap of stones. The stones were often dispersed by weather or vandals, so visitors would place additional stones to assure the grave remained marked.

Others say it could be the end result of the custom of writing notes to the deceased and pushing them into crevices in the headstone in the way notes are pushed into the Western Wall in Jerusalem. When no crevice could be found, the note was weighted down with a stone. Eventually the paper would blow away or disintegrate leaving only the stone. That led people to think it was the leaving of a stone that was the custom.

Some believe the practice has superstitious origins and is akin to leaving a calling card for the dead. In the mythology of Eastern European Jewry, souls could take on a certain terror in death and return for whatever reason to the world of the living. The "barrier" on the grave was to ensure that souls remain where they belong.

In ancient times, shepherds needed a system to keep track of their changing numbers of sheep that went out to pasture. Since memory was an unreliable way of keeping tabs on them, the shepherd would carry a sling over his shoulder, and keep inside it the number of pebbles that corresponded to the number in his flock. That way he could always have an accurate daily count and verify that the same number returned at night. The stones, therefore, may symbolize how precious each soul is to God, who, as it were, "counts" each person in the world.

Although stones conjure a harsh image, they have a special character in Judaism. After all, the sacred shrine of Judaism, the wall of the Second Temple, is considered "the foundation stone of the world," while one name for God is "The Rock of Israel."

Just as flowers that wilt may be a good metaphor for the brevity of life, stones serve as a good symbol of the permanence of memory. The pebble lets others know that someone did come and remember. Symbolically, it suggests the permanence of love and memory which are as strong and enduring as a rock. Stones do not die, just as memories and souls are meant to endure.

The *kohanim*, Jews who trace their ancestry back to Aaron, the first Jewish priest *(kohen)*, must follow strict rules of purity. These forbid, among other things, all contact with the dead and visits to cemeteries. Such contact would render the priests "impure" and disqualify them from their priestly duties.

Jewish law said that "a *kohen* may not defile himself by touching, carrying or being within eight feet of a body or the limbs, bones, blood or the flesh of a dead person." Of course, exceptions are made when the *kohen* must bury an immediate relative. And many Jews who are *kohanim* will attend a funeral or will enter a cemetery but will not come close to the grave.

Jewish law also said "the *kohen* may enter a cemetery if he remains, at all times, at least eight feet from the graves and does not pass by foot or in a vehicle under a branch of a tree which simultaneously covers both him and a grave." At Baron de Hirsch, special care has been taken to trim tree branches alongside the roadways, so that a *kohen* can walk down the centre of these roads, and not walk under trees. In the Paperman funeral complex, the *kohanim* attending a funeral service may sit in a separate building.

When Sephardic Jews from North Africa started immigrating in large numbers to Montreal in the 1960s, they began to buy plots in Baron de Hirsch Cemetery. In fact, Sephardic Jews now own the majority of plots in the Memorial Park section.

Burial practices of the Sephardim vary in some ways from their Ashkenazi counterparts. For example, Sephardic Jews will visit graves during the seven days of the shiva mourning period following the death of a loved one, while Ashkenazi Jews will not. As well, while Ashkenazi Jews will light Yahrzeit memorial candles in the home, Sephardic Jews light them at the grave. That explains the predominance of metal lanterns that can now be seen in the Cemetery. "The respect given to the dead is very strong in that community," said Gerald Silverberg. "They are constantly visiting graves of parents and dear ones."

Some disagreements over burial practices have emerged in recent years between the majority Ashkenazi and minority Sephardi Jewish population, but all have been worked out. One situation involved the handling of coffins at graveside. Although the coffins are traditionally handled by workers at graveside, they were being asked to step aside with members of the funeral

It is a Sephardic tradition to post metal lanterns in the
ground beside tombstones.
[Photo: D.R. Cowles]

פ- הילד- נ'
שלמה זלמן
בר מאיר הכהן
נפ כה אב תרפז
ת נ צ ב ה

OUR BELOVED CHILD

SOLOMON

DIED AUG 26 1927

The practice of putting pictures on tombstones was so prevalent that the
Cemetery Board sent registered letters to each burial society requesting
them not to allow pictures on monuments.
[Photo: D.R. Cowles]

party handling the task. The result, however, was not always the one sought: "There were a few accidents or near accidents when these people without the knowledge of how to do things were in a poor position," Silverberg said. In one case, "a man once fell into the grave before the coffin."

In early February 1997, a meeting was hastily called with representatives of the Communauté Sepharade du Québec to discuss problems during burials when family members have carried the casket and lowered it into the grave. To eliminate the dangerous practice of handling of the casket—while allowing mourners to follow their religious practices—an agreement was reached. All members of the Sephardic and ultra-Orthodox communities would be provided usage of the Cemetery's automatic lowering device, rather than having members of the funeral party attempt the task of lowering the casket into the grave themselves. If use of the automatic lowering device was not practical due to lack of space or mechanical problems, the burial would be handled by staff.

Clergy would do their utmost to convince families who insisted on lowering the casket themselves to allow workers to do the task, Rabbi Sholom Chiriqui recommended at the 1997 meeting. If a family was still determined to do this task themselves, the Cemetery should be notified beforehand and not be held liable. In such cases, workers would be on hand to ensure no accidents occur. Cases like these show "we are respectful of the various different customs, within the framework of Halacha," said Rabbi Glustein.

In a related development, rabbis are increasingly returning to the halachic stipulation that only Jews can touch the coffin and do the actual interment.

Although the practice was not followed for a long time, some rabbis are having graves filled by family members. The idea being espoused is that by leaving the *mitzvah* of burial entirely in the hands of paid strangers the family is being deprived of its last act of *kevod ha-met*, respect for the dead. If that's not possible, the Cemetery workers are asked to fill the grave by hand (using shovels) and not by machine, as was the case for a time. The workers can have as many as six burials in a day, which can make for exhausting work, noted Silverberg.

The term *Ohel*—literally "tent"—refers to the structure built over the grave of a *tzaddik*, or righteous person. *Ohels* are traditionally the resting places of Jewish forebears, such as Rachel's Tomb, and serve as spiritual oases.

It is believed that a *tzaddik*, one who is close to God, has the ability to bring prayers to God's attention, making it customary to pray by their gravesites and light candles. At Baron de Hirsch, *Ohels* can be seen in the form of small brick huts in some of the sections at the rear of the cemetery. However, for reasons unknown, the once popular practice of building *Ohels* has fallen out of favour, noted Rabbi Glustein, and no new ones have been built at the Cemetery for decades.

As a 1988 resolution noted, the Baron de Hirsch Cemetery is managed "with a sensitivity and respect for the precepts of traditional Judaism." However, in the past, when burial matters at Baron de Hirsch Cemetery arose that required an interpretation of Halacha, only one rabbi's opinion was sought. Since the decision of one rabbi would carry the day, "you had to be careful how you proceeded," Libby Labell, a former member of the Cemetery Board, said.

But in recent years the Cemetery has established "the rule of three" whenever any question comes up. Three rabbis are consulted on religious matters, and they issue rulings. "It's a unique and very workable system," said Rabbi Glustein, who acts as the liaison for the Rabbinical Council. The rabbis have agreed to respond within three hours of being contacted by Rabbi Glustein on any matter.

In one dramatic instance of the rule-of-three practice a few years ago, the rabbis were called to the Back River Cemetery. Workers repairing foundations accidentally hit bones and skulls while they were digging. The remains of the dead had been disturbed, in violation of Jewish law. Rabbi Glustein was paged on his beeper and was at the cemetery in fifteen minutes. "It was terrible. People were standing around just devastated." The Chief Rabbi of Montreal and other rabbis were called to the cemetery and quickly made a ruling on the procedure to follow to avoid any similar situations: workers can dig underground by machine to a certain point, and after that must dig by hand. Since then they have never found anything.

Rabbi Glustein said the existence of the Rabbinical Council "shows you there's a discipline and a respect for a process and a respect for Halacha —and a respect for the community. It's not a haphazard thing."

Rabbis have frequently been called upon to settle plot disputes: people's loved ones are not buried where they thought the plots were bought, husbands and wives are not buried together as expected, mistakes lead to people being buried in the wrong place, and so forth.

"We try not to touch the deceased," said Rabbi Glustein, "but if we had to we did. However, according to Jewish law one must wait twelve months for the body to decay until exhumation can occur."

In one case, the family of a ten-year-old child was left waiting at the Cemetery two hours for the child's Christmas-day burial because the grave had not been dug when they arrived at the Cemetery, a Cemetery Committee was told in January 1925. By contrast, in January 1993, records show that the Cemetery was congratulated for its quick response in burying a person on the same day as his death.

By 1987, the practice of people standing on graves while attending burials and unveilings was becoming so prevalent that the Cemetery Board recommended in a May meeting that rabbis be asked to remind people not to do so.

Jewish law makes it clear that Jews can not be cremated. However, when Russian Jews began to immigrate to Montreal, Baron de Hirsch quickly came face to face with that country's well-established practice of cremation. Jews in Russia were cremated because the state wanted it that way. A Russian immigrant whose parents were cremated and then buried in a Jewish cemetery in Russia wanted to have their ashes buried with her at Baron de Hirsch. The Montreal Rabbinical Council gave her permission to do so. "At a great deal of expense and trouble, she went to Russia, dealt with the government there, came back with the ashes and we subsequently buried them," said Silverberg. "And on her burial, she will be buried with them." When a person has been cremated against their wishes "then we possibly can do something for them."

While cremation is forbidden, remnants of some synagogues that were destroyed in fires are buried in the cemetery. Also, according to Jewish law, any Jewish prayer books, from Torah scrolls to the Talmud, which have been burned have to be buried.

Jews believe that all persons are put onto this world with a mission and purpose, and are meant to complete this goal in the years which God has allotted them. Since suicide is a way of saying that life is not worth living, Jewish law clamps down hard on the practice.

***

> For the sake of one individual was the world created ... he who
> destroys one's soul is considered as though he had destroyed the
> whole world.
>
> —Genesis 9:5

Accordingly, suicide victims are to be buried at the outskirts of a cemetery away from other Jews and denied normal mourning rites, such as
shiva. This ruling is believed to have been enacted mainly to discourage
would-be suicides. In practice, however, Jewish law rarely rules a self-
inflicted killing to be suicide, usually pronouncing it an accident or a case
of momentary insanity. It is very rare to find cases in which suicide victims
have been treated as second-class burials.

It is believed that imposing such a sentence would punish only the
grieving family, not the suicide, and Jewish law actually encourages rabbis
to search for any rationale to avoid declaring a person a wilful suicide.
Since the majority of suicides are indeed a result of mental or emotional
illness, rabbis are given plenty of leeway.

"If it's deemed a person was not in their right mind when they
committed suicide," the suicide victim can be buried among all others,
noted Rabbi Glustein. "The law is very, very lenient."

Halachic authorities hold that as long as no one actually saw the person
committing suicide in cold blood, the person was not responsible for his
actions. As one text puts it, if a person "is discovered choked to death, or
hanging, the act of killing should, as far as possible, be considered as murder
and not as suicide." What's more, if the person who committed suicide
did not die instantly, it is assumed the person repented in the last moments
of life.

Jewish law also says suicides should be treated as natural deaths, when
the person committed suicide through fear of suffering terrible torture,
as was the case with King Saul who feared the inhuman cruelty of the
Philistines.

Much like victims of suicide, Jews who renounce their religion are
not supposed to be given the same burials in Jewish cemeteries as other
Jews.

"To be buried in a Jewish cemetery is not necessarily a right. It's a
privilege," noted Rabbi Glustein. However, proving a person has formally
renounced Judaism is easier said than done.

First of all, a person has to publicly renounce his Jewish faith, "and there's always a question of whether the person has done so," said Gerald Silverberg.

There are a few cases of people who said they no longer wanted to be Jewish and married out of the faith, but are buried at Baron de Hirsch because the family wanted them to be buried in a Jewish cemetery. One such situation involved a Jewish woman who married a Christian, lived a Christian life and did not bring up her children as Jewish. But because she never formally renounced her religion or converted to Christianity, she was allowed to be buried at the Cemetery.

A special section of the Cemetery is set aside for cases like this. But "you wouldn't know the difference, nor would their family, in order to be sensitive to the families," said Rabbi Glustein.

Traditionally, flowers are not allowed in Jewish cemeteries because the prevailing view was that bringing flowers smacked of a pagan custom. So how can it be that there are so many flowers at Baron de Hirsch Cemetery? And how has the Cemetery been able to create its Perpetual Care Fund from the profits of flower sales? Rabbis in Montreal have given the Baron de Hirsch Cemetery dispensation from that rule "because they felt that the flowers are more for the living than in recognition of the dead," said former general manager Silverberg.

"The Cemetery is very, very sensitive to the needs of every individual," said Rabbi Glustein. Flowers in a cemetery are not expressly forbidden by Halacha, and if they were, they would not be allowed.

Ultra-Orthodox Jews don't plant flowers on graves and one section (Pinsker) has it marked in its deeds that no flowers are to be planted. As well, no flowers are allowed in the Veterans Field of Remembrance. This restriction, however, does not apply to veterans buried elsewhere in the Cemetery. In fact, the Commonwealth War Graves Commission pays for the floral arrangements of several veterans buried at Baron de Hirsch.

In 1778, an unusual problem took place: it was discovered that the uncircumcised infant son of an early settler in Montreal had been buried at the cemetery of the Shearith Israel. A meeting of "the Israelites of the Town of Montreal" was called to decide whether the son of Ezekiel and Louise (Dubois) Solomon had been buried according to Jewish rules and customs. While the burial was allowed, it was unanimously agreed "that no man or boy whomsoever shall be buried in the burying place of this congregation unless circumcised."

There was a less happy occurrence in Trois-Rivières in the early nineteenth century. Moses Hart, who was far from Orthodox in his religious beliefs, was then in charge of the family's burial plot. He violated Jewish law by not providing a proper Jewish burial service to a child. His brother Benjamin, feeling that his parents' resting place had been desecrated, reacted angrily: "Let the God of Israel judge between you and me," and vowed he would never again visit the site.

With one hundred years under its belt, there have been some strange burial requests and incidents at Baron de Hirsch over the years.

There was the licorice-loving man who requested that licorice be thrown in his casket. There was the person who wanted a written confirmation that no water would enter his grave. And there was the woman who asked not to be buried on the west side of the cemetery— close to where factories are located—because she'd be kept up by the noise!

There have been more poignant moments as well. There was the estranged family who made two orders for a monument for the same person and there were warring families who had two unveilings arranged. And there is the story of a distraught daughter, estranged from her family, who came running up to a gravesite while a burial was taking place, demanding to see inside the grave. Evidently, her father had not told her of her mother's death. The grave was opened for her.

People with tattoos have asked the Cemetery Board if they will be allowed to be buried there. They have been told to ask a rabbi. In fact, although the Torah is interpreted by some to prohibit tattoos, people with tattoos are buried in Jewish cemeteries.

It was, said Rabbi Charles Bender, a "shocking scene" seen by many who happened to be in the vicinity. In the summer of 1951, allegations flew that one of the Cemetery affiliates had buried a person illegally, by removing the body from the coffin at graveside.

This "serious irregularity" by the Tolner Congregation "places in disregard an established law of the Health Department of the City of Montreal," wrote an angry Rabbi Bender in a September 26, 1951 letter to the president of the Baron de Hirsch Institute.

It seems that at a recent funeral and interment in the cemetery of the Tolner Congregation, the body was taken out of the coffin and buried without the legal requirements. Apart from the shocking scene that this created in the presence of many people who happened to be in the vicinity at the time, the law distinctly requires that "the body shall be placed in a coffin and buried in a minimum of three feet of earth."

I am aware of a certain school of Jewish thought which states that this was done in Eastern Europe, and has become a "Jewish law" unto itself. The fact is that Jewish law is greatly governed by the law of the land as well, and in this instance, the established practice in Montreal among Orthodox groups, has been to respect the law of the land.

A similar incident was said to have occurred in June 1955, but the president and secretary of the Tolner Congregation strongly denied the allegations. They stated that the deceased had been buried in a plain box supplied by the Paperman funeral home, a box from which the body was never removed. Tolner president P. Zigman noted that Hebrew custom requires a body to be buried in a box, but that the boards of the box must not be nailed together. All that was done at the Cemetery was that the nails were removed and notches were cut out to fit the boards together. This, he said, was achieved without removing the body from the box.

That appeared to put the incident to rest, but not before the Cemetery Committee reminded the congregation of Quebec law concerning burial procedure and sent out a harsh warning. The deceased must be buried in a coffin, and any other form of burial is strictly prohibited, unless a special exemption from the Minister of Health is obtained, the congregation was told. "On several occasions in the past," their letter continued, "your Congregation has been reported to us as not having observed the burial procedures prescribed by law. Your congregation is hereby notified that, in the future, any deviation from such formalities will not be condoned."

In Baron de Hirsch and other Jewish cemeteries, books make for good neighbours. According to Jewish law, the remains of holy books that have been burned and old Jewish textbooks containing the name of God cannot be thrown into the recycling bin but have to be buried. Old Jewish textbooks are considered "good neighbours" and "it's a very very big honour to be buried next to a good neighbour," said Rabbi Glustein.

Burying Jewish textbooks in plots is not an infrequent occurrence, recalled Herbert Eisenberg, former president of the Cemetery. He'd get a call from a rabbi saying. "Eisenberg, I've got to bury a dozen Siddurs, I need a plot." He'd then ask the Cemetery manager: "You got something in the back? Open a plot for him and let him bury the books."

Limbs that have been amputated must be buried with the body, as part of the concept that bones remain after the rest of the body disappears. Rabbi Hirsch Cohen, one of the occupants of an *Ohel* at Baron de Hirsch, had a leg amputated and "I was told the leg was preserved for many years and was buried with him," Rabbi Glustein said.

"Do not graze cattle in a cemetery," is among the warnings of the *Tractate Sanhedrin*, which lists behaviours for a cemetery. Among the other little-known rules:

> Do not go to a cemetery with a light spirit.
> Do not run an aqueduct through a cemetery.
> Do not collect herbs in a cemetery.
> Do not collect tree sap in a cemetery.

And as the *Kitzur Shulhan Arukh* notes: "One who sees a coffin pass by and fails to join the procession is likened to the one who mocks and sneers at the poor, and deserves to be excommunicated."

The Baron de Hirsch Cemetery

A PORTFOLIO OF PHOTOGRAPHS BY

D.R. Cowles

Plate 1

Plate 2

Plate 3

Plate 4

Plate 5

Plate 6

Plate 7

Plate 8

Plate 9

Plate 10

Plate 11

Plate 12

8

Beyond the Tombstones
Tales of the Cemetery's Occupants

After I am dead
Say this at my funeral:
There was a man who exists no more.
That man died before his time,
And his life's song was broken off halfway.
He had one more poem,
And that poem has been lost.
For ever.

–Chaim Nachman Bialik,
From "Acharay Moti" (After My Death)

Yiddishkeit

A full century ago, Montreal had a thriving Yiddish culture and the city still has a great Yiddish cultural heritage. In North America only New York had a larger Yiddish-speaking community. The Montreal Yiddish writers were among the world's best when Yiddish was the Jewish community's *lingua franca*. Baron de Hirsch Cemetery is the resting place of many promoters of Yiddishkeit. They include writers, poets, and journalists like Yehuda Elberg, Rachel Korn, J.I. Segal, and Israel Medres, who offered accounts of nineteenth- and twentieth-century life to Yiddish readers, and educators like Shloime Wiseman and siblings, Shifre Shtern Krishtalka, Sholem Shtern, and Jacob Zipper, who fought to imbue students with a sense of the cultural worth of Judaism. In later years, as Yiddish began to fade in importance, others like Dora Wasserman, Joseph Kage, and Sara Rosenfeld have fought to maintain the language and the cultural heritage. Here are their stories.

THE YIDDISH BARD
Jacob Isaac Segal (1896-1954)
Buried March 8, 1954
Jewish National (Farband) D-20

Today his name is remembered by many for the biennial J.I. Segal Awards which celebrate Jewish writing, but Jacob Isaac Segal was known as Canada's foremost poet in Yiddish.

According to Israel Medres in his chronicles of Jewish life in Montreal for the *Keneder Adler*, the first book of Yiddish poetry to be printed in Montreal was Segal's. He would go on to pen twelve lengthy books of poetry, and receive the Louis Lamed Literary Award for Yiddish poetry. Although he spent most of his life in Montreal, only a few dozen of his poems deal specifically with the city while hundreds speak of the Old Country shtetl.

Segal was a teenager when he arrived in the city in 1910. His first job was in a factory stitching pants pockets. He later taught at the Jewish People's School. Finally, he became a journalist and editor of the *Keneder Adler* and published his poetry in the newspaper. Segal would write his poems in pencil on the long sheets of newsprint used for galleys. He signed his work with his initials, so he was known by readers for his initials in Yiddish, "Yud Yud".

Shortly after his poems appeared in the *Keneder Adler*, they began to be published in the most prestigious Yiddish literary journals of the United States and Eastern Europe. He was acknowledged as one of the most respected Yiddish poets, particularly for his depiction of the fast-disappearing Jewish way of life in Eastern Europe.

However, the tragedy of the death of his baby daughter, combined with the Holocaust and the decline of Yiddish, had a deep effect on the poet. In one of his poems, Segal questioned the future of the language:

Has autumn really come into your garden, Yiddish?
Do we with trembling hands pick the last ripeness from
  your branches?
Perhaps another miracle will yet happen, and above our tired
  drooping eyes,
Will appear the new fruits of the vine.

Loneliness was a constant theme. In 1949, he wrote an essay entitled "A Jewish Poet Speaks of Himself," in which he concluded: "I have struggled with poetry in my hand as a weapon against a heavy loneliness and a harsh despair. So far I have saved myself. May this power continue to help me. Sadness grows on me."

Interest in Segal's poetry was sparked by his death in 1954. "We Montrealers, like New Yorkers, and Chicagoans, and Philadelphians give our creative people every recognition after their death, but leave them lonely and in solitude in their lifetime," noted an obituary the day after Segal's death.

In the years immediately after his passing, hundreds of Yiddish-speaking Montrealers would gather on his Yahrzeit "in order to commune with the spirit of the departed poet, to asseverate their admiration for his works and to read his poetry." For example, two memorials were held for Segal in 1957, one by the Jewish Public Library, the other by the Jewish Writers' Association. At one of the yahrzeit gatherings, writers and poets reminisced about the Yiddish bard and read his work. At the other, a public tribute was paid to the Montrealer "whose poetry is read in all parts of the world where Yiddish is a living tongue."

In 1968, Hirsh and Dora Rosenfeld established the J.I. Segal Awards to stimulate Jewish cultural creativity in Canada and to honour the Yiddish poet's memory.

The Yiddish Journalist
Israel Medres (1894-1964)
Buried August 4, 1964
Farband – Old (D-17)

When Yiddish-speaking Montrealers were eager for information that would help demystify life in their strange adopted city, they turned to Israel Medres. For it was he, as a staff writer for the daily Yiddish newspaper the *Keneder Adler* for more than forty years, who could deliver that information in an easy-to-read language they could understand. Until he died in 1964, he chronicled the events, both big and small, that shaped a rapidly growing Jewish community.

"New immigrants who could not read the English newspapers were ignorant of what was happening in their city," Medres once observed. "For them Montreal was a closed book." But the *Keneder Adler* and journalists like Medres opened the city to them. "It revealed to them that they lived in a large metropolis with people of diverse languages, races, beliefs, and cultures."

Born in Byelorussia in the small town of Liachovici in 1894, Medres spent three years in a yeshiva, his only formal education, before immigrating to Canada in 1910. He would never see his parents or siblings again, except for a sister. She was a baby when he left Europe. They were reunited in 1960 in Argentina; she contacted him after she read one of his articles in a Buenos Aires Yiddish newspaper.

After stints as a stevedore and a tailor, Medres turned to journalism. From the time he joined the paper to his death, hardly an issue went by without his by-line. He contributed in such capacities as news editor, labour editor, court reporter, and publicist, writing a constant stream of news articles and political and social commentary. Long before social history was considered of any importance, Medres was writing on the significance of the immigrant era, when Eastern European immigration to Canada was virtually unrestricted. Medres was most admired by his readers for his light, bi-weekly essays written under the pen name Ben Mordecai. They were reprinted in almost every major Yiddish paper abroad. His articles were often hard-hitting and newsworthy. For example, in an interview with Medres before the outbreak of the Second World War, long-time Quebec Premier Maurice Duplessis expressed regret for his previous anti-Semitism and sought to make amends.

Medres was the Montreal correspondent for the New York newspaper *Morgan Zhurnal*, and edited *Dos Vort*, the official organ of the Montreal Labour Zionists.

Several of his newspaper essays were published in Yiddish and have since been translated into English as *Montreal of Yesterday, Jewish Life in Montreal 1900-1920* and *Between the Wars: Canadian Jews in Transition.* (Both are published by Véhicule Press.)

Princess of Yiddish Literature
Rachel Korn (1898-1982)
Buried September 12, 1982
Adath Israel – New (A-4)

When Rachel Korn's writing was first published in Polish, her critics were convinced that she was a man because of the toughness of her language. But the poet and short story writer would later go on to be dubbed "the princess of Yiddish literature". She produced eleven volumes of Yiddish poetry and short stories and became one of the first recipients of the Manger Prize for Yiddish Literature. Awarded by the president of Israel, the Manger Prize is the highest recognition for Yiddish writing.

Born in Podliszki, Galicia to wealthy landowners, Korn began writing in Polish at age twelve. She was in her twenties when her husband introduced her to Yiddish and she fell in love with the language. With the onset of pogroms against Jews, she decided to continue writing in Yiddish, as Polish had come to represent the language used by anti-Semitic compatriots. Her first published work, *Dorf*, appeared in 1928.

Her two younger brothers and mother were killed during the German invasion of Poland. Korn spent the Second World War in the Soviet Union, where she was the first outside guest writer invited to Russia. She returned totally disillusioned and violently opposed to communism.

In 1946, she was the first Jewish writer to be invited to be a member of the first PEN Club in Stockholm. She lived there until 1948 when she moved to Montreal, sponsored by Yiddish writer Ida Maze. However, with the Holocaust having claimed most Yiddish speakers and readers, her success and fame as a writer were subdued.

Much of her work after the war was devoted to the Holocaust and drew attention to the dangers of anti-Semitism. Still, "in spite of the fact that she writes about sorrow, loneliness, pain and hopelessness, yet in no way can one characterize Rachel Korn as the poet of pessimism and despair," wrote Mordecai Chalamish, a Yiddish writer, in the *Canadian Jewish Anthology*. "In her writings there is a vital energy which affirms life and overcomes the imminent sadness that follows her like a constant shadow."

Her works have been translated into several languages, including French, German, Polish, and Romanian. But Yiddish writer Yehuda Elberg said the translations don't do her justice: "She doesn't write in metric rhythm but her words have the rhythm of the heart that is led by emotions. She achieves drama with quiet words and she cries quiet tears."

The year she died, 1982, also saw the publication of *Generations: Selected Poems of Rachel Korn* (Mosaic Press/Valley Editions Publishers). In its foreward, Elie Wiesel wrote:

> Poet of the sufferings, wanderings and memories of the Jewish
> people, Rachel Korn impresses and moves us with the evocative

strength of her language. Each word calls out to us, each image burns itself into our minds.

No one else has her ability to paint the landscape of a buried village or her eye to portray the rapport between a mother and her daughter, between a vagabond and the sky, between a child and his longings. ... You read Rachel Korn and you discover a spellbinding world, dazzling and sombre, peopled by a humanity that has died, yet lives forever.

YIDDISH IDEALIST
Jacob (Yaacov) Zipper (1900-1983)
Buried April 17, 1983
Farband – Old (D-17)

Although he initially considered Montreal as a temporary refuge from the dangers of Europe, Yaacov Zipper would become a key figure in the development of Yiddish culture in the city.

He served as principal and teacher at the Jewish Peretz Schools for thirty-seven years until his retirement in 1971. He produced books in Hebrew and Yiddish on *shtetl* life in the Poland of his youth, tales of the founder of Hassidim, the Baal Shem-Tov, and a novel about Jewish life in Canada. Zipper "immortalized the spirit of the *shtetl*," authors Jacques Langlais and David Rome have written.

Recently, a journal which he had kept for the last thirty years of his life, unbeknownst to his family, was translated and published.

Born the son of a Hassidic rabbi, he received a traditional education in scripture, Talmud, and liturgical literature. He left his small town of Tishevitz, Poland to avoid the army and arrest. In his childhood, he and a fellow Jew almost lost their lives before a firing squad during the Polish-Russian War. "We were saved by total strangers, whose kindness I never understood and never forgot."

At nineteen, he landed in another small town, Wolin, and settled down to teach. To avoid the police, he changed his name from Shtern to Zipper, the name of the family that harboured him. But six years later, he was told by the town commandant to leave town or face arrest. An uncle in Montreal forwarded money to come to Canada and he landed in Quebec City in November 1925.

"I arrived in the winter in the snow of Quebec and there at the pier were a bunch of Jews greeting us with 'Shalom Aleichem, Yidden.' Of all the boat passengers, we were the only ones to be met like this. It was an unforgettable impression of Canada," he recalled.

He gradually brought his whole family to Canada. Still, he considered Canada as a temporary detour, a stepping stone to his ultimate goal of settlement in Palestine. Like most Yiddish writers of the era, he was torn between the Old and New Worlds.

In his writings in the years after his arrival, Zipper describes his loneliness and poverty, and the city's unfriendly environment. The secret journals convey his bitter struggle to keep Yiddishkeit in Montreal, the battles he waged to keep his financially-strapped school open, his disillusionment with Jewish community leaders who didn't provide enough support for Jewish education, and the disdain the established community had for Yiddish.

In 1982, Zipper was awarded the Manger Prize, Israel's highest prize for Yiddish literature.

Despite health problems, Zipper remained active until the end of his life in community affairs as well as writing and editing.

Yaacov Zipper described being part of a minyan among strangers not long after his arrival in Montreal. In a strange city, he listened to a man saying the Mourners' Kaddish for someone they did not know:

> A few days ago, as I was sitting in a house, a man walks in and implores, "Come to the synagogue today, young man. I have a yahrzeit. I would like to say Kaddish." What could I do? A man, unshaven, rushing about on a rainy night looking for a few Jews with whom he could say Kaddish. I went to the Shul. Cold, neglected, long benches and tables, lights burning. One at a time, men dragged themselves in, some hurrying from their work, others passing by. Having gathered them together, the mourner stood at the pulpit and recited *Maariv* [the evening prayer]. Strangers to one another, unacquainted, probably seeing each other this time alone and never again ... saying Kaddish for a stranger had brought us together. We stood about till the end of the prayer, listening to a stranger's Kaddish for the unknown dead. That dead man is not even recalled, not for a moment is the man who lived and died considered, and his son, in a distant foreign city, dashes about searching out strangers in order to recite the Kaddish on this memorial day. An orphaned and friendless Kaddish for a stranger, amongst strangers in a distant foreign city. And I felt so cold.

"Lehrer" Wiseman
Shloime Wiseman (1899-1985)
Buried April 11, 1985
Farband – New (D-15)

His first name was Shloime, but Shloime Wiseman was always called "Lehrer" (Yiddish for "teacher") Wiseman by everyone who knew him. It was a designation he carried proudly.

Wiseman came to Canada in 1916 at age sixteen from his native Ukraine, and was given his first teaching job in St. Jérôme, where the Jewish Colonization Agency had transplanted new immigrants to become farmers and small retailers. For more than fifty years, he was principal of the Jewish People's Schools in Montreal, a post he first occupied at age twenty-one in 1920 after teaching there for two years. He did not retire until the 1971 merger of the Jewish People's and Jewish Peretz schools.

The aptly-named Wiseman was also responsible for pioneering the first Jewish day school in Montreal in 1927. It became part of the Jewish People's School (*Yiddishe Folks Shulen*) in 1929. The presence of Jewish children in the Protestant public school system was tolerated, but was the subject of unhappiness, he recalled. "There were those of us who struggled for the right to establish a separate school structure." When a Jewish student was refused a scholarship, the matter went all the way to the Privy Council in London, which ruled the Protestant board could run its system as it wanted, but that Jews also had the right to establish a separate school. "The established Jewish community leaders opposed the idea, so we decided fine, we'll set up our own," Wiseman said. "So we did, first with kindergarten, then up to third grade and we kept increasing classes as the community accepted the idea of the Jewish day school."

Wiseman was also known for his translation skills. In 1953, he edited and translated into Hebrew an anthology of American short stories which was published in Israel. And in retirement he translated the *Discourses* of Epictetus, the historical philosopher, from classical Greek into modern Hebrew.

But perhaps the finest tribute paid to him was that he could always tell when homework had not been done.

Mr. JIAS

Joseph Kage (1918-1996)
Buried September 27, 1996
Farband – Old (D-17)

On the monument: "Scholar, teacher, humanitarian." On the footstone: "A man who gave tirelessly of himself to the community."

It was once said that over twenty per cent of the Jewish population of Montreal owed its presence in the city to Joseph Kage. Another estimate had it that Kage, an immigrant from Minsk, was at one time involved with facilitating the immigration of almost half of Canada's Jewish population.

For more than thirty years, Joseph Kage served as national director of the Jewish Immigrant Aid Services, the organization that oversaw Jewish immigration to Montreal. "He was Mr. JIAS. When he walked into the immigration offices in Ottawa, everyone knew him," said former Jewish Public Library president Chaim Spilberg. Kage began working for JIAS in 1947 on what he believed would be a six-month assignment to help receive Jewish immigrants from displaced persons camps. With an initial budget of $6,000, he took on the task of resettling thousands. In doing so, he took a leave of absence from his job at the McGill School of Social Work and a major pay cut. But he would stay with JIAS until 1982.

Rivka Augenfeld of JIAS recalled how Kage agonized over what to say to a boatload of Jewish orphans arriving in Halifax after the Second World War. Finally, he introduced himself, shook their hands and said in Hebrew, "Welcome and peace be with you." He often said to us,

When you're handling immigration files [remember] these are not just papers, these are human beings who cannot speak for themselves. Make sure those papers are hurting in your hands, because the people who are here can complain but the others can't. You have to remember and advocate for those who are not here yet.

Kage was also one of the founders of the Canadian Council for Refugees. And it was his convening of a national conference on Yiddish in 1969 which led to the creation of the National Committee on Yiddish of the Canadian Jewish Congress. As he put it: "I firmly believe that Yiddish has been and can continue to be one of the chief instruments in creating a bond between Jews and their Jewish traditions and an important means of combatting the waves of deculturalization that represent a grave danger to Jewish life."

For a testimonial retirement dinner held for Kage in 1983, former employment and immigration minister Lloyd Axworthy wrote that "his contribution to the evolution of immigration policy in Canada has been significant [and must be] recognized in the thousands of lives he has touched and affected in a useful and positive way."

THE WARSAW GHETTO NOVELIST
Yehuda Elberg (1912-2003)
Buried October 20, 2003
Farband – Old (D-17)

Yehuda Elberg's tales of Jewish life in Poland have been compared to the work of Isaac Bashevis Singer. Elie Wiesel said Elberg's novel *Ship of the Hunted* will "undoubtedly be counted as one of the most important contributions to Holocaust literature." He published twelve books, numerous stories, two plays, and essays and studies on Jewish affairs and history.

Three hundred members of his family, including his son, perished in the Warsaw Ghetto and in the Treblinka concentration camp. And so, in an interview in *The Canadian Jewish News* in 1992, he declared writing was a duty: "I feel an obligation to resurrect the world that Hitler destroyed. I feel there is beauty there, idealism, life shared. Good came from that despite terrible poverty, strength, idealism for a better world."

Born in Zgierz, Poland in 1912, Elberg was a descendant of a prominent rabbinical family which traced its ancestry to Rashi, the renowned French medieval commentator on the Torah and Talmud. His grandfather, Rabbi Zvi Yehezkel Michelson, the most revered official rabbi in Warsaw, perished in Treblinka. Although Elberg was ordained as a rabbi, he never followed that calling, working instead in Lodz as a textile engineer.

After the war began, he became active in the Jewish underground and wrote speeches against Nazi Germany. Elberg, one of the few survivors of the Warsaw Ghetto uprising, once described events leading to the revolt: "When we heard in the underground that the Nazis had started exterminating Jews in surrounding villages, I didn't believe it. They won't take old people, young people, women, children, and kill them. They would maybe make Jews work, but exterminate a whole community? A normal brain can't comprehend it."

Elberg said the armed resistance began only when the realization came that the Nazis were killing Jews and wanted to kill all Jews.

> To the very end, we believed in the world—that they wouldn't torch the ghetto because the world was watching. But the Germans knew better. The entire ghetto went up in flames and they smoked out the hidden Jews. What shocked me, what pained me, as much as the Holocaust, was the silence of the free world. I am convinced that if not for the indifference of the world, Hitler would not have been able to do what he did.

While the ghetto was being liquidated, Elberg, who had temporarily been outside on a mission for the underground, tried desperately to get back in, to inform people of the location of safe houses. "Resistance is going against the designs of the enemies," Elberg said. "They wanted we should die, but we went on living. And sometimes living under those conditions was harder than dying." Elberg recounted how he once found himself alone on a cold night in a forest while hunted by the Nazis. He suddenly remembered it was Chanukah. Although the few matches in his pocket were meant to assure warmth, he chose instead to fashion a primitive menorah and lit it to honour the holiday.

After the war, Elberg became one of the first organizers of Jewish community life in Poland, helping to create a Jewish newspaper and a writer's union. *Ship of the Hunted*, his most famous novel, is based on the aborted voyage of the *Exodus*, carrying Jews to Palestine in 1947, which he helped organize. He would go on to work as a correspondent for *The Jewish Morning Journal* of New York and *Davaar* in Tel Aviv. In 1947, he went to Paris to become managing editor of a Jewish literary magazine. At a congress in New York he met writer and translator Tillie Feinerman and they married in 1948. She died at age 33, leaving him with two young children. He moved to Montreal in 1956 and married Shaindle Stipelman Bloomstone.

He lectured on Yiddish literature and Jewish thought in South America, Europe, Australia, and Israel and was author-in-residence at Bar-Ilan University and Oxford University. Along with his writing and lecturing, Elberg had a parallel career in real estate development and collected antique books and Jewish artifacts.

In 1997, Syracuse University Press would publish two of his books in English. *On the Tip of a Mast*, his translation of *Ofyn Shpits fun a Mast*, is the story of a family's struggle to survive in the Warsaw Ghetto. It centres on a thirteen-year-old's ability to smuggle goods in and out to save lives. *The Empire of Kalman the Cripple* (*Kalman Kalikes Imperye*), is set in a Polish shtetl before the war, with Kalman seeking revenge for the treatment he receives. When the books appeared simultaneously in English, he said, "At the age of 85, I have given birth to twins." His writing was also translated into Hebrew, Spanish, and Hungarian.

That year, Elberg won Israel's Manger Prize for his novel *On the Tip of a Mast*. He also got literary awards from France, Canada, the United States, and Mexico. Said Elie Wiesel: "The Warsaw Ghetto has finally found its novelist—Yehuda Elberg. He writes with a rare, poetic realism … in [his] novel, madness has been raised to the level of art."

In 1991, Elberg donated several items from his personal collection of Judaica to the Montreal Holocaust Memorial Centre. "The eyes grasp more easily than the ear. It is very hard for people to grasp the enormity of what happened," he said. "Maybe this will help."

Among the heirlooms was a silver kiddush cup given to Elberg by his rabbi grandfather. He gave the cup to relatives before going into hiding during the war. He returned to the village after the war, but no one was left. He forgot about the cup, thinking he'd never see it again. In the late 1980s, a New York antique dealer called to say he had found a ceremonial cup inscribed with the names of Elberg and his grandfather. It was the cup that had disappeared more than forty years earlier.

The Woman Behind the Yiddish Theatre
Dora Wasserman (1919-2003)
Buried December 17, 2003
Memorial Park (A-1)

Before Dora Wasserman was laid to rest at the Baron de Hirsch Cemetery, a funeral cortège, led by police escort, drove past the Saidye Bronfman Centre. There, the doors were held open in a final salute to the woman who revived Yiddish theatre in Montreal. It was a fitting tribute. The Yiddish theatre that now bears her name is one of the most respected non-professional groups in the country and has survived the disappearance of most of its Yiddish-speaking audience. As the death notice in the

Montreal *Gazette* for the founder and artistic director of the Yiddish theatre noted, "She was an extraordinary woman who touched the lives of so many, and whose spirit will continue to live on through the Yiddish theatre."

Born in Chernikhov, Ukraine in 1919, Wasserman (née Goldfarb) was the youngest of five daughters in a poor family. She began acting when she was fifteen and trained with the Moscow Yiddish Academy and studied singing at the Rimsky-Korsakov Conservatory. During the Second World War, she toured with the Kiev State Theatre entertaining Soviet troops. She and her husband—Shura Wasserman, a Polish Jew she met in Kazakhstan in 1944—came to Montreal in 1950. She was hired by the Jewish Public Library in 1955.

Soon after, Wasserman founded the theatres' forerunner, the Yiddish Drama Group, in the gym of the Jewish People's School, where she taught drama to children. Its first play was *Rich Man, Poor Man.*

"Imagine what an accomplishment that was," noted a *Gazette* editorial. "There were no royal commissions in the 1950s calling for more drama in the language of Eastern European Jews. But Dora Wasserman had a dream—one that will survive her death at age eighty-four."

The east-end Comédie canadienne offered the Yiddish Theatre the use of its stage. In 1973, the Yiddish Theatre moved to the Saidye Bronfman Centre. The theatre would produce more than seventy plays in its first forty years. It toured in Israel, the United States, Russia, and Austria. One production was a Yiddish version of Michel Tremblay's *Les Belles Soeurs, Di Shvegerin.* "She understood Québécois and Jews shared a 'latin' side," said the playwright. "On opening night, it was extraordinary to see three hundred people in the theatre quaking with laughter watching five Jewish women praying on their knees."

Wasserman suffered a stroke in 1996, compromising her ability to speak. But she continued to attend as many rehearsals and performances as she could. She had been invested as a member of the Order of Canada in 1992 and was given the Order of Quebec a few months before her death. "Her contribution to our cultural life is exceptional even if she remains little known," a *La Presse* article noted.

It is now estimated about half, if not more, of the Dora Wasserman Yiddish Theatre's patrons are not Yiddish-speaking. English and French supertitles have been added since 1995. "Theatre has nothing to do with language. If language is the problem, it is not a problem," she once told a reporter. "If (a play) is good, you will feel it."

More than six hundred attended her funeral. Former federal justice minister Irwin Cotler said those gathered were not so much mourning as "celebrating the life of one who touched the lives of so many." The "ambassador of Jewish culture" was likely now "organizing a Yiddish theatre among the angels." Michel Tremblay wrote that Wasserman "is one of the human beings I admire most."

Pinchas Blitt, a long-time actor with the troupe, recalled at the funeral how she charmed angry Nobel laureate Isaac Bashevis Singer after one of his works was dramatized without permission. "Dora was never bound or fettered by the ordinary rules of life … No hour was too late, no test too difficult, no challenge too daunting, no sacrifice too great," Blitt said. "For her, the process of bringing a play to stage was almost god-like; there could be no impediment or interference."

Perhaps fittingly, she and husband Sam (or Shura), who were inseparable from the time they met, died within three weeks of one another in 2003. The couple has a single monument at the Cemetery. Hers, on the left, says, in Yiddish: "With love and magic, Dora founded the miracle of Yiddish Theatre in Montreal, a bridge to the Jewish people's continuity." In English it says: "Founding Artistic Director of the Yiddish Theatre, Montreal." His says, in Yiddish: "He shared Dora's dream and supported her in life," and in English, "A kind, strong and generous man." Between their names is a dancing Chassid, or *mentshelem*, which was used as the symbol of the drama group.

At the joint unveiling, friend and actor Anna Gonshor said Dora Wasserman was part of a generation of women who asserted "*Dos is vos ich vill*" ("This is what I want") and took their place in Yiddish culture. Daughter Ella Gaffen recalled her mother saying: 'What is time? There are twenty-four hours in a day and we have to live twenty-five!' There was no such thing as tired. There was no such thing as sick. The show must go on was not a cliché, but a way of life." The unveiling service ended with the singing of the wedding song from *A Shtetl Wedding*, one of her most popular plays.

Engaging Children in Yiddish
Shifre Shtern Krishtalka (1909-2003)
Buried December 28, 2003
Jewish Assistance (D-10)

One of Shifre Shtern Krishtalka's earliest memories was of her eldest brother Yissacher, who taught her letters, and who was killed by a shell fragment in the opening weeks of the First World War. Her memory of him served as a gateway to much of her life, leading her to a long, rewarding career in teaching.

She would spend forty years as a teacher, almost all of them in what is now known as the Jewish People's Schools and Peretz Schools in Montreal. For her innovation in teaching Yiddish, Krishtalka won the J.I. Segal Award for teaching. Her career in teaching began in Poland where she set up the first secular school for children in the small town of Tishevitz, no small feat as it meant keeping in the good graces of the suspicious community elders and authorities. Teachers College in Vilna followed.

Shifre Shtern Krishtalka and her husband Sholem came to Canada in 1933. After an apprenticeship as a sewing-machine operator, she returned to teaching, mostly children in Grades 1 and 2. She worked hard at teaching, always studying the pedagogical literature, developing her own materials, games, puzzles, plays. Soon she was contributing to the pedagogical literature, with papers and lectures in Yiddish and English, especially on how to engage children's abilities first. "When a child entered her class preceded by a confidential psychological profile as a 'slow learner' or as 'emotionally disturbed,' Shifre's invariable practice was to put the file in her desk drawer and forget about it. She moved instead to the child," her son Aaron Krishtalka said in his eulogy.

For Krishtalka, the Nazi Holocaust meant Montreal had become a North American outpost of European Jewish and Yiddish life and that teaching children Yiddish "was now a work of even greater moment, lest all should be lost, even memory," Mr. Krishtalka said. After her husband's death she channelled her grief into one grand project: putting into ordered written form her approach to teaching children Yiddish. Four years of work produced *Yiddish a Lebedike Shprakh (Yiddish, a Living Language)*. As described by her son: "It is a trip around the school year, day by day, class by class, through the procession of the festivals and the seasons, each day with its dialogue between teacher and children, their games, puzzles, songs."

The Canadian Experience in Yiddish Verse
Sholem Shtern (1907-1990)
Buried August 10, 1990
Jewish Assistance (D-10)

Through the release of his two-volume epic *In Kanada* in 1960 and 1963, which described the Jewish immigrant experience in Canada, Sholem Shtern came to be considered the most distinctly Canadian of Yiddish writers and poets.

Born in a small town near Lublin, Poland, Shtern received a traditional Jewish education and then gave private Hebrew lessons to earn a living. Soon after emigrating to Canada in 1927, he was diagnosed with tuberculosis and spent nearly two years at the Mount Sinai Hospital. There he met his Bialistok-born wife, Sonia Elbaum. After marrying, they lived in the Plateau Mont-Royal until the 1950s, when they moved to Park Extension.

He was a part of a prominent Yiddish literary family in Montreal that included his brother Jacob Zipper and their sister Shifre Shtern Krishtalka. The siblings arrived on their own, one by one, from Poland, and eventually brought their parents over.

Shtern initially sold Yiddish magazines door-to-door in Montreal. He also worked in a fruit store and as a bookstore clerk, and began to write Yiddish poems and essays which were published in literary magazines in New York, Toronto, and elsewhere.

He began teaching at the United Jewish Peoples Order Morris Winchevsky School, where he eventually became principal and stayed for twenty years. Early on Shtern became interested in Marxism. While not a Communist Party member, he was involved in many leftist organizations and wrote for the communist press. In time, he became increasingly disillusioned with communism. He is buried in the Jewish Assistance section of Baron de Hirsch. That section was once known as the Left Workmen's Circle and was formed by breakaway leftist members of the Workmen's Circle.

Shtern's greatest passion was writing and by 1945, three of his books of poetry had been published. His works were published in Yiddish publications around the world as well as in English, French, Russian, and Polish translations. His *In Kanada* was published in Yiddish verse and was also translated into English and French. The English version was called *In Canada:*

A Novel in Verse. Shtern remained an educator until the end, giving private lessons in Yiddish and Hebrew and teaching a creative Yiddish course at the Golden Age Association (now Cummings Centre for Jewish Seniors) until shortly before his death.

THE "YIDDISH CONNECTION"
Sara Rosenfeld (1920-2004)
Buried January 27, 2004
Montreal Worker's Circle #1 (D-3)

It has been said that if Yiddish language and culture survive here and abroad, it will have been because of the efforts of people like Sara Rosenfeld. If it does survive, "it will be due, quite literally, to the efforts of a handful of people, and Sara Rosenfeld will have been in the forefront of that handful," said Lorraine Singer, co-chair of a tribute to her in 2002.

Rosenfeld devoted much of her life to the promotion of Yiddish culture. Née Mlotek, Rosenfeld grew up in Warsaw, but escaped to Soviet-occupied territory after the German occupation of Poland. There she was arrested and sent to a labour camp with her future husband. Her parents and five siblings perished in Treblinka.

She came to Canada in 1948, and in 1951 founded the Workmen's Circle Choir, which performed Yiddish songs for forty-five years. For years she was also the driving force behind the Montreal Workmen's Circle Choir and Mameh-Loshn, founded mainly for Canadian-born Jews who wanted to reconnect with the Yiddish from their childhoods. In the late 1960s, Rosenfeld met strong resistance when she tried to persuade the Canadian Jewish Congress it had a responsibility to help preserve the Yiddish language. "Yiddish was looked down upon by the higher circles. It was seen as something that was not important, something people did not want to be associated with," she said a few years before her death. From 1970 to 1990, she served as founding national executive director of the Yiddish Committee of the Congress.

One of her first tasks after joining CJC was to stave off the demise of the *Keneder Adler*, the one-time daily Yiddish newspaper that had been published since 1907. For twenty years until its 1989 closure, she wrote articles, distributed the paper, and did fundraising to keep it running.

In 1974, she helped launch yet another of Montreal's summer festivals with the Yiddish Festival in the Park, an annual event in Côte Saint-Luc's

Trudeau Park featuring song, theatre, poetry, and dance. "The repertoire has to be to my liking," she told *The Canadian Jewish News*. "No cheap entertainment like they give in the Catskills." It was dedicated to her in August 2004, after her death in January that year at age eighty-three.

In 1982, she was a key organizer of the third international conference of the World Council for Yiddish, which drew Nobel Prize winners Isaac Bashevis Singer and Elie Wiesel to Montreal. Not only that, but she helped get the National Yiddish Book Center off the ground. The Amherst, Massachusetts institution has an estimated 1.5 million volumes today. She co-founded in 1996 the annual KlezKanada Jewish Cultural Festival in the Laurentians, and was instrumental in the creation of the Foundation for Yiddish Culture in Honour of Jacob Zipper and Shloime Wiseman, which supports Yiddish writers and students.

For her working "tirelessly to preserve and promote the Yiddish language in Canada," Rosenfeld was inducted into the Order of Canada in 2002. "If we don't do it, who will?" she noted of her efforts to save the language. After all, Yiddish is "the best heritage we can leave to the young."

Other Notables Buried in Baron de Hirsch Cemetery

Among the tens of thousands of Jews buried in the Baron de Hirsch Cemetery, are many who shaped life in Montreal. There are the teachers and community builders. The philanthropist whose vision and generosity continue to play a role. The artist who shaped future generations of artists but died on the opening eve of his biggest exhibition. Rabbis buried in burial huts reserved for the greats, and others who served at the pulpit for decades. There's the bagel-baker and the monument-maker. The poet who fought to die in dignity and the poet considered one of Canada's twentieth century's best. The last gambling czar. Probably the world's oldest man. The historian who chronicled Canada's Jewish community and the journalist who explained a strange new city to immigrants. Children who died tragically, a *Titanic* victim, military persons killed in war, people felled by freak accidents, and the immigrant who died during the happiest day of his life. Here are just a few stories of occupants of the Baron de Hirsch Cemetery.

THE *TITANIC* VICTIM
Leopold Weisz (1880-1912)
Buried May 12, 1912
Baron de Hirsch #1 (A-5)

Stone-carver Leopold Weisz executed the friezes on the entrance front of the Gibb Pavilion of the Montreal Museum of Fine Arts on Sherbrooke Street. People still regard them with fascination, as they do his carvings of the stone shields representing Canada's provinces which decorate the Dominion Express Building at 201 St. Jacques Street West. Ironically, while the work of the artisan can easily be found, the same can't be said for his gravesite in Baron de Hirsch Cemetery. While it is known that Weisz is buried in Baron de Hirsch #1, the exact location of his grave has not been determined.

Of the six *Titanic* victims buried in Montreal, Weisz is the only one buried at Baron de Hirsch. Believed to have been born in 1880, Weisz grew up in a Jewish neighbourhood of Pest, Hungary. When he was nineteen he went to study at the Bromsgrove Guild of Art in England. There, he met and married Mathilde Françoise Pëde, a Roman Catholic Belgian.

After working for some time in Montreal, Weisz decided in 1912 that the city, then in the midst of a building boom, "was the place to make money from art." He planned to launch a business in Canada with partner Edward Wren. So he went back to England to fetch his wife. The couple was to have sailed first class on another ship, but because of a coal strike, they transferred to the *Titanic*. They booked their berths in March 1912, paid their £26 fare and boarded the *Titanic* at Southampton on April 10.

Before they boarded, Weisz sewed his life savings, about $30,000 in currency, into the lining of his coat. He also carried about $15,000 worth of gold bullion in his pockets. On the night of the sinking he went for a walk on deck while his wife took part in the impromptu hymn-sing in the second-class dining room. Mrs. Weisz sang "The Last Rose of Summer" and thought her rendition "met with great success." Mathilde Weisz then joined her husband on deck but the temperature had dropped to minus one Celsius. "I guess we're in the ice," he said. They had just returned to their cabin at 11:40 p.m. when they felt a tremor. The ship had struck an iceberg on its maiden voyage.

Mathilde survived and was picked up by the *Carpathia*, which disembarked at New York City. Leopold wasn't so lucky. A minute after being picked up by the ship, Mathilde cried after her husband, "Mon pauvre Léopold!" She was in danger of being deported back to England as an indigent until her husband's body was recovered by the cable steamer *Mackay-Bennett*. According to the *Encyclopedia Titanica*, it was not clear whether the gold sewn inside his coat was returned to her. Weisz's body was shipped to Montreal for burial at Baron de Hirsch Cemetery. He was identified as Passenger No. 293 among the bodies recovered from the *Titanic*.

Mathilde later married her late husband's business partner, Edward Wren, and they lived in Westmount. Mathilde Wren became known in Montreal as a singer who performed in amateur theatricals and operettas with the Canadian Belgian Musical and Dramatic Club. During the First World War, she raised $57,000 for Belgian charities, efforts that were recognized by the King of Belgium with the Médaille de la Reine Élisabeth and the naming after her of a street in her birthplace of Ghent. Mathilde, who died in Montreal on October 13, 1953 at seventy-nine, is buried at the Notre-Dame-des-Neiges Cemetery. Ironically, like her husband's, her grave was unmarked. That situation came to an end fifty years after her death. In 2003, a tombstone marking her grave was donated by memorial manufacturer Rock of Ages and dedicated by members of the *Titanic* International Society, which paid for the engraving.

Sabbath Queen and Zohar Translator
Rabbi Yudel Rosenberg (1860-1935)
Buried October 23, 1935
Hadrath Kodesh – UHC

In more recent days, he became known as the grandfather of novelist Mordecai Richler. But Rabbi Yudel Rosenberg was already recognized in religious circles for his translation of the Zohar—the sourcebook of Kabbalistic lore—an arduous task that took him twenty-five years. At the Baron de Hirsch Cemetery, he is now one of the few occupants of an *Ohel*, a type of burial hut reserved for *tzaddiks*, or righteous people.

"He belongs to the group of Jewish mystics who have given warmth and spirituality to our Judaism," Harry J. Stern of Temple Emanu-El said at a 1931 special testimonial dinner for Rosenberg's seventieth birthday.

Born in Poland, Rabbi Rosenberg received a traditional rabbinic and Hassidic education. After failing at several business ventures, he began his career as a rabbi in the town of Tarlow. He came to Canada in 1913, where he served as a rabbi in Toronto from 1913 to 1918 and in Montreal from 1919 to his death in 1935. His major work was his multi-volume edition and translation of the *Zohar* from Aramaic to Hebrew. The *Zohar* (Book of Splendour), purportedly written in thirteenth-century Spain, attempts to penetrate into the inner recesses of God and is considered by many Jews to be surpassed only by the Talmud and the Tanach. In 1931, one critic dubbed the translation "the only important book contributed by Jewish Canada to cultural history."

Rabbi Rosenberg also published twenty treatises on various areas of Jewish learning, from the Kabbalah to literature. But to reach the masses of Yiddish-speaking Montreal Jews, he created a fictional narrator called the Sabbath Queen. The work was published in Montreal in 1924 with a twenty-five-cent cover price and was titled *A Brivele dun di Zisse Mame Shabbes Malkese zu Ihre un Tekhter fun Idishn Folk* (A Letter from the Sweet Mother Sabbath Queen to Her Sons and Daughters of the Jewish People). The Sabbath Queen, the "mother" of the Jewish people, berated the city's Jews for not observing the Sabbath. The Sabbath Queen tells her "dear beloved children" that Jews suffer more than other peoples and have languished in exile because so many have publicly desecrated the Sabbath, thus abandoning the peace and protection offered by the Sabbath Queen.

One thing that annoyed the Sabbath Queen was "the fact that those who publicly desecrated the Sabbath and thus demonstrated their lack of respect for the Creator, nonetheless showed great respect for the memory of their deceased parents, honouring them through the recitation of the Kaddish and Yizkor prayers." Rabbi Rosenberg felt community members feared only the dead and gave this description of their actions: "When they have a yahrtzeit on Rosh Hashanah/Yom Kippur they come into the synagogue and buy a 'fat' *aliyah* ... Is this not a desecration of God's name and a disgrace for the Torah?" He felt a forty-hour workweek, then being demanded by labour unions, would solve the problem of disrespect for the Sabbath and result in an economic boon to boot.

Rosenberg also denounced Jewish bakers who baked on the Sabbath as well as Jews who bought the goods. In a 1921 ad he placed in the *Keneder Adler*, he wrote, "It must be remembered that baked goods from a baker who desecrates the Sabbath are even more *trayf* (non-kosher) than gentile baked goods which contain lard." Rabbi Rosenberg also became involved in the battle over kosher meat, something that would rock the Jewish community early in the twentieth century, and pit him in battle against Rabbi Hirsch Cohen over control of the lucrative trade. As Israel Medres noted:

> The insistence of the Jewish immigrants, regardless of their level of observance of the laws and customs of rabbinic Judaism in other areas, to purchase and consume meat certified as ritually kosher, created a vast industry in all North American centres of Jewish life. This industry was a source of income, power and prestige, for hundreds of people, and especially for immigrant Orthodox rabbis who usually had no other viable way to make a decent living or of exercising their influence in a community which, in most other instances, tended to regard them as basically irrelevant figures.

In fact it was said that Rosenberg came to Montreal in 1919 because of opposition to Rabbi Hirsch Cohen's control of kosher slaughtering in the city. The opposition group needed a rabbi to make their battle legitimate and invited Rosenberg from Toronto. From 1919 to 1921, the two rabbis and their supporters fought each other for control of kosher meat in Montreal. Finally, they joined forces and began opposing another rabbi, Joshua Hirschorn, a new rabbi. This rabbinic cooperation ultimately led to the 1922 founding of the Jewish Community Council of Montreal, the Vaad Ha'ir.

In June 1922, Rabbi Rosenberg sent a letter to Montreal Mayor Médéric Martin, urging him to introduce a bylaw similar to one recently adopted in Toronto. It would govern the operation and sanitation of chicken-killing establishments, which would be directly under the control of rabbis and their representatives. As a result of the letter, Rabbi Rosenberg was invited to make a presentation at a city council meeting. Although not fluent in either official language, Rabbi Rosenberg submitted a written statement in English. He noted that all major Canadian cities except Montreal had established specific places where poultry could be killed under rabbinical supervision. Montreal, he said, "is still lacking in that respect like an Indian city in the Middle Ages. ... I beg, educated gentlemen, that you consider that very many diseases which exist by people, also exist in poultry." Not only that, but "myriads of flies make their residence on the blood of the chickens in the chicken stores and markets where the poultry is killed, the same flies poison the water which the live chickens drink; the same flies poison all kinds of foods which are to be found in the markets. How, I ask you learned gentlemen, can such a grave injustice be permitted in Montreal?"

A new bylaw concerning poultry, game, and fish and limiting the number of Jewish poultry slaughterhouses came into force, unfortunately leading to a new kosher meat war. This time it pitted Rabbi Cohen and the Vaad Ha'ir, who lobbied to make sure permits for poultry abattoirs would only be given under their control, against Rabbis Rosenberg and Hirschorn, who said the Jewish Community Council was not representative of the Jewish community as a whole. The *Keneder Adler* accused the latter two rabbis of being "renegades, who have sought to destroy all that is holy and dear to Montreal Jews (and) now seek to also help the chicken dealers in [their] struggle against order." Rosenberg then used the legal system. In a suit brought before the Quebec Superior Court, the Rabbi argued that a bylaw limiting the number of Jewish poultry-slaughtering establishments while allowing all other such establishments was unconstitutional. In April 1924, the court found for the plaintiffs, awarding them court costs amounting to $272.85.

A FUNERAL OF SIX THOUSAND
Zvi Hirsch Cohen (1860-1950)
November 19, 1950
Chevra T'hilim Pinsker – UHC

When Rabbi Zvi Hirsch Cohen died in 1950 at age ninety, more than six thousand people attended his funeral. Officials said it was the largest funeral ever held in Montreal for a Jew. He is buried in an Ohel at the Baron de Hirsch Cemetery.

Venerated by members of the city's Jewish community, Rabbi Cohen was dean of the Canadian Rabbinate and president of the Montreal Council of Orthodox Rabbis. He also played a role in the formation of the Canadian Jewish Congress, opening its first session in 1919 with a prayer, and was active in its forerunner, the Conference of Canadian Jews.

At his funeral, crowds of mourners filled the Adath Yeshurun Hadrath Kodesh Congregation on St. Urbain Street, near Mount Royal, while an overflow of mourners outside waited for the hearse to pass by. Representatives from the city, provincial government, police, and the Israeli consul in Montreal attended.

"In his devotion to the cause of Zionism, to the community and to the religious life, Rabbi Cohen was an example to the rest of Montreal's Jewish community," City Councillor Max Seigler said in his eulogy. "Canada has lost one of her leading citizens and is richer because Rabbi Cohen lived among us."

Born in 1860 in Budvitz, Lithuania, Rabbi Cohen studied in rabbinical seminaries in Vilna and Volozhin, before coming to Montreal in 1889. He came to Canada at "an age at which most men have determined their lives' pattern. For him it was a beginning," a newspaper obituary noted. "The extent of his work was so wide that the wonder of it is that he had time— as he always had—for study and scholarship." He was one of the founders of the United Jewish Talmud Torah School, now known as the United Talmud Torahs of Montreal. He also took a leading part in the settlement of hundreds of Jewish war orphans from the Ukraine in Montreal. And he was the Jewish chaplain to prisoners in penitentiaries.

When *schochet* Solomon Lamdan was arrested in 1908 for cruelty to chickens for slaughtering poultry kosher-style in his St. Dominique Street home near the St. Lawrence Market on Rachel Street, Rabbi Cohen saw the incident as "an intervention by municipal authorities who intend to destroy the Jewish community." He later took a prominent role in establishing a kosher meat control system and was among the organizers of the Jewish Community Council of Montreal, the Vaad Ha'ir. As an authority on Judaism, his rulings on various religious questions were sought around the world. Numerous articles of his appeared in the rabbinical press.

During the First World War, Rabbi Cohen organized the Central War Sufferers Relief Society of Canada that raised hundreds of thousands of dollars for relief of Jews in devastated areas of Europe and Palestine. He was the founder of the Ezras Torah Fund for suffering Rabbis in Europe and Palestine. As an editorial explained, Rabbi Cohen often raised his voice "in condemnation and prophetic thunder as when, seeing the persecution of his brethren overseas, he mounted tribune or pulpit to denounce, in the very accents of biblical wrath, the corruption of peoples and the iniquity of governments."

His ministry spanned a period of more than fifty years of phenomenal growth for the city's Jewish community. As Rabbi Pinchas Hirshprung of the Council of Orthodox Rabbis noted, Rabbi Cohen became a leader of the Jewish community when it consisted in large part of refugees who had fled to Canada to escape persecution. "He has guided us and inspired us during the entire period of growth. He has watched that the eternal spirit of our faith should never be absent from our midst."

ARCHITECT OF CONGRESS
Hannaniah Meier Caiserman (1884-1950)
Buried December 25, 1950
Jewish National (Farband) D-20

He was an organizer of unions in the garment trade and helped organizations like the Jewish Immigrant Aid Society and the Jewish Public Library get started. And for years, he almost single-handedly kept the Canadian Jewish Congress afloat.

H.M. Caiserman was born in 1884 in Piatra-Niamtz, Romania. He became active in the union movement, attracting the suspicion of Romania's reactionary government. Concerned about his personal safety, he left the country and came to Canada in 1910 where he went to work in a tailor shop. Witnessing sweatshop conditions, he soon left to organize the mostly Yiddish-speaking tailors to improve their work conditions. Less than two years after his arrival, Caiserman became the leader of the Tailors Union, which soon grew to four thousand members.

In 1912, the tailors officially worked fifty-nine hours a week. Unofficially they worked from dawn to dusk during the busy season. The tailors called a strike to abolish the fifty-nine-hour workweek and other unacceptable working conditions. It lasted for nine weeks and ended in victory for the workers, with the lengthy workweek abolished.

Because of its involvement in the ideal of a Jewish homeland in Palestine and its leftist leanings, Caiserman was an enthusiastic proponent of Labour Zionism. So much so that he became the candidate of the Poale Zion party in the municipal election of 1916, in the heavily Jewish St. Louis Ward. Among his campaign proposals were an eight-hour workday, the abolition of child labour, equality of rights for all national groups, and the use of Yiddish in city regulations. He lost soundly, however, even losing his election deposit.

In 1917, he was elected president of the Jewish Public Library or Yidishe Folks Bibliotek un Folks Universitet (Jewish Public Library and People's University), as it was then known. Two years later, Caiserman became one of the prime movers for the organization of the first session of the Canadian Jewish Congress. However, two years after it was created in 1919 with Caiserman as general secretary, the organization was falling apart. Caiserman left Canada in 1921 to fulfil his lifelong dream of *aliyah*, and in Palestine became managing director of the Cooperative Bank for Labour Institutions.

Two years later he was back in Montreal. While Congress remained inactive for several years, Caiserman stood at the helm as general-secretary, with his office a desk in a corner of the Baron de Hirsch Institute. There he monitored anti-Semitic incidents in Canada, and occasionally responded to anti-Semites in the name of the Jewish community.

Despite organizational obstacles and financial difficulties, Caiserman convinced Canadian Jewry in 1934 to reconvene and salvage Congress. With the institution back on its feet, Caiserman, as general secretary ensured it was involved in all major issues during that tumultuous decade. Until Samuel Bronfman became president of the Canadian Jewish Congress in 1939, Caiserman assumed almost single-handedly the role of giving Canadian Jewry a single united voice. As journalist Israel Medres wrote in an undated article from the time in *Dos Vort*: "The impression was that Caiserman is the Jewish Congress and that the Congress is Caiserman."

On the domestic front, he combatted anti-Semites like Adrien Arcand. Medres noted in the 1930s that Caiserman was recognized in the non-Jewish press as the representative of the Jewish community. Caiserman was one of three Canadian representatives of CJC at the founding of the World Jewish Congress in Geneva in 1936. In December 1945, he journeyed to Poland to survey post-war conditions. He remained there for several months. He was, according to a news release from Canadian Jewish Congress, the first representative of the Canadian Jewish community to be permitted to enter Poland. He later toured South America on behalf of the Joint Distribution Committee to organize aid for refugees. In 1947, when the Canadian government permitted the entry into Canada of one thousand Jewish orphans from Europe, he wrote articles to arouse interest in the community, appealing to Jewish homes to receive these orphans.

Caiserman also had a "burning passion" for the Yiddish language. He edited the anthology *Jewish Poets in Canada* (1934) and in the Yiddish and Jewish publications of the day, reviewed almost every Yiddish book of artistic value to appear in Canada. He ran a literary salon in his home and would organize committees to publish the work of poets and writers. Shortly after his death, poet and writer J. I. Segal wrote "the world has not been the same since. That hour Montreal became another city. But one man, yet he had transformed a continent of loneliness into a very home."

Caiserman remained secretary-general of the Congress until his death in 1950. Samuel Bronfman, then national president of the Congress, called Caiserman "one of the far-sighted architects of the Canadian Jewish Congress, a lifelong active Zionist and a devoted servant of the Canadian Jewish community. Every person in trouble found in Mr. Caiserman the friendly ear and the helping hand of a kinsman."

THE MISSED VERNISSAGE
Alexander Bercovitch (1891-1951)
Burial January 9, 1951
Tolner (D-22)

On January 7, 1951, a crowd gathered in the exhibition hall of the Snowdon YM-YWHA for the opening of artist Alexander Bercovitch's first major exhibition in a decade. When he didn't show up, people were angry, confused, and hurt. There were derogatory comments that he had deliberately snubbed the opening of the exhibition of eighty of his works, and jokes about the "late" Mr. Bercovitch.

But Bercovitch had suffered a massive heart attack en route as he waited for his streetcar at the corner of Mont-Royal and St. Laurent. He died in the street. His body went unclaimed at the morgue until the next day. He was fifty-nine, and penniless.

He "played a major role in the evolution of modern art in Canada," according to his biographer Robert Adams. Widely credited with bringing modernism into what was then Montreal's provincial and inward-looking art world, Bercovitch also taught a generation of Jewish artists, from Esther Wertheimer to Ghitta Caiserman-Roth. "After more than twenty years of works in Quebec, he had not harvested the public recognition he deserved. He died at precisely the moment when we were getting ready to give it to him," art critic Rolland Boulanger wrote at the time.

Bercovitch was born in 1891 in Kherson, a part of the Ukraine where Jewish settlement was promoted by the Czars. His family was poor—his father was a shoemaker—and he was apprenticed at age seven to a book-binder. At age nine he spent hours peering through a grill at a local monastery, watching monks painting icons, until they finally let him in. Wrote Adams: "They were amused by the little Jewish boy's fascination with icons and he became their mascot. Finally they gave him paint and a few words of instruction. Thus began an informal and irregular apprentice-ship that lasted for nearly six years."

Although he gained a reputation as a prodigy by the time he was in his teens, further training was hampered by restrictions placed on Jews. In 1907, local townspeople banded together to send him to a new art school in Jerusalem. From there, he studied at the Munich Academy of Fine Arts and at the Leningrad Institute of Arts. He also worked briefly on sets for the famed Ballets Russes.

Bercovitch was conscripted into the army but deserted and lived in hiding for the next three years. He married, had a son, abandoned his family, married again and went to teach in Turkestan, where his career took off. Eventually, however, poverty forced Bercovitch, his wife and two daughers (one of whom was named Ninel—Lenin spelled backwards—to choose Montreal in 1926.

Life wasn't much better in Montreal and he scraped by doing odd jobs. His first job was painting a picture of a boy holding a bunch of fruit on the wall of a wholesale fruit company. He later did set designs for the Yiddish Theatre, and painted the underwater scene on the lobby walls of the former Snowdon Theatre on Décarie Boulevard and the cherubs at the Rialto on Park Avenue.

Best known for his portraits and landscapes, Bercovitch was one of the first artists to explore the Gaspé coast on canvas and those works are among his best known. He also produced many of his works in Quebec City. Former Governor General Vincent Massey was among the owners of his originals. He worked with artist John Lyman to found the Contemporary Arts Society and the Eastern Group. Although his work was hailed as "powerful and innovative", he was hampered by the fact few people bought modern, locally-made artwork in those days.

Said one obituary, "He had lived with only one purpose, to be 'Alexander Bercovitch—Artist', and to that imperative he had willingly sacrificed not only others but himself. He died without recognition, treasure, or the comforting presence of his children. He died heavy with neglect and poverty and disappointment."

The January 1951 exhibition at the new YM-YWHA was to be his first one-man show since 1945. By then, however, Bercovitch was overweight and years of neglect to his health had caused irreparable damage to his kidneys. Critic Jean Dénéchaud of La Presse wrote:

> We assumed his failure to attend his own show to be just another of his eccentricities. ... His premature death leaves behind the memory of a gifted artist, a sincere artist who painted only what he sincerely felt, ... this big, terribly simple man, whose bright eye caught every detail of our streets and modern life.

Poet A.M. Klein (also buried at Baron de Hirsch) was a friend of Bercovitch. Klein said, "He will be remembered, not only by his friends who will always recall his shy, his naif personality, his mosaic hesitations in speech, his inarticulate verbal descriptions, but by all lovers of art who will cherish before their eyes the uninhibited eloquence of his palette."

A Name Synonymous with Jewish Funerals
Lazar Paperman
Buried October 22, 1954
Canadian – UHC

Until Lazar Paperman arrived on the scene, there was no formal Jewish funeral home in Montreal. Today, Paperman & Sons is synonymous with funeral services in the Jewish community.

Lazar Paperman had served as the head of a Chevra Kadisha (volunteer burial society) before members of the Jewish community urged him to open a funeral home. "He was asked by some of the leaders of the community if he would undertake to go into the business on a professional level rather than just as a volunteer," said his descendant Herbert Paperman, the current patriarch of Paperman & Sons. "That's how we started." Other attempts had failed.

Before Paperman's opened, synagogues had to find alternatives in the general community. They made arrangements with non-Jewish funeral directors for the preparation of the dead for Jewish burial. For many years, for example, the Spanish & Portuguese Congregation had such an arrangement with Joseph Wray on Mountain Street, while Shaar Hashomayim Synagogue had one with Willam Wray on University Street. "When Jewish funeral directors entered the picture, the business was gradually turned over to them, but such is the nature of human loyalty that it took a long time for the transfer to be complete," Rabbi Wilfred Shuchat noted.

Lazar Paperman is believed to have started his business in 1910. It was incorporated a few years later. He used a horse-drawn hearse in the summer and a sleigh in winter. The firm had headquarters on St. Elizabeth Street near Ontario. In the early days, preparation of the body and the funeral often took place in the home of the deceased.

In 1926, Paperman & Sons moved to larger quarters on St. Urbain Street. At the time, Lazar's sons Abe and Sam ran the major part of the operation. Abe's son, Herbert, later joined them. Burgeoning growth and a westward shift in the community eventually led to the move to larger quarters on Côte des Neiges Road.

The family has been involved in several other ventures over the years, including an ambulance service for the Jewish hospitals (Jewish General, Maimonides, Hospital of Hope), car leasing, and cemetery land ownership and management.

Paperman's was sold in 1995 to the Loewen Group, but was bought back by the family in 2001. In its new quarters on Jean-Talon Boulevard since 1995, Paperman & Sons now arranges about a thousand funerals annually, the vast majority of funerals in Montreal's Jewish community. The sons of Herbert Paperman—the fourth generation—have now joined the firm.

In their booklet, Lazar's descendants state that Lazar Paperman founded the chapel of Paperman & Sons on an ideal:

> To render last rites that will be a tribute to the dead and a solace to the living; to provide for those rites an atmosphere of dignity and tranquillity, to bring these services within the reach of all mourners; that is the funeral director's prime responsibility.

With respect to funeral services for indigents at Baron de Hirsch, "the Papermans have always been very helpful," said Jacques Berkowitz. As Rabbi Schuchat puts it, "The fact that theirs was a business operated for profit does not alter the fact that the Papermans brought order, dignity, and a high regard for Jewish law into the act and process of Jewish burial."

One of Canada's Most Important Writers
A.M. Klein (1909-1972)
Buried August 22, 1972
Montefiore (D-14)

Some have called him one of Canada's greatest poets and of "almost mythic importance" in Canadian letters and in Jewish writing. Others said he was one of the great Canadian writers of the twentieth century, the country's first distinctive Jewish voice in literature, the most influential Jewish writer of his generation, and an influence on writers from Irving Layton to Mordecai Richler. Several critics recognized him as the first writer to produce English-language poetry, essays, and fiction that reflected an authentic sense of Jewish tradition.

In *The Writers of Montreal*, Elaine Kalman Naves called Klein "arguably (one of) the most important English-Canadian writers in the first half of this century, a genius with words whose profound knowledge of Judaica was twinned by a genuinely Canadian sensibility." Mental illness stilled his voice for the last twenty years of his life. By the time he died, he had completely disappeared from the public eye.

Born in Ratno, Ukraine, Abraham Moses Klein came to Canada as a one-year-old. At Baron Byng High School he helped form the Sholem Aleichem Club, named after the Yiddish author. He later studied for the rabbinate and then graduated in law from the Université de Montréal.

Through the Depression, while struggling as a lawyer, he devoted himself passionately to Canadian and international Jewish causes and to Zionism, working as an effective fundraiser for the future State of Israel. Almost alone among his contemporaries, he foresaw the Holocaust. He began to recognize the growing threat of the emerging Nazi government in Germany in the mid-1930s and devoted much of his energy to writing articles that argued the urgency of fighting that force. Much of his newspaper writing was for the weekly *Canadian Jewish Chronicle*, which he edited from 1938 to 1955. He also wrote hundreds of articles in the *Canadian Jewish Eagle* against anti-Semitism.

He practised law, ran for Parliament as a socialist, and worked as a professor of English literature at McGill University, and as a speechwriter for Samuel Bronfman.

Klein published four books of poetry, including: *Hath Not a Jew?*, *Poems*, *The Hitleriad*, and *The Rocking Chair and Other Poems*, for which he won the Governor General's Literary Award in 1948. Often his themes were derived from his Orthodox Jewish upbringing and the Jewish community in which he lived. No poet has celebrated Montreal more originally than Klein; he was, for example, the first writer to combine Québécois joual, Yiddish, Hebrew, and English to evoke the polyglot world of his Montreal.

In the early 1940s, he began writing poems about the other communities that surrounded the Jewish community. His poems on French Canada were so successful that the Canadian Jewish Congress published them as a pamphlet to improve relations between the two communities. After the Second World War, he journeyed to Europe and North Africa, with financial assistance from Bronfman, to visit refugee camps. His only novel, *The Second Scroll*, was inspired by a trip to Israel in 1949. It has been considered among the most important works to have been written in celebration of the rebirth of the State of Israel.

In the early 1950s, Klein suffered a mental breakdown. He remained mysteriously silent for several years until he died quietly in his sleep, apparently of a heart attack. He had become increasingly disillusioned

פ נ
אברהם משה בר קלמן
נפ' י"א אלול תשל ב
ת נ צ ב ה

IN MEMORY OF
A BELOVED FATHER
AND GRANDFATHER
ABRAHAM M
KLEIN
FEB. 14. 1909–AUG. 20. 1972

[Photo: D.R. Cowles]

about a public that had little use for poetry or poets. Serious academic attention began to be paid to his work after his death and his posthumous reputation grew steadily. Many academics now believe Canadian literature courses are not complete without the inclusion of Klein's works.

"It was as if the obscurity into which he had retreated had, against all intentions, enlarged his legend," his biographer Usher Caplan noted. "The popularity of Jewish literature in North America came too late for him; had he continued writing into the sixties and beyond, he surely would have found the Jewish audience he deserved."

Master Mediator
Alan B. Gold (1917-2005)
Buried May 17, 2005
Hebrew Sick Benefit Association

When Alan Gold was named Chief Justice of the Quebec Superior Court in 1983, he became the first Jew to hold that post. But he is better known for his role as a mediator who averted a longshoremen's strike at the Port of Montreal, helped settle two postal strikes, and mediated between the Quebec government and the Kanesatake Mohawks during the Oka crisis of 1990. "It is tempting to wonder what Gold might have achieved in the Middle East," editorialized the Montreal *Gazette*.

Gold was born in Montreal in 1917 to a mother who came from a long line of rabbis in Czarist Russia and a father who was a clothing manufacturer. He spoke only Yiddish until age six. Ironically, the celebrated jurist almost didn't make it into law. When he was unable to get into law school at McGill University because of the Jewish quota system then in place, he enrolled in drama at Queen's University in 1937, where he studied acting with Lorne Greene, who would go on to have a distinguished career in film and television. He was then offered a scholarship to continue acting studies in New York and another to take political science at the London School of Economics. Gold opted for the latter. He then studied law at the Université de Montréal, graduating in 1941.

With the Second World War raging in Europe, he enlisted in the Royal Canadian Artillery and handled courts martial. After the war he went into private practice and became a part-time law professor at McGill. Gold was appointed a judge of Magistrate's Court and vice-chairman of the Quebec Labour Relations Board in 1961 and in 1970 was named a provincial court judge. He served as chief justice of the Superior Court from 1983 to 1992. He later became a senior partner at the Montreal law firm Davies, Ward, Phillips and Vineberg.

Gold first came to prominence when he prevented a longshoremen's strike at the Port of Montreal in 1968. His later roles in settling postal strikes and the Oka Crisis gained him further renown. He helped broker the settlement between the federal government and former Prime Minister Brian Mulroney in the Airbus lawsuit. He represented the Saskatchewan government in the $10 million financial settlement for David Milgaard, who spent twenty-two years in prison for a murder he did not commit. He looked into allegations of vote-counting fraud after the 1995 referendum on Quebec sovereignty. While he did not find proof of an organized conspiracy to reject No ballots on the part of the Yes side, Gold found the number of rejected No ballots was excessively high in four ridings.

In his eulogy at Paperman & Sons, his son Marc said, "He made a difference in the law, the world of the arts, higher education, and all the people he came in contact with." For Gold, law was "all about human relations, finding workable solutions, however partial, to life's enduring and eternal problems. Justice in an imperfect world was about choosing between the lesser of two evils and "not knowing where to draw the line, but knowing on which side of the line the answer fell," his son said.

He served as chairman of the Board of Governors of McGill University, chancellor of Concordia University, and associate governor at the Université de Montréal, the institution he said that "taught me French, shaped me and gave me the thrust to be a good lawyer." Quebec Premier Jean Charest described Gold as a major player in Canada's judicial world. Superior Court justice John Gomery (who in 2005 headed the Gomery Commission looking into the federal sponsorship scandal in Quebec) remembered Gold as "warm, polite, courteous, efficient, energetic, and a great jurist. He'll be remembered mostly for his talents as a mediator."

Gold was appointed an officer of the Ordre national du Québec in 1985 and an officer of the Order of Canada in 1994. He also received the Canadian Jewish community's highest honour, the Samuel Bronfman Medal. Former Quebec Premier Lucien Bouchard, who joined Gold's law firm after leaving politics, said Gold was so active he never gave the impression he was in his eighties. "He was in his office early in the morning, would leave late, go to a concert, to the theatre, drive his own car. Bottom line: affectionate, open, funny, marvellous sense of humour." Bouchard said he learned from Gold that as a mediator, all conflicts can be solved and "if you love people you will get to understand them and their point of view and why they have this position, and what can be done to bring two sides together."

Founder of the No-Hassle Money-Back Guarantee
Joseph Schreter (1905-2005)
Buried January 9, 2005
Adath Israel New (A-4)

The clothing store on the Main famous for its "no-hassle money-back guarantee" was founded by immigrant pedlar turned real estate magnate Joseph Schreter. For generations of Montrealers, the summer camp ritual has started with a stop at Schreter's. Open since 1928 and now located on St. Laurent at Marie-Anne, the store is formally known as J. Schreter Inc. "He wanted customers to have a good deal. He bought summer goods in winter and winter goods in summer and made his money on volume," Schreter's son Peter told *The Gazette*. "One of his favourite expressions was, 'The only reason I buy seconds is because I can't find thirds.'"

Schreter was born in what is now Romania, into the family of an Orthodox Jewish grain merchant. After quitting school at age eleven, he began to work for his father and was an experienced salesman by the time he was fifteen, travelling across Europe. He became adept at everything from bargaining to bribing customs officials. Schreter worked in Germany as a tinsmith when the family's fortunes took a turn for the worse after German currency tumbled, and came to Canada in 1928. Halfway across the Atlantic on a ship heading to Montreal, he realized he was forty-three dollars short of the two hundred dollars he needed to get into Canada. He spent the rest of the trip persuading passengers to change his larger bills for smaller ones. When the immigration agent in Montreal asked to see his money, he pulled out his huge wad of cash and was waved in by the agent. He opened a small clothing shop for men and boys at St. Dominique and Ontario streets, and slept on the counter of the shop for the next two years, saving money so that he could bring his girlfriend and future wife Goldie Basch to Montreal. In 1935, the store moved to what is now de Maisonneuve Blvd. He bought the building and began a real estate career.

He lost his parents and seven of his nine siblings during the Holocaust. After the war, he helped surviving relatives come to Canada and he and his wife found themselves surrogate parents of a host of Holocaust survivors. After a fire destroyed the store in 1958, it moved to its present site. Schreter sold the store in the late 1950s to his cousins and went into real estate full-time, founding Schreter Enterprises and Nordic Development. He and his partners bought land all over the city, including property next to one of the cemeteries in the city's east end. "At least the neighbours will be quiet," he said.

Schreter was a director of the Hebrew Free Loan Association for fifty years, and its president for three years. In 2005, Schreter's opened a second store in the West Island of Montreal, replicating just about everything from the Main except for the squeaky wood floors. Joseph Schreter, who died just months short of his hundredth birthday, often said, "If I'd known I was going to live this long, I'd have taken better care of myself."

FIRST COMMUNIST CITY COUNCILLOR
Michael Buhay (1889-1947)
Buried August 12, 1947
Jewish Assistance (D-10)

Michael Buhay ran for city council in 1918 in Montreal's St. Louis ward and lost. But his next attempt, in 1942, was successful and he became the first communist to be elected to Montreal's city council. He was re-elected in 1944 and died in office in August 1947. Buhay was an active member of the Labour Progressive (Communist) Party. He is buried in Jewish Assistance, a section of the cemetery that was originally created by leftists who broke away from the Workmen's Circle. It was known, in one of its incarnations, as the United Jewish Peoples Order.

As described in the *Keneder Adler*, the funeral procession to the Cemetery included a few dozen city councillors who followed two automobiles packed with flowers. They, in turn, were followed by the hearse which was surrounded by an honour guard composed of members of the Labour Progressive Party. One of the eulogies was delivered by the General Secretary of the Labour Progressive Party.

The World's Oldest Man?

Dr. Joseph Joffre (*circa* 1875-1988)
Buried November 9, 1988
Nusoch Hoari – Old (C-13)

Before Dr. Joseph Joffre died in November 1988, he may have been the world's oldest man. There was no way to prove it, for it was rare to register the births of Jewish children in nineteenth-century Latvia. But if there had been proof, Joffre would definitely have made it into the *Guinness Book of World Records*.

Born in Lebow, Latvia, Joffre was an amateur boxer who earned a doctorate in chemistry from a German university. He did further studies in London and was ordained a rabbi. After coming to Canada he worked in hospitals as a chemist and founded an artificial limb firm in Ottawa. He also served as a medical officer with the Royal 22nd Regiment in Europe during the First World War. In Canada, Joffre married a fellow Latvian, Sarah Miller; they were together for sixty years before her death at eighty-six.

In Montreal's Jewish community, he was best known for leading the annual March to Jerusalem, something he did from 1973 until he was about one hundred and five. "I'll be there as long as I can walk," he once said.

Aside from a bout of appendicitis in 1945, Joffre said, he was never sick in his life. "Give to others and believe in God," was another one of his formulas for living. "I have always tried to help people, especially children, and I believe that is why God has given me life."

The Joffres had six children and adopted another nine. They had fourteen grandchildren and twenty-one great-grandchildren. He was a fixture at the Golden Age Association (now Cummings Centre for Jewish Seniors) until a few years before his death and a member of the Knights of Pythias for ninety years. A resident of Maimonides Hospital Geriatric Centre from November 1987 until his death, Joffre read the newspaper and went to the hospital synagogue every day. Arm wrestling was a long-time passion; Joffre claimed he once took on Louis Cyr, the Quebecer called the strongest man in the world, in an arm wrestling match. He frequently challenged men young enough to be his great-grandsons to arm wrestle.

He loved salt and sugar in his food and his occasional ill spirits stemmed only from being surrounded by people he considered too old or deaf to talk to, said his daughter, Tillie Downer. Until the end, he could walk a bit, although he usually used a wheelchair, only used reading glasses, and was lucid. "The most important thing is to believe in mankind," he said.

THE BERMAN FAMILY
Joseph Berman
Buried May 11, 1989
Adath Israel – New (A-4)
On the monument:
"A man's wisdom maketh his face to shine." (Eccles. 8:1)

Norman Berman (1932-1961)
Elyce Joy Berman (1956-1961)
Jonathan Berman (1954-1961)
Adath Israel – New (A-4)
On the monument:
"...lovely and amiable in their lives, even in their death they were not divided." (Samuel 2, Ch. 1)

Joseph Berman was an industrialist and philanthropist. He died at ninety, but his name and those of grandchildren who predeceased him, live on. Berman's life, career, and contributions paralleled the evolution of the twentieth-century Montreal Jewish community.

His beginnings were difficult. Berman was born in Russia. His father died when he was a baby. At fourteen, he went to Bialystok to work in his uncle's hardware store. A literary and linguistic scholar, Berman read Shakespeare in Russian, studied Hebrew and Yiddish literature, and became a teacher at eighteen—opening a small school and teaching reading, writing, and religious studies. However, Berman, who described himself as "a good salesman and a fast decision-maker in business," was soon travelling from town to town buying and selling hardware, furs, and anything else he could peddle.

After arriving in Montreal in 1925, Berman worked in a dry-goods store and studied English at night. After surviving the Depression, he found a partner and went into the knitting manufacturing business. The knitting mill ran full tilt during the war and by the time Berman was forty, he had the time to write stories and poems.

He was able to combine his wealth and literary interests. At Bar-Ilan

University in Israel, he established, in his and his late son's names, the first department of Jewish literature encompassing all Jewish literature written by, about, or for Jews in all languages. And at Hebrew University, he established the Berman Chair in Yiddish Literature and Folklore. For his longstanding support, both universities granted him honourary degrees.

In September 1961, after returning from a world tour, Berman and his wife were confronted with the tragic loss of their son and two grandchildren. Norman Berman, thirty-two, Norman's daughter Elyce Joy, five, and son Jonathan, seven, were killed when their light Beachcraft Bonanza plane crashed shortly after takeoff from Dorval Airport (now Pierre Elliott Trudeau International Airport). Norman was described by friends as a capable pilot. The plane flipped twice in the air and crashed nose-first in a field used for pony rides near Pointe Claire. It burst into flames as it hit the ground.

Literature and poetry helped Joseph assuage his grief. He said he felt an overwhelming need to perpetuate his and his son's names. "I know people whose life is business. It is their entire gold, their god, their reason for living—there is no room for anything else. Myself, I do not feel this way. I don't want to be known only as a businessman. I want rather to be con-nected with education, with poems, with learning."

As profile-writer Lou Seligson once put it, "The name Berman is planted in Israel in so many places that generations to come will one day wonder about it." At Hebrew University in Jerusalem, there's the Berman Family Building, the Berman Hall in the University Library, and the Berman Dormitory. A youth orchestra near Tel Aviv bears his name. In Montreal, the Jewish Public Library, for which he was treasurer and honourary president, named its auditorium after him and his wife. Today, Norman Berman's name lives on in Montreal at the Norman Berman Children's Library of the Jewish Public Library. The children's library continues to play an important role in the community. In 2004, for example, it coordinated volunteer efforts of librarians to help with the rebuilding of the United Talmud Torah's school library, destroyed in a firebombing on the eve of Passover. The Library also gave free memberships to all two hundred and fifty students of the Ville St. Laurent school. The grandchildren's names also live on. Although they never lived to see e-mail, the Jonathan and Elyce Joy Berman Multimedia Centre gives computer courses to a clientele that includes recent immigrants, seniors, and students.

TRAGIC ENDS

The lives of several other children buried at Baron de Hirsch Cemetery were cut short by tragedy over the years. Here are a few examples:

Charles Rubin
Steven Rubin
Age nine and age five
Accidentally drowned February 23, 1953
Kehal Yeshurun (C-7)
On the monument: "Our beloved sons."

As a newspaper account put it: "Two small white coffins were lowered into the wintry ground of Côte des Neiges Cemetery West," marking the tragic ends of brothers Charles and Steven Rubin. On a February day, they were playing at the excavation site of what is now Ste. Justine Hospital when they fell through ice covering deep water. Their bodies were found sixteen hours later. The reporter described the funeral at Paperman's: "The crowd thickened, but only the sound of an occasional passing car and the quiet sobbing of women and more than a few men disturbed the almost palpable quiet."

William (Wolf) Merson
Buried April 13, 1931
Montefiore (D-14)

On a windy afternoon in 1931, sixteen-year-old William Merson and about two hundred other pupils were playing in the yard of Baron Byng High School on St. Urbain Street. Suddenly, at 1:15 p.m., tragedy struck when a fifty-foot flagpole was blown down by the wind. The pole struck Merson on the head and he was pronounced dead a few minutes later.

"THE END OF AN ERA"
Rabbi Chaim Denburg (1918-1991)
August 7, 1991
Beth Yehuda – New (C-2)
On the monument:
"The words of a wise man are enobling and a man who labored with wisdom, knowledge and ability."

It was, many of the more than one thousand people who attended his funeral said, "the end of an era." Rabbi Chaim Denburg was one of the longest-serving pulpit rabbis in Montreal, as rabbi for seven years at Chevra Kadisha Synagogue from 1949 to 1956 and at Shomrim Laboker Synagogue for the next thirty-five years.

A rarity among Montreal rabbis, Rabbi Denburg had been born in Montreal. Ordained in 1942, he was a professor of Medieval Jewish Philosophy at the Université de Montréal, where he received a Ph.D. He was chair of the university's philosophy department for twenty years. As well, he translated into English *The Code of Hebrew Law*, a commentary on the Jewish code of law, the *Shulchan Aruch*.

He could make his opinion known forcefully. In 1964, when the Catholic Church finally moved to clear Jews of Christ's death, Rabbi Denburg said Jews "need not be grateful or overwhelmed." Speaking at the Jewish Public Library, at what was believed to be the first public open forum to feature jointly a rabbi and a Roman Catholic priest, Rabbi Denburg said, "We Jews will not owe the Church one iota of gratitude if we are cleared. On the contrary, it is the Church that owes us the apology for the centuries of their dark record towards us. Anti-Semitism is not a Jewish problem; it is the Christians' problem."

Denburg was frequently consulted by other rabbis on the fine points of Jewish divorce law. His skill and compassion in applying the *get*, the religious divorce, led Jews from as far away as England, France, and Israel to seek his help. One of the first graduates of the Rabbi Isaac Elchanan Theological Seminary of Yeshiva University in New York, Rabbi Denburg was honoured by the school in 1990, shortly before his death. He received the Distinguished Rabbinican Alumnus Award at the RIETS Annual Dinner of Tribute for his "devoted spiritual leadership in propagating the values of the Judaic heritage, exemplary service to the Jewish community, and erudition and scholarship in Jewish learning."

"He was a human being of the first rank and a great, great scholar, one of the great rabbis of Montreal," said retired Shaare Zion Congregation Rabbi Maurice Cohen. Rabbi Meyer Kizelnik of Beth Hillel Synagogue described him as a "giant of a man" and "a rabbi's rabbi."

The One-Man Gray Panther
David Weiss (1914-1992)
Buried July 17, 1992
Memorial Park

David Weiss promoted the concept of an active retirement long before it became fashionable. In the 1960s, when the concept of gerontology was a mystery to most, Weiss was teaching a course in social gerontology. He long advocated the preparation for creative retirement and at a show for the fifty-plus set, offered up the 5Ms of successful aging: Use your mind, use your muscle, be motivated, use your mouth, and have a mission.

In his eulogy, Rabbi Leigh Lerner of Temple Emanu-El Beth Sholom Congregation called him "Montreal's one-man Gray Panther group, asking what we plan to do with retirement." Before his "retirement", Weiss was executive director for twenty years of the Baron de Hirsch Institute (now Jewish Family Services of the Baron de Hirsch Institute) and headed Montreal's Jewish family and child casework agency.

Weiss went to school in the Bronx and was a star tackle on the football team as well as student body president. "I always lived in two worlds. Athletic and intellectual, integrating body and mind. These are the two facts of your being—in fact, a duality of personality—and my teaching goals are to develop sound minds in healthy bodies in a sane society." He graduated from City College of New York and Columbia University's School of Social Work and also studied at the Jewish Theological Seminary. In 1943, he took on a job at the YMHA in Rochester, New York, where he created a sensation, by organizing a "trial by youth", a mock court trial in which he charged parents with indifference and carelessness.

Weiss joined the Baron de Hirsch Institute in 1947, a job he described as "a broker between the haves and the have-nots, endlessly having to juggle what was decent and moral with what the community would accept and could pay for." By 1966, having become somewhat of an institution himself, he decided "it was no longer my suit ... This kind of thing is an endless crisis and needed newer warriors." Still, he stayed on another four years.

Over the following years, Weiss taught a course in community recreation at Dawson College, and also taught in the School of Social Work at McGill University, at College Marie-Victorin, and at Sir George Williams University (now part of Concordia University). The Dawson course eventually developed into a full-time program in community recreational leadership, which he chaired. He authored *Principles of Administration in Social Agencies* (1956), *Existential Human Relations* (1975), *Advice Not Judgment* (1963) and a book of poetry, *The Human Quotient* (1977). At the time of his death at age seventy-seven, he was working with sculptor Stanley Lewis on another book of poetry and art.

CHARLIE CHAPLAIN
Rabbi Charles Bender (1896?-1993)
Buried April 25, 1993
Adath Israel – New (A-4)

When he was well into his nineties, Charles Bender continued to officiate as a rabbi, making him possibly the oldest active rabbi in Canada. "The word 'retire' has two meanings," he would say. "Retire means you take the old tire, you recap it and you put it back again on your car. That's the retirement that I have." He was still conducting daily services at the Montefiore seniors' home where he lived until three weeks before his death at age ninety-seven in 1993.

Bender was born in London, the youngest boy in a family of ten children. In 1899, when he was three, the Bender family went to Palestine but was stopped by the Turks. Instead they lived in Cyprus for several years trying to be farmers, an experiment that didn't work. They eventually returned to England and lived in Liverpool. Charles came to Montreal via Rochester, New York in 1928.

His first position was with the Spanish & Portuguese Synagogue, which was then on Stanley Street near St. Catherine Street. He was the rabbi there until 1940, when he was appointed by Adath Israel Congre-gation, then in Outremont, where he stayed until 1975.

Every two weeks for eighteen years, Bender would visit Jewish inmates at St. Vincent-de-Paul Penitentiary where he served as the Jewish chaplain. In 1942, he became a chaplain with the Royal Canadian Air Force. He didn't go overseas, but attended six stations at home. People used to call Rabbi Bender the "Jewish Padre" and because his first name was Charles, "Charlie Chaplain".

For twelve years, Rabbi Bender was the national president of the Jewish National Fund of Canada, travelling from Halifax to Vancouver. He was the editor of *The Jewish Chronicle*, dean of the Jewish Teacher's Seminary, and founder and first president of the Board of Jewish Ministers.

At Adath Israel, Rabbi Bender oversaw the opening of a Hebrew Day school, at the time a daring undertaking for a North American congregation. When the synagogue made its move from Outremont to Hampstead, he continued to officiate in a room in the old high school the synagogue had owned. It was a way of serving elderly and observant Outremont-based members who couldn't drive to the synagogue's new home.

Known by his "pince-nez" eyeglasses, Rabbi Bender lived for about sixty years with his younger sister Mabel and never married. However, he officiated at nearly two thousand weddings, including those of many couples whose parents he had married. "I had one wedding booked where I had officiated at the grandparents' wedding, but unfortunately I took ill at that time," he recalled.

Archivist and Historian to the Community
David Rome (1910-1996)
Buried January 16, 1996
Farband #4 (B-32)

David Rome wore several hats: chronicler of Jewish life, librarian, press officer, archivist, writer, and editor. He was a lifelong advocate of improved relations between anglophone Jews and Quebec francophones, a major reason why he was named in 1987 as a Knight of the Order of Quebec.

Born in Vilna, Lithuania in 1910, his family arrived in Vancouver, via Halifax, in 1921. "The whole story of our family and every other family of these decades of getting into Canada from Europe after 1914, was a saga because of the very tight and tightening immigration rules that were coming into effect in Canada," he once reminisced in an interview. "After we did manage to reach Canadian soil legally with passports and visas and everything, [we] were detained incommunicado in a Halifax jail for seven weeks."

Rome studied English literature at the University of British Columbia and at the University of Washington in Seattle. However, he was determined to become a librarian, despite being warned by a gentile librarian at UBC of the difficulty of entering the profession as a Jew. The University of Toronto turned him down for library studies because it maintained that, as a Jew, he would be unable to obtain a job anywhere in the field and would thus spoil their employment record for graduates. Fortunately McGill

The 100 Club

Baron de Hirsch Cemetery is home to growing numbers of people who have lived a century or more. Among them:

Esther Malka Meltzer, died February 5, 1971, age one hundred and three. On her tombstone: "Many daughters have done virtuously, but thou excellest them all."
Buried February 5, 1971. Chevra Mishnayes—UHC

Tillie Propos, died January 23, 2001, age one hundred and twelve. On her tombstone: "Lived to 112."
Buried January 25, 2001. Hebrew Sick –A (C-1)

Rose Belson, age one hundred and one.
Buried July 9, 1993. Shomrim Laboker – Old (D-2)

Sara Wolloch, age one hundred and one.
Buried April 16, 1997. Farband – Old (D-17)

Samuel Rosenbloom, died October 15, 1961,
age one hundred and one.
Buried October 15, 1961. Russian Polish – UHC

Annie Bordoff, April 1, 1901 – October 4, 2001, age one hundred
Buried October 7, 2001. King George – UHC

Faigel Yanofsky, April 25, 1880 –September 16, 1980,
age one hundred.
Buried September 18, 1980. King George – UHC

Dora Smolar, died December 10, 1991, age one hundred and one.
Buried December 11, 1991. Chevra T'Hilim Pinsker – UHC

Freda Mayoff, April 17, 1894 –April 8, 1996, age one hundred and one.
Buried April 9, 1996. Chevra T'Hilim Pinsker – UHC

University accepted Rome and he set off to Montreal in the 1930s, hitching rides on freight trains because of a lack of funds. He earned additional degrees from McGill and the Université de Montréal and worked as a writer for *The Jewish Standard*, before becoming the first press officer of the Canadian Jewish Congress in 1942 and first national director of the Labour Zionist Organization. While working at Congress as press officer for eleven years, he was credited with creating its national archives.

Shortly after arriving at Canadian Jewish Congress, Rome was appointed secretary to the Congress' committee on Jewish-French-Canadian relations. In the early 1950s he founded the Cercle Juif de la langue française. At the time, it provided the community with a rare forum for dialogue that would extend beyond the clergy to reach the intellectual élite of French Canada. In 1986, he would collaborate with long-time friend, priest Jacques Langlais, on the critically acclaimed *Jews and French Quebecers: Two Hundred Years of Shared History* and in 1992 on an illustrated history of Jewish life in Quebec, *Les Pierres que parlent/The Stones That Speak.*

Rome went on to become director of the Jewish Public Library from 1953 to 1971, before returning to CJC as its archivist. In his years as archivist, he would write or edit well over fifty historical books on Canadian Jewish subjects for the *Canadian Jewish Archives* series. That once earned him the title "the most published writer in Canada."

"His chronicling of Jewish life in Canada and his outreach to the general community were unparalleled," said Jack Silverstone, national executive director of the Canadian Jewish Congress. A room of his Mountain Sights duplex once overflowed with books which are now part of the National Library of Canada's Jacob M. Lowy Collection of rare Hebraica and Judaica.

THE BEDRIDDEN POET
Kenneth Hertz (1945-1996)
Buried January 30, 1996
Baron de Hirsch #4 (E-20)
On the monument:
"For a burst of light, I shall love you forever"
"The death's head smiled at me. I smiled not back."
"My body is my burial tomb

my body is my mourners

my body is my stone."

From *The Cracked Cellar* (Aleph House)

Ken Hertz was once described as one of the most promising poets of his generation. Sadly, he became best known not for his poetry but for his disabling illness and his lengthy battle to obtain experimental treatment. By the time of his death at age fifty in 1996, Hertz had been bedridden for twelve years with an advanced case of Parkinson's disease.

As a youth, Hertz had been a free spirit; at seventeen he was living in a shack along railroad tracks and later became a denizen of the bohemian McGill student ghetto and a small publisher. In the mid-1970s he ran a newsstand at Pine Avenue and St. Laurent Boulevard, which he described as "the most polluted corner on earth." In 1982 he was diagnosed with Parkinson's. Dreading hospitals, he fought a long public battle to stay in his Town of Mount Royal home. With his atrophied body needing round-the-clock care and constant moving, Hertz raised money from private donors, and was also assisted over the years by a local community clinic and the Jewish Family Services of the Baron de Hirsch Institute.

In 1987, about $35,000 was raised to send Hertz to Mexico for an experimental operation, but doctors judged his condition to be too weak, for him to make the trip.

In 1991, there was some rare good news: *The Cracked Cellar*, an anthology of one hundred and one poems written between 1958 and 1964 while Hertz was in his teens, was launched at the Jewish Public Library. The book was supposed to have been published over twenty years earlier but the publisher had gone out of business. "I don't know of any other book in the annals of Canadian history that took so long," poet and University of Ottawa literature professor Seymour Mayne told the audience of two hundred at the launch. The launch proceedings were relayed by phone to the bedridden Hertz. "Ken Hertz's work established him as one of the most promising young poets of his generation," Irving Layton wrote in the preface. "When he took ill, it was as if somebody was conspiring against me, trying to rob me of the pleasure Ken's work has brought me."

In 1995, he was forced into public curatorship. In January 1996, with his condition rapidly deteriorating, Hertz was taken to Royal Victoria Hospital, against his will. Friends objected, saying he had a written refusal of treatment. But Urgences Santé said the written refusal was too old and that the poet was too ill. He died a few hours following admission to the hospital. At his graveside funeral at Baron de Hirsch Cemetery, friends remembered Hertz as a brilliant poet and generous publisher.

THE SAVIOUR OF FAIRMOUNT BAGEL
Jacob Shlafman (1926-1997)
Buried February 26, 1997
Hebrew Sick M

When it comes to bagels, most Montrealers agree those from Fairmount or St. Viateur are best. Long "holey" wars erupt over which of the two are better. But had it not been for Jack (Jacob) Shlafman, there would have been no bagel supremacy disputes. St. Viateur would have reigned alone. For it was Shlafman, who along with his family, resurrected The Original Fairmount Bagel Factory on Fairmount Avenue in 1979, after it had spent twenty years in bagel limbo. Given that it was his father who reputedly opened the first bagel bakery in Canada, it was a noble return.

Montreal bagel bakeries began in 1919, when Isadore and Fanny Shlafman, immigrants from Kiev in the Ukraine, opened a tiny bakery on Roy Street near Waldman's fish market. The bagels were made using a recipe brought from home, where Isadore's father had been a baker. By 1919, Montreal Bagel Bakery was just off St. Laurent Boulevard in a lane a few doors from Schwartz's Hebrew Delicatessen. The bakery was in a wooden shack and they transported the bagels by wheelbarrow to a vending stand on St. Laurent. They remained there until 1949, when Isadore bought a two-storey cottage at 74 Fairmount, replacing the living room wall at the back with a bagel oven. Son Jack joined him in the business.

In 1957 Jack Shlafman teamed up with Holocaust survivor Meyer Lewkowicz to open Montreal Fairmount Bagel Bakery at 263 St. Viateur Street. After his father's death, Shlafman decided to close the Fairmount shop and concentrate on the St. Viateur shop, where Shlafman and Lewkowicz were joined by a third partner, bagel-maker Isaac Shneider.

In 1960, Shlafman and Shneider left to open another bagel bakery on Darlington Avenue. The following year Shlafman started the first Van Horne Bagel Bakery on Van Horne Avenue near Victoria Avenue, before getting out of the bagel business for many years.

During the Fairmount store's twenty-year closure, it was occupied by Jesuits "who kept a big Bible in the window," then by a baby-sitting service, and later a steam-iron rebuilding service, among other things. But in 1979, Jack's son Irwin, who was only a toddler when the bakery shut down in 1959, noticed a For Sale sign on the building. He raced home and told the family. They discovered that the original bagel oven, although hidden behind a false wall, was still intact and that there were many bagel-making utensils inside. The family even found an ancient bagel, which they kept. In Montreal bagel lore, these findings were akin to the discovery of the Dead Sea Scrolls.

After convincing his now cabdriver father to return to the back-breaking, time-consuming business, Jack Shlafman agreed "due to the whining of my children and wife," but only on the understanding that it would be a family operation. They bought back the building and the Original Fairmount Bagel Bakery was reborn.

By now, bagels were a mainstream food and the shop quickly became a hit. It took six months to learn how to control the wood fire when it reopened and, Shlafman noted, "if I don't put in eighty or ninety hours a week of work, I don't put in any." Learning to control the fire was the hardest part. His hands would be constantly swollen from the hard work of kneading the dough, shaping the bagels, and working in front of a hot wood-burning oven, moving the bagels around on long wooden planks. The results, however, were worth it: "Each bagel is an individual piece. When I bake a dozen you won't find any burnt or unevenly done. They're all beautiful."

Now run by his children, Fairmount Bagel bakes more than twenty varieties of bagels, including those made with organic whole wheat flour, along with the traditional sesame and poppy seed types. Meanwhile, with the fight still raging over which city's bagels are best, perhaps Shlafman said it best about the Montreal bagel in comparison to the New York version: "Everybody else has heavy bagels. They're like cement. They don't put anything in them. The American-style bagel is lousy."

THE SPECIAL
Bernard Wilensky (1946-2000)
Buried November 17, 2000
Hebrew Sick A (C-1)

Wilensky's Light Lunch on Fairmount Avenue has been immortalized in Mordecai Richler's *The Apprenticeship of Duddy Kravitz*. Generations of Montrealers have lunched on the Wilensky Special—a combo of grilled salami and bologna with mustard on a toasted roll—and old-fashioned cherry cokes. Articles posted in the restaurant from around the world attest to the Special's greatness. But for several days in November 2000, no Specials were to be had when third-generation counterman Bernard Wilensky passed away just a month short of his fifty-fourth birthday. He had been a fixture behind the grill since age thirteen.

His brother Saul said Bernard had kept a congenital heart defect a secret. "His heart simply gave out on him in the end, but none of that ever stopped him from working or enjoying life, or even playing hockey. He was just a genuine good person who loved his world and who refused to complain about his lot."

The Boy Plunger
Harry Ship
Buried June 21, 1998
Ship Family Circle (B-20)

When Harry Ship died of lung cancer in 1998, newspapers dubbed him "the last gambling czar." Ship was considered synonymous with gambling in the city in the era before government-owned casinos became the norm. Ship built a small empire of gaming houses—one on a farm on Côte Saint-Luc Road in Côte Saint-Luc, another in Greenfield Park, and one downtown. He owned the Chez Paree nightclub when it featured such acts as Frank Sinatra, Dean Martin, Jerry Lewis, and Sammy Davis Jr.

As the city's most famous bookie, he was a household name in the 1930s, '40s, and '50s. He was immortalized in the Mordecai Richler novels, *The Apprenticeship of Duddy Kravitz* and *Barney's Version*. The late *Gazette* columnist Nick Auf der Maur remembered that when he was in high school, kids would speak his name with awe: "They say he bets a million bucks a week." To the 1965 *Who's Who in Canadian Jewry* he was a "business executive and restaurateur". Ship's White House Casino in Côte Saint-Luc is described by William Weintraub in *City Unique: Montreal Days and Nights in the 1940s and 1950s*, as offering "good whiskey and filet mignon on the house, as well as six blackjack tables, two roulette wheels and two crap tables. Its patrons included politicians, lawyers and even judges."

He was said to be a mathematical wizard who could calculate the odds better than anyone. He had studied mathematics for two years at Queen's University, not the usual background for those in the business.

"It was crazy," he recalled in later years. "I had no conception of what money meant. I was a millionaire one week, a bum the next. I don't know where I got the nerve. People couldn't figure out how I stayed alive."

His most famous operation came to be his bookmaking establishment on St. Catherine Street East, where primarily working-class gamblers could bet on any horse race in North America, with results obtained instantly by telephone. While riding high in the 1940s, Ship vowed to bring to his Chez Paree the biggest star of the era, Frank Sinatra. However, Sinatra refused to come to Montreal unless Ship gave him an enormous-for-the-time advance of $10,000. Ship reluctantly gave in to Sinatra's demand and was amply rewarded by the crowds lined up along Stanley Street in frigid weather to see the singer.

Ship met his nemesis under Mayor Jean Drapeau, who was trying to clean up the city, and morality crusader Pacifique (Pax) Plante. He was sentenced to six months in Bordeaux Jail.

Toward the end of his life, Ship had harsh words for the casinos that were then being planned by the Quebec government, words that ring true with experience:

> The way they're doing it, it looks like they'll get the little guy. A guy whose business can't get money from the bank and he's desperate. People who are short of money. Those are the people who get hurt. And that's no fun. Gambling is meant for fun, not for hurting people.

Millions Saw his Artwork
Norman Kucharsky (1914-1999)
Buried September 9, 1999
Russian-Polish #3

It is likely that millions of Canadians saw Norman Kucharsky's artwork on CBC Television, but few knew the man behind the fleeting images on their screens. From TV's debut in the early 1950s until his retirement in 1979, Norman Kucharsky (the author's father) was a graphic artist for the CBC and Radio-Canada in Montreal. There, he helped produce all manner of visuals for the two networks, long before the computer replaced the paintbrush as the graphic artist's tool.

For years, Kucharsky created cartoons and stage sets for the long-running children's show *Chez Hélène*, which taught French to generations of English-speaking kids. As a courtroom artist for *The National* and local news, he hurriedly sketched witnesses testifying in the MacDonald Commission on RCMP wrongdoings, the Morgentaler abortion clinic trials, and the Malouf Inquiry examining the cost overruns of the Montreal Olympics. But he was best known locally for his station identification breaks, broadcast every half hour. Many of these breaks portrayed scenes of Montreal's distinctive neighbourhoods, street life, and architecture, "bringing out the colour of the city," as he put it. He would paint the scenes on the spot, balancing his sketch pad, pillboxes of colours and water, and often freezing his fingertips in the winter, despite wrapping his drawing hand in a sock with a brush protruding from a hole he'd cut in the wool.

When he began his career, "you wouldn't stand much of a chance with a name like Kucharsky," so he adopted the pen name Norman Kirk "and had no difficulties."

Following a brief career in advertising after the war, he came to the CBC when it had only a French-language station in Montreal. "I was not just the only anglophone, but the only Jew at the time. Because of that I became a sort of consultant on Jewish matters, despite my rather hit-and-miss Jewish education." He felt strongly about depicting aspects of Judaism in his artwork and convinced producers to let him draw station identification breaks of major Jewish holidays, and not just of Christian holidays. As a result, the network's mostly Christian viewers saw biblical scenes ranging from shofar-blowing during the High Holidays, to Moses being confronted by the Burning Bush during Passover.

As a soldier in the Canadian Army during the Second World War, he put his artistic skills to good work. Before being wounded in the leg by a bullet during a 1944 battle in Holland, he did reconnaissance work, sketching towns for use in army intelligence. He also won awards for his depictions of soldiers' lives, and his wartime scenes were shown in National Gallery and Montreal Museum of Fine Arts exhibits of Armed Services competitions.

Since limited finances made it next to impossible for him to attend university after graduating from Baron Byng High School, he was mostly self-taught as an artist. But after the war he set out for New York, and studied under such well-known artists as Raphael Soyer and William Gropper. As a father, he would encourage his children to eat by drawing faces on hard-boiled eggs, or amuse them with dry tales of his experiences growing up in Montreal's cold water flats.

After retiring from the CBC in 1979, he taught courses in art and calligraphy, produced hand-drawn diplomas for such clients as the Jewish Public Library and United Talmud Torahs and personalized *ketubahs* for marrying couples. And he continued to sell his series of pen-and-ink scenes of Old Montreal and the downtown area, which were sold in greeting card, print, and bookmark formats to gift shops and galleries throughout the city.

He also delighted in drawing Montreal's old-fashioned dépanneurs (corner stores), many of which have fallen victim to the wrecker's ball or have been replaced by bland franchised outlets. "It's part of our history, our life in the neighbourhood," he said. Twenty of his watercolours and acrylics of corner grocery stores were exhibited in Montreal in 1985. Alas, his artistic talent proved to be limited only by his modesty. Far less skilled artists with better marketing prowess saw a greater measure of recognition during their careers.

He fell ill while vacationing in Halifax. Even while awaiting heart surgery in hospital, he drew and gave some of the nurses flattering portraits of themselves.

Everyone Called Him Mendy
Mendy Berson (1931-2002)
Buried January 3, 2002
Shomrim Laboker – Old (D-2)

"As long as people die, Berson & Son will be in business," Mendy Berson once said.

For more than eighty years, Berson & Son Monuments has been creating burial monuments for the Jewish community, making it one of the longest-running businesses on the Main. From 1973 to 2001, the familiar face fronting the family business was Mendy Berson, the grandson of its founder. His Jewish name was Menachem Mendel, his English name Marvin, but "everyone called him Mendy," said daughter Brandee Berson.

Berson went to Baron Byng High School but left with one semester to go. Still, "he had skills you don't learn in school. His wisdom came from the street," Brandee said.

For years, Mendy Berson worked as a taxi driver while his father ran the monument business, unwilling to relinquish control to his son. When Mendy Berson entered the business in 1973, he used his own system, just like his father did before him, when his grandfather Louis Berson left the business.

His philosophy was that while the business had to make a living, it also had to serve the community, Brandee Berson said. "My father had a belief that if someone comes with their hand out to you, you give them. No matter who (would) come in here asking for money, whether it is a yeshiva, one of these homeless people or a food basket, my father would never say no. Whether it was a couple of dollars or hundreds of dollars, he would not say no." When B'nai Brith packed Rosh Hashanah, Chanukah or Passover baskets, "my father would be there every night. It was his way of giving back to the community."

But none of that was of concern to the Quebec government when it came after Berson over the size of the Hebrew lettering on his business sign in 1997. The Office de langue langue française sent Berson what he described sarcastically as a "love letter". The crime: the sign had the firm's name and the word monuments with five Hebrew characters slightly larger than the French. Language inspectors said the French letters should predominate. Said Brandee Berson: "My father was terribly hurt by that. He was born here, he grew up here, he gave back to the community and then to have the language police come after him for a sign that probably was older than my father, it hurt him. He couldn't believe it was happening to him." So Berson made the situation as public as possible and was soon fielding calls from newspaper and TV reporters from Europe to Israel. All the media coverage made the Parti Québécois government "look like a bunch of idiots." The monumental sign flap even reached the National Assembly, with Louise Beaudoin, the minister in charge of the language law, saying, "I don't think it's reasonable." The language office backtracked. The sign remains.

In his final years, Mendy's daughter entered the business. (His son said the business wasn't for him—all he saw was things for dead people. In response, Mendy Berson said: "What do you think I'm running here? A tennis court?")

Berson died less than a month after he was viciously pistol-whipped and robbed while alone at his St. Laurent Boulevard office. Police did not treat the case as a homicide. The business is now run by Brandee Berson.

Mendy Berson once mused there was a possibility the company name would eventually change from Berson & Son to Berson and Daughter. Not a chance, said daughter Brandee Berson. "I have absolutely no intention of changing it ever. It's my family legacy."

Matzohgate
Bill Winikoff (1920-2004)
Buried September 19, 2004
Montreal Worker's Circle – UHC

In 1996, the Office de la langue française warned supermarkets they would be contravening Quebec's language laws if they sold imported kosher products without French on the labels during the eight-day Passover holiday. Winikoff, who was president of Allied Food Distributors, fought back, noting the government was violating a tacit agreement it would lay off imported kosher products during Passover. His business complied year-round with the labelling requirements of the French Language Charter, although he once had a run-in with a language inspector who told him to stick labels on tiny packets of jam that were to be delivered to the Jewish General Hospital. But it was too complicated to do so during Passover, when demand for kosher foods surges.

When Quebec's "language police" told Bill Winikoff his matzoh didn't pass the language muster, he wasn't prepared to just let the crumbs fall. In an affair that would come to be known as Matzohgate, the kosher food importer and distributor fought against bureaucrats' attempts to deprive Jews of Passover food.

The controversy gained attention from international media. The Board of Trade of Metropolitan Montreal accused the language watchdog of sabotaging efforts to attract international business. "The same English label goes out on all the shipments, and I've never heard of France complaining," said Winikoff, who was in the food business since the Depression. Finally, the language office and Canadian Jewish Congress struck an agreement to exempt Kosher-for-Passover products bearing only English labels: merchants were allowed to sell kosher products with English labels for forty days before Passover and twenty days after.

MR. PROFILE
Lou Seligson (1914-2002)
Buried July 25, 2002
Hebrew Sick A (C-1)

He was known as Mr. Profile. For close to twenty years, Lou Seligson profiled and sketched about eight hundred Montreal Jewish community personalities in his column in *The Canadian Jewish News*. Before that, he wrote about and drew hundreds of dignitaries in politics, arts, business, and sports for a variety of newspapers in Montreal, the United States, Israel, and Europe.

Born in Argentina of rancher parents, James Louis "Lou" Seligson grew up in Milwaukee, after his parents fled anti-Semitic violence. He initially wanted to be an artist but saw artists were starving at the height of the Depression. Instead, he pursued a journalism degree. Once, while covering heavyweight boxer Joe Louis in Los Angeles, he made a sketch and the rest, as they say, was history. Albert Einstein, Harry Truman, and Douglas MacArthur were among the people he sketched.

After serving in the U.S. Merchant Marine during the Second World War, Seligson became involved in leftist activities and was friendly with writers with similar political views like humorist Dorothy Parker. Using the pen name Luis, he caricatured people like Richard Nixon and Charles de Gaulle for the Socialist Workers Party's newspaper, *The Militant*. Although he was blacklisted during the McCarthy era, Seligson continued to write under pseudonyms until he left for Israel. There he worked as a foreign correspondent and for the Israeli daily *Ma'Ariv*, where his interviews of English-speaking dignitaries would be translated into Hebrew. A three-year stint as editor of Switzerland's only English newspaper followed, until he came to Montreal in 1970. He worked for the *The Gazette* and wrote the Line ByLine column in the the *The Montreal Star*, until it folded in the late 1970s. Then came the weekly caricatures in *The Canadian Jewish News*. Former editor Maurice Lucow described Seligson as an "old type" newsman, "the kind of guy you may have seen in movies like *The Front Page*."

In 1993, a collection of 179 of his columns was published in the book *Mr. Profile*. Proceeds from sales and donations made by many of the people profiled in the book went to Canadian Friends of Tel Aviv University. In the foreward, Lucow wrote: "What amazed me was that Lou was able to grind out a fascinating column week after week. Somehow he always managed to find somebody of interest to write about—from the establishment to the rank-and-file members of the community."

The Happiest Day of His Life
Elazar (Lalazer) Goel (1933-2003)
Buried July 7, 2003
Independent #1 (C-9)

His children called it the happiest day of his life. In July 2003, Elazar Goel, who had arrived from Iran only a few weeks earlier, collapsed at his son's Montreal wedding. He died that night in hospital. Goel, seventy, had not seen the groom or his other son since they had left Iran for Montreal fifteen years earlier with their mother. He never saw his wife again—she predeceased him. But he was also reunited with three daughters whom he had not seen for twenty-one years, and he saw his five grandchildren for the first time. It was his first time out of Iran, and his first trip on an airplane. Restrictions on emigration, the Iran-Iraq War, and difficulty in disposing of his property, were to blame for his long-delayed departure.

About two hundred people attended his son's wedding at the Spanish & Portuguese Synagogue. "Our father was so proud, so happy, so much at peace. He held his head so high. He kissed the Torah three times," his daughter Sima told *The Canadian Jewish News*. After the ceremony he danced the hora for about three-quarters of an hour with one of his grandsons on his shoulders. Soon after he collapsed, and was pronounced dead at the Jewish General Hospital. Guests were only told of his death when they were leaving the festivities. His children decided to spare the newlyweds the bad news on their wedding night and only told them the next morning. Groom Kevin said his father "had a smile on his face when he left us."

A Doctor's Holocaust Memoir
Dr. Mina Deutsch (1911-2004)
Buried October 6, 2004
Beth Hamedrash Hagodol #1 (B-14)

Dr. Mina Deutsch was a psychiatrist who published some twenty academic papers during her career as well as an account of survival during the Holocaust. A review of her 1994 book, *Mina's Story: A Doctor's Memoir of the Holocaust*, called it "a chilling account of the years spent in hiding, trading possessions and medical knowledge in return for safety."

She was born Mina Kimmel in a small town in Galicia, now part of the Ukraine. She attended university in Prague, the first in her family to attend high school and university. While in medical school in Prague, she met her future husband Leon, a fellow medical student. They moved to Poland where they were married in 1938. To avoid being deported after the Germans invaded Poland in 1939, the couple and their infant daughter went into hiding in the countryside of Galicia.

An obituary notice published in *The Gazette* explained: "Drs. Mina and Leon Deutsch were heroic survivors of the Holocaust who were co-opted by the Nazis to fight a typhoid epidemic and were later forced into hiding in an underground bunker for almost two years." The story of the couple's survival with their child involved risk, fortitude, and incredible luck, *Jewish Book World* noted. Finally liberated by the Russians, they immigrated to Canada in 1948, after both lost their parents and several siblings.

In Canada, the couple completed specializations in psychiatry. For twenty-two years, Mina worked at the Douglas Hospital in Verdun with Dr. Heinz Lehmann, a pioneer who introduced antipsychotic medications. Deutsch spoke ten languages and collaborated on studies for the World Health Organization. In retirement, she sat on the International Board of Governors of the Hebrew University in Jerusalem, where she endowed a chair in psychopharmacology. That chair would go on to lead to the development of the Alzheimer's disease drug rivastigmine.

The *Keneder Adler* Obituaries

Funded by a grant from the Jewish Genealogical Society of Ottawa, the Obituary Project has arranged the translation of more than three thousand obituaries and articles that appeared in the Montreal Yiddish daily *Keneder Adler* from 1907 to 1931. Here's a sampling of *Keneder Adler* obituaries of people buried at the Baron de Hirsch Cemetery.

Jacob Rosenbloom
Buried February 26, 1928
Montreal Worker's Circle – UHC
The one-year-old Henri Julien Avenue resident "died as a result
of an accident while playing Ring Around the Rosey."

Fatal car accidents seemed to be commonplace:

Sam (Shlomo) Duchoeny
Buried September 13, 1925
Chevra Shaas #3 (C-11)
"Died as a result of an automobile accident on Main Street, Montreal.
Residents of Lachine are invited to attend funeral."

Joseph Dansky
Buried November 18, 1915
Chevra Mishnayes – UHC
"He was run over by an automobile on Nov. 16. He was the beadle
[synagogue sexton] at Beth Abraham Synagogue."

Morris Spector
Buried January 7, 1930
Montefiore (D-14)
The St. Denis Street resident "rode a bicycle without a light and was
run over by an automobile on Pine Avenue East."

Drownings occurred in Cartierville at the Rivière des Prairies beach for urban dwellers (now closed):

Israel Rokita
Buried July 18, 1926
Chevra T'Hilim Pinsker – UHC
"He drowned in Cartierville."

Many of the notices listed an affiliation with a sick benefit society or synagogue, and invited members to the funeral:

Hirsch Dvarin
Buried March 30, 1928
Canadian – UHC
"Former residents of Boguslav are invited to attend the funeral."

Esther German (Herman)
Buried November 3, 1924
Baron de Hirsch #1 (A-5)
The fifty-year-old Coloniale Avenue resident "was a 'Green' (new immigrant) woman, arrived from Europe a month previously. All her 'Green' friends are invited to attend the funeral.
Funeral from Royal Victoria Hospital."

One 1920 notice read: "All members of the King George Sick Benefit Association must attend the funeral. Those who do not wish to attend will be assessed the penalty of 1 dollar."

Accidental deaths occurred:

Mashe Myers
Buried July 15, 1930
Hebrew Sick – Old (C-1)
"She died after accidentally inhaling acid fumes."

Sidney Yarmulnik
Buried January 22, 1928
Beth Israel & Samuel (C-14)
The twenty-seven-year-old Clark Street resident (previous places of residence: Mezbizs, Kamenets, Podolsk), "was mistaken for

a bank robber and shot by a police detective. He was employed
by Canadian Hat Manufacturing Co. as a designer.
He came to Canada seven years ago."

Michael (Yichel Michl) Heller
Buried June 21, 1931
Beth Yehuda – Old (C-3)

Heller died in Val David at age nineteen. The funeral was from his father's
residence on Joyce Avenue in Outremont. "What at first appeared to have
been an accident is now suspected to have been murder," the notice reads.
"In fact, he was killed accidentally by Michael Machlovitch who was
practicing with a small-bore rifle."

There seemed to be little hesitation in discussing death by suicide,
something that is rarely done today:

Israel (Yitshak) Hochstein
Buried September 27, 1931
Young Israel #1 (D-4)

The forty-nine-year-old father of four was found hanged in his dry
goods store on Wellington Street in Verdun. In a note he attributed
his suicide to ill health and poor business.

Some of the notices are inexplicable:

Samuel (Shmuel Aryeh) Strean
Buried November 3, 1920
Chevra Shaas – Old (C-12)

Strean, the "longtime president of Chevra Shaas Congregation," and
"prominent contributor to the Jewish community… died as a result of
unjust criticism by a small group of Chevra Shaas members."

Others note occupations with pride:

Solomon (Zalman) Belinsky
Buried March 19, 1928
Chevra Shaas – Old (C-12)

The seventy-five-year-old father of six and grandfather to thirty-two "arrived in Montreal in 1904 as an experienced *shochet* [a professional in the kosher slaughter of animals]. He was the city's most respected *shochet* for the next 24 years."

Or occupations that no longer exist:

Aaron Finkelstein
Buried July 11, 1919
Hebrew Sick – Old (C-1)
The sixty-three-year-old was the father of five, most notably "father of Finkelstein the Coal Dealer."

Abraham Aronovitch
Buried October 1, 1918
Kehal Yeshurun (C-7)
Aronovitch, who lived on City Hall Street, but died in Windsor, Nova Scotia, "was at the training centre for the Jewish Legion for Palestine when he died. He was a legionnaire. Died of pneumonia."

Killed in Action: Baron de Hirsch's War Dead

It was long the policy to bury soldiers killed in action where they fell. Only in recent decades have the bodies of soldiers killed abroad been brought back to Canada. Thus, of the 116,000 Canadian men and women who died in the First and Second World Wars, the Korean War, the Boer War and the Nile Expedition, only about fifteen per cent (around seventeen thousand) are buried in Canada.

Most of the war graves in Canada are for military personnel who died during wartime in accidents while serving at home. There are others for people who were wounded and returned to Canada and then died, within a prescribed time, of their war injuries. The Baron de Hirsch Cemetery marks the final resting place of sixteen Jews who died in action in the armed forces. Most of them were killed during the Second World War, a conflict that cost the lives of 120 Jewish Montrealers. Florals for these soldiers are paid by the Commonwealth War Graves Commission, which maintains the graves of Commonwealth forces who were killed in the two world wars. The Cemetery is also the resting place of many Jews who served abroad and returned home alive. The sixteen are:

Jack Kugelmass and Frank Schwartz
Hebrew Sick – Old (C-1)

Leading aircraftman Jack Kugelmass, Royal Canadian Air Force, was killed in a flying accident on July 1, 1941. He was in a Cessna training plane on a navigational cross-country flight from his flying school in Saskatoon when his plane crashed one hundred miles north of Saskatoon. He was buried beside the grave of his friend, Leading Aircraftman Frank Schwartz, RCAF, who was killed in a flying accident near Dunnville, Ontario, on May 26, 1941. Kugelmass attended Mount Royal Public School and Baron Byng High School and studied pharmacy at McGill University before entering the service. Employed as a salesman prior to enlisting, Schwartz attended Baron Byng, Devonshire School, and United Talmud Torahs. A double tombstone marks the graves of the lifelong friends.

Abraham Steinberg
Jewish Assistance (D-10)

A member of the Canadian Army Dental Corps, Captain Abraham Steinberg was killed in a plane crash near Lake Bérubé, Quebec while on his way to Ancienne Lorette from Bagotville on January 21, 1944. Steinberg, who enlisted with the Dental Corps in January 1942, obtained his degree in dentistry in 1927. He was on his way home on leave when the crash occurred.

Samuel Meyer Levine
Memorial Park (A-1)
While a student pilot at No. 9 Service Flying Training School in Summerside, Prince Edward Island, Sergeant Samuel Meyer Levine, RCAF, was the lone occupant of a Harvard trainer which crashed off the south coast of P.E.I. near Charlottetown, on November 11, 1941. His body was recovered in the Northumberland Strait. Before enlisting, Levine had been employed by a clothing manufacturer.

Bennie Stromberg
Yishitzer #1 (C-22)
Sergeant Bennie Stromberg, RCAF, was killed when his plane crashed into the Miramichi River at Bay du Vin, on May 7, 1943, while on a routine flight. At the time, he was stationed in Chatham, New Brunswick.

Hyman Revzen
North End Wilkomirer – UHC
Aircraftman Hyman Revzen, RCAF, died in a plane crash during target practice at the Bombing and Gunnery School at Mont Joli, Quebec on July 27, 1943.

Harold Resnick
Montreal Workers Circle – UHC
Ordinary Telegraphist Harold Resnick, Royal Canadian Navy Volunteer Reserve, died in Halifax on June 17, 1941 from injuries suffered on active service.

Sidney Newman
Chevra T'Hilim Pinsker – UHC
Private Sidney Newman, Royal Canadian Infantry Corps, died of natural causes on July 20, 1945.

Private Abraham Zeven, Canadian Infantry
Baron de Hirsch #1 (A-5)
Buried December 24, 1919

Sapper Samuel Bloom, Canadian Railway Troops
Baron de Hirsch #1 (A-5)
Buried February 20, 1920

Sergeant Abie Kirsch, Royal Canadian Air Force
Montreal Worker's Circle – UHC
Died October 23, 1941

Private Sydney Garber, Royal Canadian Army Medical Corps
Hebrew Sick – Old (C-1)
Died November 24, 1943

Aircraftmen First Class Sydney Desmond, Royal Air Force
Volunteer Reserve
Memorial Park (A-1)
Died August 22, 1944

Sergeant Ivor Ralph Platt, Royal Air Force Volunteer Reserve
Memorial Park (A-1)
Buried June 30, 1945

Corporal Louis Levine, Royal Canadian Corps of Signals
Memorial Park (A-1)
Died January 22, 1946

Gunner Jacob Betnesky, Royal Canadian Artillery
Hebrew Protective (C-6)
Buried May 14, 1947

Holocaust Memorials

A number of tombstones at Baron de Hirsch memorialize not only those who are buried in the Cemetery, but family members who were killed in the Holocaust. These tombstones can be found throughout the Cemetery. It is recommended that Holocaust survivors include that information on their tombstones, as a reminder for future generations.

"In memory of our beloved parents and brothers who perished in 1944 during the Nazi occupation of Poland," reads the text from one such monument. "Finally joining their mothers, fathers, sisters and brothers who died at the hands of the Nazis. Survivors of the Warsaw Ghetto uprising," says another.

A monument unveiled in 1952 by Adath Israel Congregation is a memorial "to the martyrdom and heroism of our brethren who perished at the hands of Nazi tyranny 1933-1945." The monument is a simple one. It's one of the few in the Cemetery that do not commemorate victims from a specific region or town.

A monument was erected by the Czenstochower Society of Montreal in 1966. It is significant in that it marks the burial site of a coffin with ashes from the Treblinka concentration camp. The remains are those of "the cremated martyrs of Czenstochow and vicinity". The monument is in memory of the fifty thousand martyrs and heroes of Czenstochow, Poland and neighbouring towns "who perished together with the six million victims in martyrdom in perpetuation of the Jewish faith in the years of Nazi rule."

"O earth! Cover not their blood!" reads the text on the monument.

Unveiled in 1978 by the Vilno and Vicinity Association, another Holocaust monument recalls the Jews of Vilno, Poland and vicinity who perished in the ghetto, concentration camps and partisan battles. In 1941, about fifty thousand Jews of Vilno, Poland were led to a nearby forest, shot to death and thrown into pits. Survivors remained in the Vilna ghetto until it was liquidated in 1943 and they were shipped to concentration camps.

In 1972, the Hebrew Sick Benefit Association consecrated a simple martyrs' monument. The monument reads: "This monument is consecrated as a memorial to our six million brethren who perished in martyrdom 1939-1945. We shall never forget."

On a monument at the entrance to one of the Russian Polish Hebrew Sick Benefit Association areas of the Cemetery is the simple phrase: "Lest we forget, the six million martyrs, among them the Russian Polish Jewish communities, who perished at the hands of the Nazis."

Unveiled in 1964, a monument memorializes "our beloved six million brothers and sisters and the Jewish communities of Koluszki and Brzeziny in Poland who were slaughtered by the hands of the Nazi Murderers 1938-1945."

Dedicated in 1964 by the Association of Jews from Pinsk, Belarus, and vicinity, there is a monument in sacred memory to the martyrdom and heroism of thirty thousand Jews from Pinsk and neighbouring towns who perished at the hands of Nazi tyranny from 1941-1943.

There is a monument dedicated by the United Ozerover Aid Societies in memory of the men, women, and children whom the Nazis deported and massacred from the city of Ozerov, Russia on October 22, 1942.

Dedicated in 1954 by the Rovner Lutsk Landsmanschaften, this monument was built in memory of the martyrs of the district of Wolyn, today part of Poland. It remembers "our beloved brethren and their families of Rovna, Lutsk and surrounding communities who were exterminated by the Nazi beast in 1942 thereby sanctifying their name of God."

"Remember the 6 million," reads one of the columns of a large, stylized Star of David on a Holocaust memorial erected in 1982 by the Stolin and Vicinity Memorial Association. Stolin is a small town in the south of Belarus. "Let us not forget our martyred brethren from these towns and villages," reads a monument next to the bronze Star of David. The monuments list the names of forty-two victims. "In sacred memory of the martyrs of Stolin and vicinity who were murdered by the Nazis and their collaborators on the eve of Rosh Hashanah 5703-1942," is the text from a second monument at the site.

A handful of ashes from the death camps lies buried under a monument built in 1987 by the *Landsleit* (immigrants from the same home-town) from Zamosc. The granite Holocaust memorial, featuring a bronze menorah, is one of the largest in the Cemetery. "In eternal memory of the Jewish martyrs of the city of Zamosc (Poland) who perished under the Nazis and their collaborators, in the ghettos and death camps of Belsen, Majdanek and other places," reads the monument. "Forget not. Forgive not."

"In sacred memory to the martydom and heroism of our thirty thousand
brethren from Pinsk and neighbouring towns who perished at the hands
of Nazi tyranny, 1941-1943."
Erected by the Association of Jews from Pinsk and Vicinity, 1964.
[Photo: D.R. Cowles]

Another monument bears the incription: "1942. I will give them an everlasting name that shall not be cut off. Dedicated to the sacred memory of the martyrs of Shebreshin—May 1965."

A monument was put up by the United Bucoviner Association of Canada "in lasting tribute to the countless number of men, women and children brutally massacred in Bucovina, Bessarabia, Roumania and Transylvania – 1940-1945."

Erected by United Hebrew Cemeteries in 1951, a monument is "in everlasting memory of the six million Jews killed in cold blood by the Germans, Nazis and their helpers in the years 1939-1945." Another reads, "In everlasting memory of the prestigious Lithuanian Jewish community who perished in the Holocaust 1941-1945."

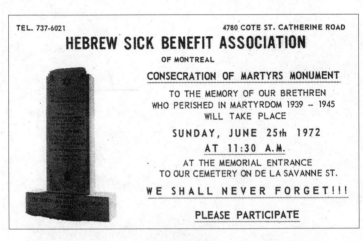

TEL. 737-6021   4780 COTE ST. CATHERINE ROAD

HEBREW SICK BENEFIT ASSOCIATION

OF MONTREAL

CONSECRATION OF MARTYRS MONUMENT

TO THE MEMORY OF OUR BRETHREN
WHO PERISHED IN MARTYRDOM 1939 – 1945
WILL TAKE PLACE

SUNDAY, JUNE 25th 1972
AT 11:30 A.M.

AT THE MEMORIAL ENTRANCE
TO OUR CEMETERY ON DE LA SAVANNE ST.

WE SHALL NEVER FORGET!!!

PLEASE PARTICIPATE

Advertisement.
In 1972, the Hebrew Sick Benefit Association consecrated
a simple martyrs' monument.
[Canadian Jewish Congress Archives]

9

The Words on the Monuments

As for man, his days are as grass; as the flower of the field, so he flourisheth. For the wind passeth over it, and it is gone; and the place thereof knoweth it no more.
—Psalm 1

Some of the words on the monuments at Baron de Hirsch Cemetery are from the Bible, others from songs and poems. Many are original, many unattributed. Here's a sampling:

ARON FRYDMAN (1906-1987)
In the winds of war
You ran for your life
Memories of horror
Was your grim life
After the Holocaust
You found a new life
Our birth was your daily light
But so late in your life
Now under the wings of God
Is your everlasting life
We miss you.

ERROL CUTLER (1948-1994)
He played the game with dignity and grace

SOL ABRACEN (1916-1994)
A truly unusual man

ANN ABRACEN (1912-1990)
Of a thousand words and a million deeds
HOWARD ABRACEN (1943-1978)
Alone with his heart at last

ANNA BORCZUK (1910-1987)
LEON BORCZUK (1906-2000)
Finally joining their mothers, fathers, sisters and brothers who died at
the hands of the Nazis. Survivors of the Warsaw Ghetto uprising.

SOPHIE GOLDFARB (1928-1977)
"Wisdom hath buildeth her house" (Prov. 9: 1)
"Strength and dignity were her clothing" (Prov. 31: 25)

MOE CAPLAN (1918-1999)
A good name is better than the finest of oils

LEONIE SARAH LEIFFER (1907-1989)
Your smiling face
And gentle humor
Gives us all the strength
To carry on, as you did
Against all odds ...
We salute you!

MAURICE SINGER
(Died December 11, 1964, age ninety years)
He that walketh uprightly and worketh righteousness and speaketh
the truth in his heart.

ROSE RIFFLE KUCKOFF (Died July 22, 1958)
You fell asleep without saying goodbye
But our memories of you will never die

NICOLE NICKY SOMLO (Born May 18, 1959)
Died accidentally in Jerusalem, Israel at the age of 20 years
Sunshine child, flutist, poet

All the winds of the world come and blow in Jerusalem
And each wind comes to bow before the Lord in Jerusalem

Who holds the key
Over the hills
Beyond the skies
Where life and death
Begins and ends for us
By Nicky

DR. FRANÇOIS SOMLO (1912-1995)
"... you had a beautiful destiny
With the art of healing and as a poet in your world of fantasy,
We all love you."

EVA COHEN (1923-2002)
My Chu-Chu

TONY ROSENTHAL (Died June 11, 1975)
How can a piece of earth
So small, so narrow
Hold your love and our sorrow?

LEE FARR (1908-1947)
Dearest, to live in hearts you leave behind, is not to die.

ANN RESIN (1907-1968)
Time dims not the achievements
Of the brave
But worth shines steadfast
Ever from the grave

SARINA MIZRACHI LEVY (1896-1982)
Tu nous as enseigné comment aimer sans rien demander en retour.
Merci.

PETER DAVID BERGER (1948-1968)
To my brother
Last night I looked for you
Darkness said that you were gone
To that sacred land of
Which you always spoke
Had long been poised
Against the hearts that
Dared, so painfully
To love you.
Last night I called for you
Silence told me of your flight
Down twisted passageways
Of drug-filled dreams
To meet the mystic
Moulder of your passion
And live at last beyond
Polluted bounds of
Wasted life.
Last night I reached for you
But emptiness reminded me
And longing plucked a
Bitter tune inside
My yearning heart
Which ached to say
For one last time
I love you.
Last night I lost you too, my brother. *–Nomi*

NOCHIM LEWIN, M.D., F.C.C.P. (1892-1953)
This memorial was erected by the patients of the Mount Sinai
Sanitorium in fond memory of their beloved doctor and as a tribute to
his many years of unselfish service.

DAVID ROSENBERG (1908-1962)
Dedicated his life for the welfare of the patients of
Mount Sinai Sanitorium

LEIB BACHARIER (1904-1985)
Here lies an honest man
His simplicity belied his depth
His humility his worth

IRVING POSTELNIK (THE BARBER) (1910-1969)
In his life known as Irving the Barber
His days filled with friendship and laughter
His life was full of kindly deeds
A helping hand to those in need
A pleasant word, a heart of gold
Words can't express the sorrow we share
Or truly tell how much we care
Deep in our hearts a memory is kept
We loved you dearly and will never forget

HENRY FIELD (1913-1988)
Happy is the man who departs the world with a good name

TAMMY ROSENBERG UNGAR (1917-1998)
Oh, to be together in your kitchen once more …

EMMY STEINERT (1887-1963)
She openeth her mouth with wisdom,
The law of loving kindness was on the tongue.

OTTO STEINERT (1915-2000)
Who is wise? He who learns from everyone. Who is rich?
He who is content with his lot in life.

AGNES KLEIN (1936-1995)
The fractured heart
She tenderly consoled
The fluttering fur
Of a species forlorn
If eloquence could dance
And entrance the sublime

Such grave has inherited
A love for all time

JOSHUA PLOTNICK (1954-1975)
JACK PLOTNICK (1925-1975)
In loving memory of Jack and Josh—who were brutally
murdered together

LORRAINE GREENBERG (1954-1996)
Sunshine fades
And shadows fall
But sweet remembrance
Outlasts all

HANNA GETA TEFERA (1972-1988)
My breath is corrupt
My days are extinct
The graves are ready for me (Job 17: 1)
At sixteen I am already in the ground

MICHAEL STEVEN MARMEROS (1982-1992)
So full of life
Always with a smile
Our very special boy
Forever loved

BERTHA WEITZMAN (1921-1993)
She strove to touch the stars.

JULIETTE MOSS
(Died August 8, 1931, aged eighteen years)
Died too soon to know life.

BENNIE ABERGSON (October 17, 1927, age seventeen)
Remembrance is a flower that never dies
When watered by the tears of
Love of his mother and sister.

Oren Grunbaum (1976-1996)
Excerpt from Oren's writings:
We are visitors
In a place where we once belonged
We are strangers
In a land we once walked on
Our sister – The moon
Our mother – The earth
The sun – Our healer
We hide from all
And they hide from us.
We reach for stars
While our greed self destructs ...
The journey of young dreams has come to its end.
Footstone:
To live in the hearts we leave behind is not to die.

Gerald G. Freed (1937-2000)
I'd rather be skiing

Lyubov Slepvan (1911-1996)
Do not stand by my grave and cry. I am not here ... I did not die.

Mina Weber (1899-1995)
You left farewells
Unspoken
You suffered silently
You quietly
Slipped away
Your fight for life
Never did bend
Until the very end
A woman excellent
In deeds. A warm heart
Devoted and generous
Sadly missed by her
Son and loving family

As long as life
And memory last
We will remember you
Forever in our hearts

JACOB LIPNOWSKI (Died November 15, 1998)
Survivor, protector, hero
Incredible physical might
And athletic prowess
In a constitution
Forged by steel and
Tempered by strength of
Character, love of life and
Commitment to family.

JACQUES ZAFRANY (1920-2001)
Être unique
Fier, généreux
Plus grand que nature
Amoureux des plantes
Des animaux et des humains
Dont tu étais
Le défenseur acharne
Nous ta famille
Te saluons et t'aimons
De tout notre coeur

EMILE ZELIGMAN (1911-2003)
Il y a d'innombrables rues dans chaque âme

BRIAN VICTOR SILVERMAN (1967-1985)
Those who have gone before us
Who showed us the way
To those who travel with us
Who brighten the way
And to those
Who will come after us

[Photo: D.R. Cowles]

Who we pray will
Continue the way

ROSE ROTHMAN (1907-1997)
The flame in her heart
Radiated unforgettable
Warmth to family, friends
And all who came into
Its glow

Your ideas…Fireworks
Your thoughts…Music
Your actions…Miracles
Your words…A Prayer
Your Life…An Example to Mankind

ELLA SAMUELY ROTHSCHILD
(Died June 4, 1922, age twenty-six)
The grief that is in our
Hearts
No human eye can trace
For many a tear is hid
Behind a smiling face

CLAUDE DAVID TAPIERO (1941-1999)
Comme l'eau réflète le visage
Le coeur de l'homme le fait également
Proverbes, XXVIII, 19

ISAAC JACQUES DANAN (1905-2003)
"It's a long way to …" [With musical notes]

JACK MINTZBERG (1923-1987)
Bluebird

BERNARD FIGLER, QC (1900-1983)
May his memory live on as a blessing

IDA BERMAN (1908-1990)
Strength and honour are her clothing Prov. 31:25

DR. HYMAN RUBINSTEIN (1906-2002)
Uncle Hymie to Everyone

MELVYN HOCKENSTEIN (1944-1976)
Live while there's life to give
Love while there's love to give
This man's gentle spirit and kindness
Will flourish in the memories of those who love him

BEN BARUCH ISRAEL BULTZ (1914-1983)
Out of a lump of clay
God created a man
Who cleaved a wife
Sculpted two sons
Molded grandchildren
And carved friendship,
Dignity and love.

PAL KÜRSCHNER (1901-1997)
I lived a long life because I honored my parents
His love and teachings will inspire us always.

JOEL WOLMAN (1983-1998)
The Lord shall guard your soul
He shall guard your departure
And your arrival from this time and for evermore

DOBA BOYER
(Died August 18, 1965)
Give her the fruit of her hands
And let her own works praise her in the gates

SARAH CAISERMAN (Died January 9, 1967)
Do not go gentle
Into that good night
Old age should burn
And rave at close of day
Rage, rage against
The dying of the light
(Dylan Thomas)

LENA FINEBERG (1894-1990)
The Lordly spirit within me
Is my light and the stronghold
Of my life. Of whom shall I be afraid?

TILLIE BURDMAN (1904-1997)
Nature has planted another flower

ROBERT MARX (1884-1958)
All the generations of mortal man
Add up to nothing
Show me the man whose happiness was
Anything more than illusion followed by
Disillusion.

JACK OVERLAND (Died March 20, 1949)
Here's where all men's dreams come true
No class, no arrogance, no prejudice
All things undone or meant to do
Are shared alike in this paradise.

EMIL KOLTAI (1919-1994)
EVA KOLTAI (1924-1983)
In memoriam: My brother and sisters fell victim to the Holocaust that
ravaged our family. Iren, her husband and four children, Margit, her
husband and three children, Berta and Imre all fell at Auschwitz

HARRY HANDEL (1912-1970)
Good night, sweet prince

LEON ACKERMAN (1912-1969)
Laibish, my dearest you loved me so much ... Now I
miss you so much...Your loving Eva.

ROSE LEIBOVITCH (1898-1977)
Here will I await thee
'Till thou comest again
And if thou wait up yonder
Then there we'll meet my dear

LOUIS LEIBOVITCH (1897-1995)
To see a world in a grain of sand
And a heaven in a wild flower
Hold infinity in the palm of your hand
And eternity in an hour

DR. HAROLD ROSEN (1921-1990)
Scholar, physician, teacher
Who can know thy worth
May his memory ever be
A blessing and an inspiration

PERCY LIONEL RASHCOVSKY (1935-1989)
A founding member of the Hope and Cope self-help group program.
Percy devoted many years inspiring others during his own affliction.
We will sorely miss him.
Footstone:
Time the great healer of grief and sorrow. Trust in
thoughts of a brighter tomorrow.

ADELA ROSENBERG (1903-1991)
ISAC ROSENBERG (1902-1989)
Blessed be this land and its people for they restored
Our dignity and we have lived in peace.

MARTIN REGENSTREIF (1903-1975)
And the elements so mixed
In him that nature could stand up to all the world and say,
"This was a man."

MARY ITESCU (1951-1970)
"Uca" Our beloved daughter and sister who lost her life
accidentally by asphyxiation, while on vacation in Cavendish, P.E.I.
She will never be forgotten.

NAOMI HOLTZMAN (1952-1969)
Dearly beloved daughter and sister. Accidentally killed in
Israel at the age of 17 yrs.

ADELLA STIPELMAN (died July 27, 1965)
Strength and dignity were her clothing

BRINA MEDICOFF (died January 29, 1968)
She looketh well to the ways
Of her household and eateth
Not the bread of idleness
Footstone:
—Mama—
Her hardships many
Her pleasures few
She loved us dearly
'Til her life was through

BELLA-YAFA FORMAN ETZIONY (1908-1964)
The stars have deceived me
There was a dream—But it too is gone
Nothing have I now in this world
I have none.

MACKENZIE BELSON (2002-2006)
Where there is love, there is life.

ANNA SHIRLEY HEIDENFELD NÉE SPIGELMAN
(Died December 19, 1969 at the age of nineteen)
Israel
Where our fathers lived and wept
Where foreign tyrants calmly slept
Time hid in sand and dust
Was born a dream that fear couldn't rust
Where seed grew from waste
And flowers from dust
A dream was unfolded
To be treasured with trust
Where our brothers reap and sow
A haven upon earth
Our mothers can now rest in peace
Their children nurse their dream from birth—Anna Shirley

FRANK DAVID WHITE (1897-1970)
Lord, who shall abide in thy tabernacle? Who shall dwell in thy holy
hill? He that walketh uprightly and worketh righteousness and speaketh
the truth in his heart.

CHAIKE BELCHATOWSKA SPIEGEL (1919-2002)
Fighter in the Warsaw Ghetto uprising

TODD ADAM SANDLER (1980-1999)
A shining light to all who knew him

SAMMY KRUL (1956-1975)
Our beloved young son and brother.
Torn away from us so soon in life.
Footstone:
He knew how much we loved him.
He knows how much we will miss him.

LEON KOKIN (1910-1994)
Partisan, defender of Jewish lives and honour, 1942-1944

EVELYN CHEIFETZ (1919-1988)
I remember the days of old
I meditate on all that thou hast done
I muse on what thy hands have wrought
I stretch out my hands to thee
My soul thirsts for thee like a parched land (Psalm 143)

WILLIAM CHEIFETZ (1920-1991)
Take my hand as I falter
There is little left for me
With you at my side
I have touched eternity (Wm.C.)

ARTHUR LERMER (1908-2001)
Optimistic Arthur
Lifelong Bundist
Champion of Yiddish

MIRIAM LERMER (1914-1986)
Brave Manya
A tower of strength
Wisdom and love

RACHEL EISEN BERGNER-RAVITCH (1906-2000)
First librarian of the JPL

JACK POST (1919-1986)
I am a thousand winds that blow
I am the diamond glints on snow
I am the sunlight on ripened grain
I am the gentle autumn rain
Do not stand at my grave and cry
I am not there. I did not die.

Hoops Dubow (January 1, 1989)
I will rise after a thousand years
Lipping flowers
And set my teeth
In the silver of the moon—EEC
[ee cummings]

Elishka Korpner
(November 29, 1951, age thirty-nine)
Only once during life did you hurt me and that was
when forever you left me

Cyril Kaspi (1958-1993)
Biochemist, humanist, teacher, scholar, taken in his prime

David Serour (1974-1989)
Avec une chandelle aussi courte tu as su illuminer les 15 belles années
de la vie de ceux que tu aimais.

Helen Schnapp
(Died November 22, 1928, age nine)
In sad and loving memory of my only beloved daughter
Inserted by her heartbroken mother

Alexis Anna Judith Crelinsten (1992-2001)
Now we are lit by her only from within.

Sara Rotchin Policoff (1907-1996)
Miss me … But let me go
When I come to the end
Of the road
And the sun has set for me
I want no rites
In a gloom filled room
Why cry for a soul set free?
Miss me a little
But not forever and

Not with your head bowed low
Remember the love that
We all have shared
Miss me, but let me go

RAE SHAPIRO
(Died May 15, 1926, age twenty years and seven months)
Peacefully sleeping, resting at last from life's weary trials
and suffering past.

PHILLIPP SPRINGER
(Died October 15, 1918, aged forty-four)
Secretary of Local 659 Journey Barbers Union of America

FANNY PHILLIPS GOODMAN (1887-1941)
A loving mother so gentle and kind
What a wonderful memory she left behind
Long days long nights, she bore her pain
To wait for cure, but all in vain
Till God himself knew what was best
He took her home and gave her rest

JEANETTE SILVER (1923-1988)
There's many a lonely heartache
And often a silent tear
But always precious memories of
The days when you were here.

CORPORAL CHARLES GOLDIN, RCASC
(Died January 17, 1949)
Gave his life for his country, for a better world to live in.

NANCY OSTROFF
(Died December 17, 1942, age nine)
In our hearts your memory lingers
Sweetly, tender, fond and true
There is not a day, dear Nancy
That we do not think of you

GERTRUDE CUBITZ
(Died May 20, 1926, age nineteen)
The paths of glory lead but to the grave.

Cemetery superintendent's residence, formerly the head office
of United Hebrew Cemeteries.
[Photo: D.R. Cowles]

A Walking Tour of
Baron de Hirsch Cemetery

The grounds of the Baron de Hirsch Cemetery are well worth exploring. A walking tour is an opportunity to show respect to the dead and to reflect on the history of our community.

One can start a tour by entering the Cemetery at the main gate (Gate #2) on de la Savane. Continue along the path, known as Path A. The *Cemetery office* is just to the left of the gate.

The Stone Fence

The *stone fence* is home to two time capsules. One was inserted in 1937 when the original stone fence was built. It contains copies of the defunct Yiddish daily *Keneder Adler*, *The Canadian Jewish Review* (headlined "Present Regime Cannot Continue in Palestine"), the Montreal *Gazette* of July 29, 1937, minutes of meetings, and annual reports. Workers repairing the stone in 1993 stumbled on to the time capsule by fluke; nobody remembered that it existed. It was reinstalled, and another time capsule was added at the time of the repairs in 1993.

Sculpture of the Baron de Hirsch

The *sculpture of the Baron Maurice de Hirsch* outside the office honours the man for whom the Cemetery is named. Born in 1831 into a distinguished family, before he was forty he was a captain of industry and a leading financier in Europe. Influenced by his wife, Clara, he became a major philanthropist. With Montreal's Jewish community facing an influx of immigrants at the turn of the twentieth century, the community implored him for help and the Baron responded immediately. In recognition of the Baron's generosity, the Baron de Hirsch Institute was formed in Montreal in 1891. In fact, almost all of the community organizations in today's Jewish community of Montreal owe their start to the Institute. When the monument was unveiled at the Cemetery in 1941, Max Finestone, president of the Baron de Hirsch Institute, said it would be "an everlasting memorial

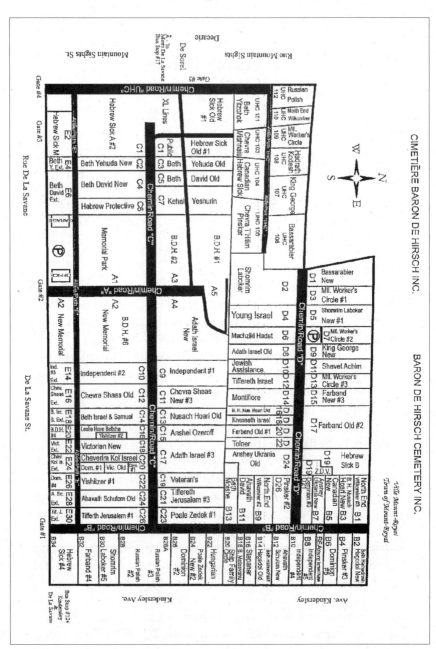

Map of the Baron de Hirsch Cemetery.

to a great Jew and a great humanitarian." Although his wealth was vast, "his heart was with the little people, the oppressed and the disinherited, and his whole life is a record of his care for those whose lives needed to be rebuilt."

Yahrzeit Lanterns

Continuing along Path A, where it intersects with Path E, to the right is *New Memorial Park*, one of the newer sections of the Cemetery. The many metal lanterns next to the tombstones are for Yahrzeit memorial candles. While it is traditional for Ashkenazi Jews to light Yahrzeit candles in the home, Sephardic Jews light them at the graves of loved ones. Although Sephardic Jews are buried throughout the Cemetery, many are buried in New Memorial. The section was opened in the early 1970s, which correlates roughly with the arrival of large numbers of Sephardim in Montreal.

Trees

Note the tall *trees that line the path* and throughout the Cemetery. There were once as many as 1,300 poplars in the Cemetery. They were originally planted to soak up water. The poplars have been dying off and are being replaced with long-life columnar oaks. The new trees don't grow as high as poplars, but they don't require as much water and have small root systems that don't spread greatly.

Special care has been taken with trees at Baron de Hirsch Cemetery so that the *kohanim* can enter the burial grounds. Jewish law says that the *kohanim*, who trace their ancestry back to Aaron, the first Jewish priest *(kohen)*, cannot pass under the branch of any tree branches over a grave. Branches along the paths are trimmed so the *kohanim* can walk along the centre of the paths without walking under trees.

Children's Graves

> Few in years
> Sweet and dear
> Like water, flow our tears
> For their young lives
> In loving memory of three hundred children
> Who lie here in unmarked graves.

Three hundred unmarked children's graves were discovered in recent decades when digging began in an area that was thought not to have been used for any burials. This monument was donated by monument-maker Smith Bros. and unveiled in 1983.
[Photo: D.R. Cowles]

At the end of Path A you'll find those poignant words on a monument in memory of 300 *children buried in nearby unmarked graves*. The monument was donated by monument-maker Smith Bros. and unveiled in 1983 at a ceremony attended by several rabbis and Cemetery Board members. The children's graves had been unmarked. They were discovered only in recent decades when digging began in an area that was thought to not have been used for any burials. Their presence can be explained. While the Baron de Hirsch Institute has always covered the cost of burials of the poor, it was not always the fashion in the Cemetery's early days to include tombstones for such burials. (That situation has long changed and now the Cemetery provides full service for all indigent burials.) The rows of unmarked graves, designated by numbers in stone markers on the ground, are located to your left in Baron de Hirsch #1, the oldest Baron de Hirsch-owned section of the Cemetery. They can be found, simply enough, by searching for the area of the section that does not contain tombstones.

Titanic Victim

Somewhere in Baron de Hirsch #1 is the body of the only victim of the *Titanic* disaster who is buried in the Cemetery, and one of only six *Titanic* victims buried in Montreal. Sculptor Leopold Weisz, who had lived for years in Montreal, went back to England to fetch his wife, Mathilde. The couple was to have sailed first-class on another ship, but because of a coal strike, they bought tickets on the maiden voyage of the ill-fated *Titanic*. Before they boarded, Weisz sewed his life savings, $30,000 in currency and $15,000 worth of gold, into the lining of his coat. Mathilde survived and was picked up by the *Carpathia*, which disembarked at New York City. He wasn't so lucky. His body was recovered and shipped to Montreal for burial at Baron de Hirsch. The gold sewn inside his coat was returned to Mathilde, a move that saved her from being deported to England as an indigent. Mathilde later married her late husband's business partner, Edward Wren. Weisz's carving of a frieze on the old Montreal Museum of Fine Arts building on Sherbrooke Street West remains today, as do his carvings of the stone shields representing Canada's provinces which decorate the Dominion Express Building at 201 St. Jacques Street West.

Walking Westward from Path A

After Path A comes to an end at Baron de Hirsch #1, make your way in the same direction (westward) by walking gingerly between the graves. You will reach what was the *United Hebrew Cemeteries*. Like the Baron de Hirsch Cemetery itself, United Hebrew Cemeteries served a variety of burial societies and congregations. With the gradual disappearance of burial societies, the Baron de Hirsch assumed control of the United Hebrew Cemeteries in the early 1980s. It also took over United Hebrew Cemeteries' former office at de la Savane and Mountain Sights (next to Gate #4), transforming it into a *home for the Cemetery's caretaker*, making the caretaker and his family the Cemetery's only living residents.

Ohels

Once you've reached the former United Hebrew Cemeteries area, you'll see a few tiny huts that look like miniature homes or garden sheds. These are, in fact *Ohels*. An *Ohel* (literally, a tent) is traditionally a structure built over the resting place of a *tzaddik*, or righteous person. At Baron de Hirsch, a handful of rabbis were given the honour of having these brick and concrete structures to mark their final resting places. It is believed by some that a *tzaddik* is closer to God, and thus has the ability to bring prayers to God's attention. It is customary to pray by their gravesites and to light candles. Thus, if you enter any of the *Ohels* at Baron de Hirsch, you'll see *yahrzeit* candles on the sandy ground.

Among those buried under *Ohels* are Rabbis Yudel Rosenberg (1860-1935) and Zvi Hirsch Cohen (1860-1950). Rabbi Rosenberg, whose *Ohel* is in the Hadrath Kodesh section, was known in religious circles for his translation of the *Zohar*—the sourcebook of Kabbalistic lore—an arduous task that took him twenty-five years. To reach the masses of Yiddish-speaking Montreal Jews, he did so through a fictional narrator called the Sabbath Queen, who urged them to observe the Sabbath.

When Rabbi Zvi Hirsch Cohen died in 1950 at age ninety, more than six thousand people attended his funeral. Officials said it was the largest funeral ever held in Montreal for a Jew. He was dean of the Canadian Rabbinate and president of the Montreal Council of Orthodox Rabbis and had been one of the organizers of the Jewish Community Council of Montreal, the Vaad Ha'ir. As an authority on Judaism, his rulings on various religious questions were sought around the world. His *Ohel* is in the Chevra T'Hilim Pinsker section.

No new *Ohels* have been built for about half a century at the Cemetery.

In 2000, Ben Weider of body-building fame financed the repair of the *Ohels* at Baron de Hirsch, although strong winds have since unhinged the doors on some of them.

Wilkomirer Monuments

At nearby North End Wilkomirer and adjoining sections you'll notice *old monuments that stand upright*, in comparison to tombstones in other older sections of the Cemetery that are leaning in all directions. This is because, starting in 2003, tombstones in sections like these are progressively being repaired and restored. Money is being taken from the Cemetery's Perpetual Care Fund as part of a multi-year program to bring the sections up to an acceptable standard. Tests done in sections like North End Wilkomirer found that foundations were not dug deep enough. The only way to solve the problem is to temporarily remove the tombstones, rebuild foundations by digging to at least the frost level (five feet) and using reinforcement rods and top-quality cement, and then put the tombstones back into place.

Similar repairs have been made in several sections including the King George, Hadrath Kodesh and Montreal Workers' Circle sections of the former United Hebrew Cemeteries. Purists may argue that the action to restore tombstones results in less esthetic appeal in the older sections, but it's the only alternative to having tombstones falling on the ground.

Holocaust Memorials

Holocaust memorials, monuments commemorating victims of Nazi brutality, are scattered throughout the Cemetery. They have been erected by various Montreal organizations in memory of persons from their towns or districts of Central Europe.

Veterans Field of Remembrance

Located on Path C, which runs east-west, this section can be reached either from Path A or B. From Path A, turn right when you reach Path C and walk toward the end. On the left is the *Veterans Field of Remembrance*. If you take Path B (located at the gate on de la Savane near Kindersley), turn left at Path C and walk to the third section on the right.

In 1953, the Baron de Hirsch Institute contributed the ground for the Jewish Veterans Field of Remembrance. The section is now the resting place for those who fought overseas for Canada in the World Wars, as well as persons who served in the Israeli, Czechoslovakian, Free French, Polish and Russian military, former members of the Slovak Partisans and others.

An entranceway monument on the right hand side of the Field of Remembrance is "dedicated to the glory of God and the sacred memory of the Jewish men and women of the province of Quebec who gave their lives in the service of their sovereign and country 1914-18, 1939-45."

In the centre of the section are two flagstaffs with dedications next to them. On the right side, is one to the memory of Vladimir Jabotinsky (1880-1940), founder of the Jewish legion (1916-1919) and "In tribute to the millions of Jews exterminated by the Nazis 1939-1945."

To the left of the flagstaff is a 1959 tribute to the men and women who died in the service of their country, erected in memory of Charles Sherman Rubin, 1874-1959.

Unlike the rest of the Cemetery, the monuments here are no more than eighteen inches in height.

One of the highlights of this section is a Roll of Honour that includes the text:

> They were lonely
> And pleasant
> In their lives
> And in their death
> Were not divided
> Swifter than eagles
> Stronger than lions
> To do the will
> Of their master
> And the desire
> Of their rock

Throughout the Cemetery...

The *flowers* a visitor sees in summer are not a traditional feature of Jewish cemeteries, because the prevailing view was that bringing flowers smacked of a pagan custom. But the Baron de Hirsch has been given permission to plant flowers because it is felt the flowers are more for the living than in recognition of the dead. However, flowers are not permitted in ultra-

Orthodox sections of the Cemetery (Chevra Mishnais and Chevra T'Hilim Pinsker) as well as in the Veterans' Field of Remembrance.

Keep your eyes open for *animal life*, especially during Cemetery visits on weekdays when there are fewer visitors. The Cemetery is home to foxes, groundhogs and a wide variety of birds.

In older sections of the Cemetery, note how *babies and children* are often buried together either in the first row or last row. Burial societies and congregations would often reserve a section for infants, given Montreal's high infant mortality rates early in the twentieth century.

Contrary to the belief of some, the last row of any Cemetery section is *not* reserved for persons whose deaths may have been considered suicide, nor does it indicate lower status.

Cemeteries and gravesites are considered sacred in Judaism. One way of preventing people from unintentionally desecrating gravesites by walking on a grave was through the use of *cement* or *granite ledges* (commonly known as slabs) over gravesites. But the slabs have caused a lot of problems in the Cemetery, including broken foundations and monuments. In 1961, the Cemetery stopped allowing the slabs but many remain today, particularly in older sections of the Cemetery.

Photographs are not allowed on tombstones at Baron de Hirsch, athough the practice used to be popular, following a European tradition. So prevalent was the practice tht in 1917 the Cemetery sent registered letters to each burial society requesting them not to allow pictures on monuments. Still, in older sections of Baron de Hirsch, it's not uncommon to find tombstones with poignant photographs, usually printed on porcelain. Although some have been worn away by the elements, many, amazingly, have stood the test of time. These include bar mitzvah boys dressed in tallis and holding their prayerbooks, and others who died at an early age.

In the early years of Baron de Hirsch Cemetery there were no *height restrictions*, and some monuments in the older sections at the rear of the Cemetery are eight or nine feet high. Monuments today can be no more than three feet high (not including a one-foot base).

Almost all monuments in the Cemetery include the English and Hebrew names of the deceased (with the traditional Hebrew "son of" or "daughter of"), the dates of birth and death (according to the Jewish calendar and usually by the Christian calender), and the relationship to other family members (such as father or mother). As well, there are the

Hebrew letters *pay nun*, standing for *po nikbar(ah)* ("here is buried)" and the letters *tav, nun, tzadek, bet, hay*, standing for the phrase "*teheye nishmato tsrurah b'tsror ha-chayyim*" ("May his/her soul be bound up in the bond of eternal life.") Aside from those traditional inclusions, there are no regulations for what goes on the monument.

Throughout the Baron de Hirsch Cemetery, you'll see hands in the shape of a V on tombstones, as well as a number of other Jewish symbols. While most do not reveal anything about the deceased, *two hands in the shape of a V* indicate that the deceased was a member of the *kohanim*, because this is the hand position that is used when the *kohanim* bless the congregation.

A *pitcher* or *jug* signifies a member of the Levite tribe.

The Magen David, or *Star of David*, is not only the flag of the State of Israel, but the symbol of the Jewish people. It is also considered a symbol of redemption.

Traditionally, a Magen David is used for men while a *menorah* is used for women. Since women *bent shabbes licht* (prayed and lit the Sabbath candles on Friday night), they get the menorah. The Star of David was on King David's shield.

The *Ner Tamid* or *eternal lamp* is often seen. The eternal lamp is constantly lit in synagogues. The menorah or seven-branched candelabra, the emblem of the State of Israel, has its origin in Exodus. Since it had seven branches in the Temple and identical copies were forbidden, it often has six branches or a Star of David in the middle.

Also keep a lookout for a *broken tree trunk* or *candle*. These symbolize a life tragically cut short by accident or illness.

Children's tombstones are often indicated by *lambs*. Other pictures of animals may refer to specific names, such as an *eagle* for Adler, a *lion* for Judah or Aryeh or Leo, and a *rooster* for Hahn. An *ark* and *Torah scroll* is often found on the monuments for a rabbi, a *violin* for a musician, a *pen* for a writer, and a *row of books* suggests a learned person.

Personalities

The Baron de Hirsch Cemetery is the burial site of numerous personages who contributed to Jewish life in Montreal and elsewhere. The gravesites of a few are noted here.

In Montefiore (D-14) is poet and novelist A.M. Klein.

In the Ship Family Circle (B-20) lies Harry Ship, the "last gambling czar". Several of the Yiddish greats are buried in the two Farband Old sections of the Cemetery. They include Jacob Isaac Segal, Israel Medres, Jacob (Yaacov) Zipper, Joseph Kage, Yehuda Elberg, Rachel Korn, Dora Wasserman, and Sara Rosenfeld.

Writer Israel Medres, Montreal, Quebec, shortly before his death in 1964.
[Photo: Abe Madras]

Acknowledgements and Sources

Thanks are due to numerous individuals and institutions that have contributed to this book.

Individuals who granted interviews: Jay Aaron, Barbara Akerman, Joe Alter, Suzanne Belson, Jacques Berkowitz, Brandee Berson, Martin Brook, Bella Caplan, Frema Engel, Rabbi Moishe Glustein, Eiran Harris, Herbert Isenberg, Libby Labell, Herbert Paperman, Morris Pascal, Gerald Silverberg, and Steve Tabac.

Archives
Canadian Jewish Congress National Archives, Montreal; American Jewish Archives, Cincinnati; Jewish Public Library, Montreal; City of Montréal Archvies, and Library and Archives Canada.

Websites
Canadian Broadcasting Corporation – www.cbc.ca
The Canadian Encyclopedia – www.tceplus.com
Encyclopedia Titanica – www.encyclopedia-titanica.org
Fairmount Bagel – www.fairmountbagel.com
Jewish.com
Jewish Encyclopedia.com – www.jewishencyclopedia.com
Jewish People's Schools and Peretz Schools – www.jpps.ca
Judean Memorial Gardens – www.judeangardens.com
Kolel: The Adult Centre for Liberal Jewish Living – www.kolel.org
Library and Archives Canada – www.collectionscanada.ca
Mount Sinai Hospital – www.sinaimontreal.ca
PBS – www.pbs.org
Rachel Korn – www.rachelkorn.com
Shaar Hashomayim Synagogue – www.shaarhashomayim.org
Tandem – www.tandemnews.com
The Tenement Museum, New York – www.tenement.org

Periodicals
Canadian Jewish Archives, Canadian Jewish Chronicle, The Canadian Jewish News, Canadian Jewish Review, Le Devoir, The Gazette, The Globe and Mail,

Hour, The Jewish News Weekly of Northern California, The Jewish Standard, The Jewish Times, Keneder Adler, Kiplinger Magazine, The Link, The Montreal Daily Star, The Montreal Star, Montreal Mirror, National Library News, Our Community News, La Presse, The Scribe (Journal of the Jewish Historical Society of British Columbia), *The Suburban, The Vancouver Sun, The Weekly Herald.*

Books

Irving Abella, *A Coat of Many Colours, Two Centuries of Jewish Life in Canada* (Lester & Orpen Dennys, Toronto, 1990).

Robert Adams, *The Life and Work of Alexander Bercovitch, Artist* (Marlowe Editions, 1988).

The Baron de Hirsch Institute: History of a Great Institution (1913).

J.L. Becker, "Reuben Brainin in Montreal", in *Tzum Hundersten Geboirntog fun Reuben Brainin* ("On the centenary of the birth of Reuben Brainin"), (ed. N. Meisel, Ikuf, New York, 1962).

Simon Belkin, *Through Narrow Gates: A Review of Jewish Immigration, Colonization and Immigrant Aid Work in Canada (1840-1940)* (Eagle Publishing Co., Montreal, 1941).

B'nai Brith Canada, *From Immigration to Integration. The Canadian Jewish Experience: A Millennium Edition* (2000).

Usher Caplan, *Like One That Dreamed: A Portrait of A.M. Klein* (McGraw-Hill Ryerson, Toronto, 1982).

Anita Diamant, *Saying Kaddish: How to Comfort the Dying, Bury the Dead, and Mourn as a Jew* (Schocken Books, New York, 1998).

Rabbi Aaron Felder, *Mourning and Remembrance in Halachah and Jewish Tradition* (C.I.S. Publishers and Distributors, New Jersey, 1992).

Finding a Burial Place (Center Genealogy Institute, New York, 2002).

Rela Mintz Geffen, ed. *Death and Mourning: A Time for Weeping, A Time for Healing,* from *Celebration and Renewal: Rites of Passage in Judaism* (Jewish Publications Society, 1993.)

Hyman Goldin, *The Jew and His Duties, the Essence of the Kitzur Shulhan Arukh* (Hebrew Publishing Company, New York, 1953).

Eli Gottesman, *Who's Who in Canadian Jewry* (Jewish Institute of Higher Research, Central Rabbinical Seminary of Canada, 1965).

Arthur Daniel Hart, ed., *The Jew in Canada* (Jewish Publications, 1926).

Edward Hillel, *The Main: Portrait of a Neighbourhood* (Key Porter Books Ltd., Toronto, 1987).

Alan Hustak, *Titanic: The Canadian Story* (Véhicule Press, Montreal, 1998).

Barbara Binder Kadden and Bruce Kadden, *Teaching Jewish Life Cycle: Insights and Activities* (A.R.E. Publishing, 1997).

Joe King, *From the Ghetto to the Main: The Story of the Jews of Montreal* (Jewish Publication Society, Montreal, 2001).

Joe King, *Three Score and Ten: A 70-Year History of the Jewish Federation (now known as Allied Jewish Community Services) of Greater Montreal* (Montreal, 1987).

Rabbi Maurice Lamm, *The Jewish Way in Death and Mourning* (Jonathan David Publishers, New York, 1969).

Lewis Levendel, "Centenary of the Canadian Jewish Press" (*National Library News* 29/12, Ottawa, 1997).

Rabbi Tom Louchheim, *Jewish Customs of Mourning* (Congregation Or Chadash, Tucson, 1997).

Israel Medres, *Montreal of Yesterday: Jewish Life in Montreal 1900-1920* (trans. Vivian Felsen, Véhicule Press, Montreal, 2000).

Israel Medres, *Between the Wars: Canadian Jews in Transition* (trans. Vivian Felsen, Véhicule Press, Montreal, 2003).

Elaine Kalman Naves, *Putting Down Roots, Montreal's Immigrant Writers* (Véhicule Press, Montreal, 1998).

Guy W. Richard, *Le Cimitière juif de Québec, Beth Israël Ohev Sholom* (Septentrion, Sillery, 2000).

Jack Riemer, ed. *Wrestling with the Angel: Jewish Insights on Death and Mourning* (Schocken Books, New York, 1995).

Ira Robinson and Mervin Butovsky, eds., *Renewing Our Days: Montreal Jews in the Twentieth Century* (Véhicule Press, Montreal, 1995).

Ira Robinson, Pierre Anctil, and Mervin Butovsky, eds., *An Everyday Miracle, Yiddish Culture in Montreal* (Véhicule Press, Montreal, 1990).

David Rome, *House of Life, A History of Jewish Cemeteries in Canada* (Canadian Jewish Congress National Archives, Montreal, 2004).

David Rome, *Jacob's Opponents, The Immigration Story II* (Canadian Jewish Congress National Archives, Montreal, 1986).

David Rome, *On the Early Harts: Their Contemporaries* (Canadian Jewish Congress National Archives, Montreal, 1981).

David Rome, *On the Early Harts* (National Archives, Canadian Jewish Congress, Montreal, 1980).

David Rome and Bernard Figler, *Hannaniah Meir Caiserman: A Biography* (Northern Printing and Lithographing, Montreal, 1962).

David Rome and Jacques Langlais, *Les pierres qui parlent : deux cents ans d'enracinement de la communauté juive au Québec (The Stones That Speak, Two Centuries of Jewish Life in Quebec)* (Septentrion, Sillery, 1992).

David Rome and Jacques Langlais, *Jews & French Quebecers, Two Hundred Years of Shared History* (Wilfrid Laurier University Press, Waterloo, Ontario, 1991).

Stuart Rosenberg, *The Jewish Community in Canada* (McClelland & Stewart, Toronto, 1970).

Rabbi Wilfred Shuchat, *The Gate of Heaven: The Story of Congregation Shaar Hashomayim of Montreal 1846-1996* (McGill-Queen's University Press, 2000).

MacKay L. Smith, *Jews of Montreal and Their Judaisms: A Voyage of Discovery* (Aaron Communications, Montreal, 1998).

Ville de Montréal. *Les rues de Montréal : Répertoire historique* (Les Éditions du Méridien, Montréal, 1995).

Rabbi Joseph Telushkin, *Jewish Wisdom: Ethical, Spiritual, and Historical Lessons From the Great Works and Thinkers* (William Morrow and Company Inc., New York, 1994).

Morton Weinfeld, *Like Everyone Else...But Different, The Paradoxical Success of Canadian Jews* (McClelland & Stewart, Toronto, 2001).

William Weintraub, *City Unique: Montreal Days and Nights in the 1940s and '50s* (McClelland & Stewart, Toronto, 1996).

Ronald Wolfson, *A Time to Mourn, A Time to Comfort* (The Art of Jewish Living Series, Jewish Lights Publishing, Woodstock, VT, 1993).

Yaacov Zipper, *Yaacov, The Journals of Yaacov Zipper, 1950-1982; The Struggle for Yiddishkeit* (trans., ed. Mervin Butovsky and Ode Garfinkle, McGill-Queen's University Press, Montreal, 2004).

Index

Page references in bold indicate illustrations.

35th Anniversary Year

1973-2008

Véhicule Press
www.vehiculepress.com